LINGUISTICA ANTVERPIENSIA NEW SERIES

Themes in Translation Studies

8/2009

LINGUISTICA ANTVERPIENSIA

NEW SERIES

Themes in Translation Studies

8/2009

ARTESIS UNIVERSITY COLLEGE ANTWERP
DEPARTMENT OF TRANSLATORS & INTERPRETERS

2986656

EVALUATION OF TRANSLATION TECHNOLOGY

Edited by

Walter Daelemans & Véronique Hoste

418.020285635
EVA

Contents

Walter Daelemans & Véronique Hoste
Introduction. Evaluation of Translation Technology 9

I Evaluation of Machine Translation

Andy Way
A critique of Statistical Machine Translation 17

Paula Estrella, Andrei Popescu-Belis, Andrei & Maghi King
The FEMTI guidelines for contextual MT evaluation:
Principles and resources 43

Vincent Vandeghinste
Scaling up a hybrid MT System: From low to full resources 65

Bogdan Babych & Anthony Hartley
Automated error analysis for multiword expressions: Using BLEU-type scores for automatic discovery of potential translation errors 81

Nora Aranberri-Monasterio & Sharon O'Brien
Evaluating RBMT output for –ing forms: A study of four target languages 105

Lynne Bowker
Can Machine Translation meet the needs of official language minority communities in Canada? A recipient evaluation.. 123

II Evaluation of Translation Tools

Iulia Mihalache
Social and economic actors in the evaluation of translation technologies. Creating meaning and value when designing, developing and using translation technologies.. 159

Alberto Fernandez Costales
The role of Computer-Assisted Translation in the field of software localisation 179

Lieve Macken
In search of the recurrent units of translation 195

Miguel A. Jimenez- Crespo
The effect of Translation Memory tools in translated Web texts: Evidence from a comparative product-based study 213

Book Reviews

Díaz Cintas, Jorge (Ed.) (2008). *The didactics of audiovisual translation.* Amsterdam: John Benjamins. 263p.
(Jimmy Ureel)
.... 235

Ferreira Duarte, J., Assis Rosa, A., Seruya, T. (2006*) Translation Studies at the Interface of Disciplines.* Amsterdam / Philadelphia : John Benjamins Publishing Company, 207 p.
(Isabelle Robert) 238

Lewandowska-Tomaszczyk, Barbara and Marcel Thelen (Eds) (2008). *Translation and Meaning. Part 8. Proceedings of the Łódź Session oj the 4th International Maastricht-Łódź Duo Colloquium on "Translation and Meaning", 23-25 September 2005.* Maastricht: Zuyd University, Maastricht School of International Communication, Department of Translation and Interpreting. 441p.
(Sonia Vandepitte) 243

Martínez Sierra, Juan José (2008), *Humor y traducción: Los Simpson cruzan la frontera.* En: Collecció "Estudis sobre la traducció", núm. 15, Universitat Jaume I. 271p.
(Anne Verhaert) 248

Milton, John & Bandia, Paul (Eds) (2009). *Agents of Translation.* Amsterdam/Philadeplphia: John Benjamins. 329p.
(Sara Verbeeck) 250

Pöckl, Wolfgang & Schreiber, Michael (Eds) (2008). *Geschichte und Gegenwart der Übersetzung im französischen Sprachraum.* Frankfurt am Main-Berlin-Bern-Bruxelles-New York-Oxford-Wien: Peter Lang Verlag. 200 p.
(Frédéric Weinmann) 252

Alphabetical list of authors & titles with keywords 257

Alphabetical list of contributors & contact addresses 259

Evaluation of Translation Technology

Walter Daelemans
University of Antwerp

Véronique Hoste
University College Ghent/ University of Ghent

Lacking widely accepted and reliable evaluation measures, the evaluation of Machine Translation (MT) and translation tools remains an open issue. MT developers focus on automatic evaluation measures such as BLEU (Papineni et al., 2002) and NIST (Doddington, 2002) which primarily count n-gram overlap with reference translations and which are only indirectly linked to translation usability and quality. Commercial translation tools such as translation memories and translation workbenches are widely used and their developers claim usefulness in terms of productivity, consistency or quality. However, these claims are rarely proven using objective comparative studies. This collection dissects the state of the art in translation technology and translation tool development and provides quantitative and qualitative answers to the question how useful translation technology is.

Evaluation of translation technology requires a multifaceted approach. It involves the evaluation of the textual output quality in terms of intelligibility, accuracy, fidelity to its source text, and appropriateness of style and register. But it also takes into account the usability of supportive tools for creating and updating dictionaries, for post-editing texts, for controlling the source language, for customization of documents, for extendibility to new languages and for domain adaptability, etc. Finally, evaluation involves contrasting the costs and benefits of translation technology with those of human translation performance.

This collection comprises 10 original contributions from researchers and developers in the field. The volume is divided into two parts. The first addresses evaluation of Machine Translation, the second evaluation of Translation Tools.

Part I opens with an invited position paper of Andy Way (*A critique of statistical machine translation*) in which he analyzes the divide between on the one hand the developers of Statistical Machine Translation (SMT) systems, and on the other hand translators. In spite of the technical success of SMT, with phrase-based SMT dominating research and development, translators largely ignore it. According to Andy Way, the reason for this is the fact that the approach is perceived as being extremely difficult to understand, as its proponents are not interested in addressing any community other than their own. After a fascinating account of the early history of

SMT, the author argues convincingly that SMT has much to learn from other paradigms, including more linguistically sophisticated ones. He also criticizes the danger of over-optimizing systems when using only automatic MT evaluation methods.

The topic of evaluation methodology is further taken up by Paula Estrella, Andrei Popescu-Belis, and Maghi King (*The FEMTI guidelines for contextual MT evaluation: principles and resources*) in their introduction to the Framework for the Evaluation of Machine Translation in ISLE (FEMTI). This methodology takes into account the context of the use of an MT system and is based on ISO/IEC standards and guidelines for software evaluation. The methodology provides support tools and helps users define contextual evaluation plans. Context in terms of tasks, users, and input characteristics indeed plays an all-important role in evaluation. The web-based FEMTI application allows evaluation experts to share and refine their knowledge about evaluation.

Despite the high correlations with human judgements (e.g. Zhang et al., 2004), automatic metrics such as BLEU and NIST do not necessarily result in an actual improvement in translation quality (Way, Callison-Burch et al., 2006). Furthermore, a limitation of current automatic scores developed within SMT is the fact that they give only a very general indication of translation quality. Both the article of Bogdan Babych and Anthony Hartley, and the contribution of Nora Aranberri-Monasterio and Sharon O'Brien focus on more fine-grained MT evaluation, aiming at a more thorough error analysis which can help MT developers to focus on problematic categories. Bogdan Babych and Anthony Hartley (*Automated error analysis for multiword expressions: using BLEU-type scores for automatic discovery of potential translation errors*) adapt the BLEU metric to allow for the detection of systematic mistranslations of multiword expressions (MWE), and also to create a priority list of problematic issues. Two aligned parallel corpora serve as the basis for their experiments and they experiment both with rule-based and statistical MT systems. They show that their approach allows for the discovery of poorly translated MWEs both on the source and target language side. Even more specific is the evaluation of output of rule-based MT systems when translating –ing forms by Nora Aranberri-Monasterio and Sharon O' Brien (*Evaluating RBMT output for –ing forms: a study of four target languages*). These forms have a reputation for being hard to translate into e.g. French, Spanish, German, and Japanese and are therefore frequently addressed in controlled language rules which seek to reduce the ambiguities in the source text in order to improve the machine translation output. For the evaluation of the translation quality of the -ing-form, the authors opted for a human evaluation and show that Systran, a rule-based MT system, obtains reasonable accuracy (over 70%) in translating this form. Due to the labour-intensive nature of human evaluation, they also assess the agreement between the human scores and automatic metrics such as NIST, GTM, etc. and show good correlations. The authors conclude on the basis of their experimental work that the problem of the -ing forms is overstated and explore a few possibilities for further improving these results.

Part I closes with yet another perspective on the evaluation of Machine Translation: recipient evaluation. This study is another nice application of the context-based evaluation of MT. In order to determine the usefulness of MT as a cost-effective way of providing more material in the language of minorities, Lynne Bowker (*Can Machine Translation meet the needs of official language minority communities in Canada? A recipient evaluation.*) investigates the reception of MT in the Canadian context where bilingualism is officially legislated. The reception of MT output by the two studied Official Language Minority Communities (OLMCs) was investigated by presenting four translation versions, viz. human translations and raw, rapidly post-edited and maximally post-edited MT output to members of the two OLMCs. Bowker's study reveals that whereas (rapidly and maximally post-edited) MT output could be acceptable for information assimilation in cases where there is a lack of ability to understand the source text, only high-quality translations are acceptable for information dissemination where translation is seen as a means for preserving or promoting a culture. Another interesting finding was that the 'average' recipients are more open to MT output than language professionals.

Part II of this volume addresses the evaluation of computer-aided translation tools (see e.g. Bowker, 2002 for an introduction). These tools include Translation Memories (TM), (bilingual) terminology management software, monolingual authoring tools (spelling, grammar, style checking), workflow management tools etc. A first question to be answered is whether current state of the art tools are perceived as useful by translators, and how they can be improved. Iulia Mihalache (*Social and economic actors in the evaluation of translation technologies. Creating meaning and value when designing, developing and using translation technologies*) discusses the advantages for companies as well as for translators of encouraging public evaluation of tools in on-line communities, and develops evaluation criteria from the perspective of translators communities, making use of different technology adoption models. She also discusses the 'how' of evaluation: a more complete understanding of translation technologies evaluation criteria is obtained if translators' attitudes, perceptions and behaviours related to technologies are studied in a multidisciplinary way from sociological, economic, psychological, and cultural perspectives. Alberto Fernández Costales (*The role of computer assisted translation in the field of software localization*) analyzes the effectiveness of computer assisted translation tools in Localization, the adaptation of a product to a particular locale. By empirically studying the usability and reliability of a particular tool (Passolo) for localizing a program, insight is provided into how translation tools can alleviate some of the challenges of localization. Besides improving text consistency and terminological coherence (but see Miguel Jiménez-Crespo's paper for contradictory results), the main advantage is that these tools can save time, and thereby improve the productivity of localization experts.

Possible improvements in current Translation Memory technology are studied in the article of Lieve Macken (*In search of recurrent units of translation*). Translation Memories are currently sentence-based. This means that new text to be translated can only be matched with sentence-like segments, leading to limited recall in many cases. However, the number of matches can be increased if input is allowed to match sub-sentential segments. In a series of experiments, the degree of repetitiveness of different text types is compared, and performance of a sentential Translation Memory system is compared with a sub-sentential one. The results show that whereas sub-sentential memory systems are certainly a move in the right direction, they also sometimes lead to distracting translation suggestions. For solving the latter problem, better word alignment algorithms are necessary.

TM tools have changed the nature of translation by imposing a number of technological constraints that can in principle lead to either positive results (increased consistency) or negative results (increased decontextualization). Miguel Jiménez-Crespo (*The effect of translation memory tools in translated web texts: evidence from a comparative product-based study*) provides an empirical study on the often-debated question whether TMs improve or degrade translation quality. In a corpus-based study of 40,000 original and localized Spanish websites, he shows that the localized texts (translated using TMs) show higher numbers of inconsistencies at the typographic, lexical, and syntactic levels than spontaneously produced, non-translated texts, and therefore lead to lower levels of quality. While this article does not provide the last word in this discussion, it paves the way to interesting follow-up studies controlling for different variables that may influence the difference observed.

Acknowledgements

The authors would like to take this opportunity to thank all the authors for their contributions. The final contributions have undergone a detailed review followed by a thorough revision step. Our sincere thanks also go to the reviewers who helped us to assure the highest level of quality for this publication: Joost Buysschaert, Gloria Corpas Pastor, Alian Desilets, Andreas Eisele, Frederico Gaspari, David Farwell, Eva Forsbom, Johann Haller, David Langlois, Lieve Macken, Karolina Owczarzak, Jörg Tiedemann, Harold Somers. We also thank Aline Remael for her advice throughout the publication process and for some of the final formal editing with Jeremy Schreiber.

Bibliography

Bowker, L. (2002). Computer Aided Translation Technology: A Practical Introduction, University of Ottawa Press, Ottawa, Canada.

Callison-Burch, C., Osborne, M., and Koehn, P. (2006). Re-evaluating the Role of Bleu in Machine Translation Research. *Proceedings of the 11th Conference of the European Chapter of the Association for Computational Linguistics (EACL)* (pp.249-256).Association for Computational Linguistics. Trento, Italy.

Doddington, G. (2002). Automatic Evaluation of Machine Translation Quality using N-gram Co-occurrence Statistics. *Proceedings of the Second Human Language Technologies Conference (HLT)* (pp.138-145). Morgan Kaufmann. San Diego, USA.

Papineni, K., Roukos, S., Ward, T., and Zhu, W.J. (2002). BLEU: a method for automatic evaluation of Machine Translation. *Proceedings of the 40th Annual Metting of the Association for Computational Linguistics (ACL)* (pp.311-318). Association for Computational Linguistics. Philadelphia, USA.

Zhang, Y., Vogel, S. and Waibel, A. (2004). Interpreting BLEU/NIST scores: How much improvement do we need to have a better system? *Proceedings of the International Conference on Language Resources and Evaluation (LREC)*.(pp.2051-2055). European Language Resources Association. Lisbon, Portugal.

I EVALUATION OF MACHINE TRANSLATION

A critique of Statistical Machine Translation

Andy Way
Dublin City University

Phrase-Based Statistical Machine Translation (PB-SMT) is clearly the leading paradigm in the field today. Nevertheless—and this may come as some surprise to the PB-SMT community—most translators and, somewhat more surprisingly perhaps, many experienced MT protagonists find the basic model extremely *difficult to understand. The main aim of this paper, therefore, is to discuss why this might be the case. Our basic thesis is that proponents of PB-SMT do not seek to address any community other than their own, for they do not feel any* need *to do so. We demonstrate that this was not always the case; on the contrary, when statistical models of translation were first presented, the language used to describe how such a model might work was very conciliatory, and inclusive. Over the next five years, things changed considerably; once SMT achieved dominance particularly over the rule-based paradigm, it had established a position where it did not need to bring along the rest of the MT community with it, and in our view, this has largely pertained to this day. Having discussed these issues, we discuss three additional issues: the role of automatic MT evaluation metrics when describing PB-SMT systems; the recent syntactic embellishments of PB-SMT, noting especially that most of these contributions have come from researchers who have prior experience in fields other than statistical models of translation; and the relationship between PB-SMT and other models of translation, suggesting that there are many gains to be had if the SMT community were to open up more to the other MT paradigms.*

1. Introduction

It is clear that Phrase-Based Statistical Machine Translation (PB-SMT) is by far the most dominant paradigm in our field today, at least with respect to the research community. Younger readers, newcomers to the field and 'dyed in the wool' practitioners of SMT may not realise it, but 'twas not ever thus. In the early 1980s, the struggle to become *the* way that MT was done focused on two rule-based (RBMT) strategies: transfer (e.g. Arnold & des Tombe, 1987; Bennett & Slocum, 1985), and interlingual MT (e.g. (Carbonell et al.,1992; Rosetta, 1994). Even before SMT was propounded as a possible competitor to RBMT, Example-Based MT (EBMT) had been proposed in (Nagao, 1984).[1]

At the time SMT was proposed in Brown et al. (1988a), therefore, RBMT was the prevalent paradigm, which according to some researchers was under pressure from EBMT, which "set out to supplant ('traditional') rule-based MT" (Nirenburg et al., 1993).

Interestingly, when we asked recently whether at the time he had really thought that EBMT could take over from RBMT, Nagao (1984) noted:

> Yes. I thought that RBMT had a limitation because we cannot write a complete grammar of analysis, transfer and generation consistently and completely, and that improving an RBMT system is quite difficult because no one is confident about what grammar rules are to be changed in what way to handle a particular expression, etc. in order to improve a system.In contrast, EBMT has a kind of a learning function by adding new translation pairs to handle new expressions. It is a very simple process.

With RBMT being dominant, and EBMT having had a few years' headstart, SMT was, therefore, truly the new kid on the block back in 1988.

In Section 2, we address the issue of the nature of the language used by the IBM team in seeking to put across their views, starting with the 1988 paper, and moving via Brown et al. (1990) and Brown et al. (1992) to Brown et al. (1993), perhaps *the* most cited paper on (S)MT even today. As an aide-memoire, we have taken the liberty of asking some of the MT protagonists of the time for their recollections of the presentations which accompanied some of these papers, and as a result contrast the content of the papers with the more provocative language used in the accompanying conference presentations. It is apparent that the MT community at the time were less than welcoming to the newcomers, and that the language used to purvey their displeasure regarding the proposed techniques was itself somewhat rich!

Nonetheless, at this juncture, it suffices to say that we believe there was a real sea change in the language used between the earliest paper of Brown et al. (1988a), and the well-known Computational Linguistics article of Brown et al. (1993). It is by no means surprising that Brown et al. (1992) was presented at a conference subtitled "Empiricist vs. Rationalist Methods in MT". That is, the tide was already turning at this point, and by the time the 1993 paper was published the SMT developers had (largely) won the day. From this point on, SMT was mainstream, and no longer had to appeal to the remainder of the MT community to justify its acceptance; if you couldn't keep up, you were left behind. We contend that this pertains right up to the present day, where for many PB-SMT is completely impenetrable.

Of course, when you are a member of any dominant group, you don't need to appeal to outsiders; you may choose to, or instead you may look inwardly and preach to the converted using a language only they understand. With respect to PB-SMT, it is by no means clear that today's protagonists are even *aware* that a sizeable community exists for whom their research is unintelligible; nor is it clear that even if they *did* know this that they would necessarily know how to communicate their ideas to non-SMT people.[2]

We aim to make three further contributions in this paper. Firstly, in Section 3 we outline the basic models of SMT, followed by a short discussion of MT evaluation. In particular, given the influence of automatic MT evaluation metrics nowadays, we address the question as to whether the tail is wagging the dog; instead of looking at the automatic evaluation scores *per se*, not enough emphasis is placed on whether translation quality is *actually* increasing. We conclude this section by examining what's good and not so good when it comes to SMT.

Secondly, in Section 4 we provide comment on the recent syntactic embellishments of PB-SMT, noting especially that many of these contributions have come from researchers who have prior experience in fields other than statistical models of translation.

Thirdly, in Section 5 we relate PB-SMT to other models of translation. We expect this to be of interest not only to the previously mentioned constituencies, but also to the PB-SMT community itself, many of whom do not seem to be aware that there are indeed other ways, and a vast untapped literature for them to avail of; things are not necessarily 'novel' just because they've been 'discovered' in an SMT framework.

Finally, in Section 6 we conclude with what are, in our opinion, the lessons to be learnt by all of us as a community from our observations.

2. (In)accessibility of Statistical Models of MT

It is clear from the previous section that we are critical of how SMT researchers present their work. In this section, we set out our argument about why we believe appropriate explanations of today's mainstream statistical models of translation are currently lacking for the constituencies mentioned at the outset of this paper.

2.1. Adopting a Conciliatory Tone

In the original exposition of SMT (Brown et al., 1988a),[3] the language used in places is noteworthy for its conciliatory tone (our italics):

> "We wrote this *somewhat speculative* paper hoping to stimulate interest in applications of statistics to translation and to *seek cooperation* in achieving this difficult task,"
>
> "*the proposal may seem radical*"
>
> "Very little will be said about employment of conventional grammars. This omission ... may only reflect ... our uncertainty about the

> degree of grammar sophistication required. *We are keeping an open mind!*"
>
> "Not to interrupt the flow of *intuitive ideas*, we omit the discussion of the corresponding algorithms".

That is, in the written records, at any rate, the intention seems to be one of appealing to the remainder of the (mostly rule-based) community, pointing out that this is new and that they might not like this competing approach (the authors are aware of the "*many weighty objections to our ideas*"), but also that they would not be able to achieve the goal of high-quality translation without the help of the (mostly) linguistics-based experts already operating in the field. Perhaps most apposite for today's practitioners is the final sentence, where they state that they feel their results are hopeful "for future statistical translation methods *incorporating the use of appropriate syntactic structure information*" (cf. Chiang, 2005).[4]

If we are permitted a quick aside, it is remarkable that the paper was accepted at all for Coling in 1988. Peter Brown, first author on the IBM papers, kindly forwarded to us the original review of the paper that appeared as Brown et al. (1988b), which, despite his working for the past 14 years in statistical finance, still takes pride of place on his office wall:

Original Review of SMT for Coling 1988

> The validity of statistical (information theoretic) approach to MT has indeed been recognized, as the authors mention, by Weaver as early as 1949. And was universally recognized as mistaken by 1950. (cf. Hutchins, MT: Past, Present, Future, Ellis Horwood, 1986, pp 30 ff. and references therein).
>
> The crude force of computers is not science. The paper is simply beyond the scope of COLING.

Given the content of this review,[5] the programme chair Eva Hajičová (as well as, interestingly, Makoto Nagao, who as one of Eva's "five advisors" presumably was responsible for reading the MT abstracts) must have been at least a little reticent in allowing the paper to proceed to publication; given the situation today, we must as a community compliment them retrospectively on their open-mindedness in accepting the paper and helping kick-start the new paradigm.

Brown et al. (1988a) was presented as part of a panel at TMI on "Paradigms for MT", with contributions from Jaime Carbonell, Peter Brown, Victor Raskin and Harold Somers. The recollection of those present is very interesting. Pierre Isabelle recalls:

> Peter Brown is pretty good at being provocative and at TMI-88 he was at his best. If I remember correctly, he went as far as saying that

> statistical approaches were just about to eradicate rule-based MT research (the bread and butter of everyone except him in the room) in the same way it had already eradicated rule-based speech research. Peter Brown definitely made that particular statement in public, but I am not 100% sure it was at TMI-88. In any event, his talk at TMI did indeed start and end with hugely provocative statements (for the time). As for the technical substance of the talk, few if any people in the room were then in a position to understand it in any depth.
>
> We were all flabbergasted. All throughout Peter's presentation, people were shaking their heads and spurting grunts of disbelief or even of hostility.

Pierre goes on to say that the usual question and answer session was "a big mess", because:

> 1) Nobody had understood Peter's talk well enough to come up with technical questions or objections; and 2) in the heat of the moment, nobody was able to articulate the general disbelief into anything like a reasonable response to Peter's incredible statements.

Harold Somers, sitting next to Peter Brown on the panel, notes:

> My recollection is that he knew very well that people would be shocked, and his presentation was more "you ain't gonna like this but…".
>
> The audience reaction was either incredulous, dismissive or hostile. Someone probably said "Where's the linguistic intuition?" to which the answer would have been "Yes, that's the point, there isn't any".

Walter Daelemans recalls that "the Leuven Eurotra people weren't very impressed by the talk and laughed it away as a rehash of 'direct' (word-by-word) translation, which was probably a fair comment at the time."

With respect to the above comments, Peter Brown unsurprisingly has a somewhat different recollection of these early presentations:

> While it is my style to be provocative, a statement such as "eradicating rule-based MT" would not be provocative but simply antagonistic and that is not my style. I was very much aware that what we were saying would be controversial, and that our goal was to show that mathematically what we were doing was correct. However, what I believed then and believe today is that while there is an enormous role for linguistics in translation, the actual translation itself should be done in a mathematically coherent framework. Our goal was to present that framework and to show how far you could get with only

> minimal linguistics and then to excite people into imagining how far we could get with more linguistics incorporated in a mathematically coherent system.
>
> As for starting and ending with "hugely provocative" statements, my goal was to provoke debate and discussion not to be antagonistic. Trying to antagonize others just isn't my style. I checked with with my colleagues who attended the TMI conference and they agreed that it is just not something I would have done.

In order to better understand the tensions between competing paradigms at the time, ten Hacken (2001) contains a few appropriate observations regarding the climate around this period:

> In the research programme predominant at Coling 1988 a number of signs of a crisis can be recognized. *In MT, one of the main problems was that despite large-scale investment in terms of time and money, projects considered as state-of-the-art failed to produce solutions which could be used in actual practice. As far as MT was available, the technology it used was outdated.* (p.11, our italics)

Of course, what ten Hacken says about the lack of useable systems (it's fairly obvious that he's speaking about Eurotra here, partly from his own experience on the project) is completely true. However, today's rule-based proponents would take issue with the latter point, presumably.

He also, somewhat more controversially still, observes that "most of the MT researchers at Coling 1988 belonged to the first group", namely "a group of scientists who refuse to consider the problem seriously". Ten Hacken (2001) notes further that

> By the mid 1990s the crisis had reached such proportions that we even find an explicit description of it in (Melby, 1995). The tone of this work is highly pessimistic in the sense that *MT as it had been attempted for a long time was a hopeless enterprise and should be given up*. (*ibid*., our italics)

Of course, in the intervening period, it largely *has* been abandoned.

With respect to Brown et al. (1988b), ten Hacken (2001) includes them in "a group of scientists who explore the borderlines of the research programme in order to find out whether non-mainstream versions might be better" (*ibid.*). Their approach was in direct contrast to the common view of the time that "the obstacles to translating by means of the computer are primarily linguistic" (Lehrberger & Bourbeau, 1988, p.1).[6] Ten Hacken (2001) observes that already by 1998, "the statistical approach to MT ha(d) gained prominent status at the cost of the previously dominant linguistic approach" (p.2), so the 'non-mainstream' had very much become the *de facto* standard. We address some of the reasons why statistical models of translation became so dominant in section 3.2 below.

2.2. Describing SMT for Non-Specialists

Moving on, the first of the two Computational Linguistics articles (Brown et al., 1990) introduces most of the terminology we all use today in SMT: word alignment, language and translation models, parameter estimation, decoding, fertility, distortion, and perplexity, among others. The ideas in this paper are decidedly more fully worked out, and far from omitting "complete mathematical specification(s) to a future report", as in the 1988 papers, this 1990 paper provides the basic equations necessary for SMT to be carried out. Nonetheless, these are explained in language likely to be understood by newcomers to probability theory. And again, the last sentence offers the hand of friendship to the rule-based practitioners: "We hope to... construct grammars for both French and English and to base future translation models on the grammatical constructs thus defined" (p. 84).

In Brown et al. (1992), the IBM team provide a somewhat weak attempt at casting SMT as transfer. Notwithstanding our evaluation of this paper, it is obvious that even trying to couch SMT in terms of transfer may appeal to rule-based protagonists. Indeed, Peter Brown's recollection is that "by that time people were interested in the statistical approach and were listening to the talk without simply writing it off as something completely inane". This is confirmed by Somers (2003, p. 323), who observes that by now SMT "was seen (by some) as a serious challenge to the by now traditional rule-based approach, this challenge typified by the (partly engineered) confrontational atmosphere at TMI-92 in Montreal".

It was in such an atmosphere that around this time, Fred Jelinek, the head of the IBM team, uttered his (in)famous remark "Every time I fire a linguist, my system's performance improves". While many people believe this to have been uttered in the context of MT, it seems instead to have been quoted in the area of speech recognition.[7] Nonetheless, it was clear that linguistic proponents of MT could see that they were next in the firing line.

2.3. Mathematical Formulation of SMT

Clearly by this time the tide was turning in favour of corpus-based models of translation, including EBMT. Somers notes (*ibid.*) that EBMT was also seen (as we have noted above) as a significant challenger to RBMT. Interestingly, Way (2009) notes that similar trends in the language used can be seen in EBMT papers at the time:

> At the very same conference where SMT was first proposed in Brown et al. (1988a), Sumita and Tsutsumi (1988) note that for them, two items for future work involved using "deeper analysis" and focussing on "rule acquisition". However, within three years,

> one of the same authors felt able to write that the fact that "EBMT has no rules" was one of the main advantages over RBMT (Sumita & Iida, 1991).

Nonetheless, given that the nature of EBMT sub-sentential alignments are more linguistically motivated than those of SMT, EBMT has remained more approachable to those of a less statistical bent (cf. the last paragraph before section 3.1 for other reasons why this might be the case).

Returning to SMT, in Brown et al. (1993), any pretence at staying in touch with the nonstatistical disappears completely. While they note that

> Today, the fruitful application of statistical methods to the study of machine translation is within the computational grasp of anyone with a well-equipped workstation," (Brown et al., 1993)

this is soon followed by:

> We assume the reader to be comfortable with Lagrange multipliers, partial differentiation, and constrained optimization as they are presented in a typical college calculus text, and to have a nodding acquaintance with random variables.

Of course, we are taking these quotes somewhat out of context, and the title of the paper by Brown et al. (1993) is, after all, "The mathematics of statistical machine translation: Parameter estimation". To provide a more balanced view, therefore, Peter Brown noted in a recent email conversation:

> As for the language, our goal was to explain what we were doing as clearly as possible. None of us had any background in linguistics, just like we have no background in finance, so we just wrote it using the language and terminology of statistics with which we are familiar. I imagine that were we to write a paper on finance today, some of the finance guys might complain about our terminology also. For what it's worth I think it's very important to get the mathematics straight when doing linguistics but once it is straight then linguistic knowledge will be what matters. In other words, it's not math *or* linguistics, but math *and* linguistics. Our goal was to establish the mathematical framework for MT so that the linguistically-minded could proceed with the research. I gather from your note that that has not happened and it's unfortunately either math guys or linguistic guys working on MT but not both working together.

Given the title and topic of the paper, it would be churlish to heap all the blame on the pioneering IBM group; indeed, one of the reasons why this paper is so well-regarded nowadays is that it's particularly clearly written. As a successful paper, perhaps Brown et al. (1993) was seen as *the* way to put across ideas from the SMT community, rather than being just one way in which this innovative research could be communicated.

Whether this was done intentionally or not, it's true that from 1993 onwards, attempts to engage the established MT community had indeed fallen by the wayside, and certainly by the new millennium SMT had become the dominant paradigm with no incentive to engage with researchers from older/other paradigms.[8]

Finally, while we can accept Peter's words at face value, it's clear that neither the SMT community (at least not until recently, and only then when researchers from outside the mainstream SMT community started to demonstrate the effectiveness of syntax) nor the more linguistically-oriented researchers - who along with the linguists, have to take their fair share of the blame for allowing SMT to become so dominant despite the contents of these early SMT papers - took from the IBM research the fact that once the mathematics had been properly sorted out, "then linguistic knowledge will be what matters"; if they had, we'd probably have had ten years earlier the syntax-based systems that are coming onstream now.[9]

3. Phrase-Based Statistical Machine Translation

We have complained that papers on PB-SMT are somewhat less than perspicuous for the general MT audience. It's well outside the scope of this paper to try to explain the various components of such systems (corpus preparation, word alignment, phrase extraction, language and translation model induction, system tuning, decoding and post-processing) in a manner that is not overly loaded with terminology and formulae, and short on intuition. However, we will point the interested reader to two companion papers: firstly, in Hearne and Way (2009a), we *do* try to achieve exactly that, by providing an explanation of SMT for non-specialists; secondly, in Hearne and Way (2009b), we discuss the important role of translators and linguists in the SMT process, whose contribution is often overlooked by SMT developers, but nonetheless remains an absolute prerequisite for SMT as we know it today, as well as for any extensions going forward.

In a nutshell, the goal of PB-SMT is to find the most likely translation T of a source sentence S. We say "most likely," as many possible candidate target language translations may be proposed by the system. The most likely translation is the one with the highest probability (hence "argmax") according to $P(S \mid T).P(T)$, as in (1):

(1) $argmax_T \; P(S \mid T).P(T)$

where $P(S \mid T)$ is the *translation model*, which attempts to ensure that the meaning expressed in S is also captured in T, i.e. that T is an *adequate* translation of S; and $P(T)$ is the *language model*, which tries to ensure that the candidate translation T is actually a valid sentence in the target language, i.e. that T is *fluent*. This is the 'noisy channel' model of SMT (Brown et al., 1990; Brown et al., 1993), and the language and translation models are (usually) inferred from large monolingual and bilingual aligned corpora respectively.

It is commonplace today to use phrases rather than words as the basis of the statistical model (hence 'phrase-based'). A phrase is defined as a group of source words s□ that should be translated as a group of target words t□ The 'log-linear' model of PB-SMT (Och & Ney, 2002) (rather more flexible than the 'noisy channel' model) is that in (2):

(2) $argmax_T \sum_m^M =_1 \lambda_m \cdot h_m (T, S)$

The uninitiated reader should note that the leftmost parts of the equations in (1) and (2) are identical, i.e. the task is the same; the only difference is how each candidate translation (out of the T possible translations) output by the SMT system is to be scored.

In (2), there are M feature functions, whose logarithms should be added together (hence the Σ in (2), as opposed to the multiplication in (1); the typical values for each feature are in practice so small that multiplying them becomes impractical, as the product of each of these probabilities approaches zero quite quickly) to give the overall score for each translation. Typical feature functions for a PB-SMT system include the phrase translation probabilities in both directions (i.e. source-to-target *P (t□ | s□)* and target-to-source *P(s□ | t□))* between the two languages in question, a target language model (exactly as in (1)), and some penalty scores to ensure that sentences of reasonable length vis-à-vis the input string are generated.[10] Note that if only the translation model and language model features were used, then the log-linear model in (2) would be identical to the noisy channel model in (1). Typically the λ_m weights for each feature h_m in (2) are optimized with respect to some particular scoring function (usually a specific evaluation metric, cf. section 3.1 for further discussion of this topic) on a development (or 'tuning') set using a technique called Mimimum Error Rate Training (MERT) (Och, 2003) to try to ensure optimal performance on a specific test set of sentences, which is hopefully as 'similar' as possible to the development set. We again refer interested readers to Hearne & Way (2009a) for more detailed description of the components of these models in language we hope is more intuitive to them than is usually seen in SMT papers.

In Hearne & Way (2009b), we make the following (hopefully useful) observation:

> RMBT and EBMT dwell on the process via which a translation is to be produced for each source sentence, whereas SMT dwells on how to tell which is the better of two or more proposed translations for a source sentence. Thus, RBMT and EBMT focus on the best way to

> generate a translation for each input string, whereas SMT focuses on generating many thousands of hypothetical translations for the input string and working out which one is most likely. In seeking to understand SMT in particular, this is a key distinction: while the means by which RBMT and EBMT generate translations usually look somewhat plausible to us humans, the methods of translation generation in SMT are not intuitively plausible. In fact, the methods used are not intended to be either linguistically or cognitively plausible (just probabilistically plausible) and holding onto the notion that they somehow are or should be simply hinders understanding of SMT.

Not everyone would agree with us regarding this latter point, and we return to this in section 3.3.

3.1. Evaluation

While we've excluded discussion of the pre-processing and runtime stages in PBSMT, one stage that warrants a few words here is evaluation.
Ten Hacken (2001) makes the following observation:

> Whereas the architecture of the system and the choice of a linguistic theory as a source of knowledge to be applied are the subject of controversial discussion, the assumptions on the nature of translation and the proper evaluation of the MT system are not questioned in the late 1980s (p.13).

We argue below that while the introduction of automatic evaluation metrics in MT - where MT system output is compared against one or more reference translations produced by humans - has largely been beneficial, they have to a large extent taken on too much importance, especially since real translation quality is what we should be concerned with.

In our view, today's automatic MT evaluation metrics are basically useful for three tasks:

1) for system developers to check that different incarnations of the *same* system are improving over time;
2) to compare *different* systems when trained and tested on the same data sets, as in today's large-scale MT evaluation campaigns such as NIST,[11] WMT[12] (Callison-Burch et al., 2007; Callison-Burch et al., 2008; Callison-Burch et al., 2009), IWSLT[13] (Paul, 2006; Fordyce, 2007; Paul, 2008) etc.;
3) for MERT (Och, 2003), i.e. customising (tuning) one's system to perform as well as it can on the current data using *one* particular MT evaluation metric (e.g. BLEU (Papineni et al., 2002), NIST (Doddington, 2002), WER (Levenshtein, 1966), Meteor (Banerjee & Lavie, 2005), F-Score (Turian et al., 2003), etc.).

In the original exposition of BLEU, the main use envisaged by such automatic evaluation metrics concerned the first task above, namely incremental testing of one particular system on a defined test set of example sentences. There is no doubt, especially on small-scale evaluation tasks (such as IWSLT, where only 20,000-40,000 training examples of parallel text are available), that these evaluation metrics are especially useful, as changes to the code base can be evaluated very quickly, and quite often.

What they are *not* so useful for is telling potential users which system is best for their purposes, i.e. if someone were considering purchasing an MT system, and wanted to know how to discern the performance of one system against the other, we would not necessarily advise their doing so on the basis of the systems' comparative BLEU scores. While that's exactly what's done in the second task above, users should realise that those scores represent the systems' scores trained on *one* data set for *one* language pair in *one* language direction and tested on *one* (small) set of sentences, all of which may or may not bear any relation to the *actual* scenario that the user has in mind in which the system is to be deployed. *Caveat emptor*!

With respect to the third scenario outlined above, there are any number of automatic evaluation metrics, from string-based (e.g. BLEU, NIST, F-Score, Meteor) to dependency-based (Liu & Gildea, 2005; Owczarzak et al., 2008). MERT is concerned with the optimisation of one's system performance to *one* such particular metric on a development set, and hoping that this carries forward to the test set at hand. What is *not* (usually) performed in this developmental phase is any examination as to whether increases in scoring with the particular automatic MT evaluation metric *actually* improve the output translations as measured by real users in real applications.

While most developers of MT evaluation metrics cite some correlation with human judgements, many real improvements in translation quality do not result in improved BLEU (or any other) score. For instance, consider the example in (3) from Hassan et al. (2009).

(3) **Source:** واكد الجانبان على دور منظمة التجارة العالمية

Reference: *The two sides highlighted the role of the World Trade Organization,*

Baseline: *The two sides on the role of the World Trade Organization (WTO),*

CCG: *The two parties reaffirmed the role of the World Trade Organization,*

Omitting verbs turns out to be a problem for baseline PB-SMT systems. Given the amount of morphological variants possible, the language model only has a few occurrences of each possible verbal inflected form in order to try to decide which output string it most prefers. Accordingly, very often it prefers an *n*-gram which does not contain *any* verb, as opposed to including a verb that has been observed only rarely. That is, with respect to (3), the baseline system prefers the bigram *sides on* over any combination with *sides* plus some (relevant) verb (*highlighted*, here).

Hassan et al. (2009) note that this is particularly the case when translating the notorious verbless Arabic sentences, as in (3); while the reference translation contains the verb *highlighted*, as there is no verb in the Arabic sentence it is hardly surprising that the baseline system outputs a translation with no verb. However, the system of Hassan et al. (2009), which incorporates supertags[14] (Bangalore & Joshi, 1999) from Combinatory Categorial Grammar (CCG: Steedman, 2000), contains a more grammatically strict language model than a standard word-level Markov model, and so exhibits a preference for the insertion of a verb with a similar meaning to that contained in the reference sentence. Nonetheless, as *reaffirmed* is not contained in the reference translation, this clear improvement in translation quality does not carry over to an improvement according to any string-based evaluation metric. However, in the recent IWSLT-07 evaluation, the supertag-based Arabic-English system described in Hassan et al. (2007) was adjudged to be ranked first by some margin in the human evaluation, despite this clear advantage of more readable output not carrying over to the automatic evaluation scores.

In sum, increased automatic evaluation scores do not necessarily reflect any actual improvements in translation quality. Furthermore, He and Way (2009) note that there is no guarantee that parameters tuned on one metric (e.g. BLEU) will lead to optimal translation scores on the same metric; rather, the score can be improved significantly by tuning on an entirely different metric (e.g. METEOR), especially where just a single reference translation is available (in WMT evaluation tasks, for instance). He and Way (2009) also observe that tuning on combinations of metrics can lead to more robust performance. Of course, for general-purpose MT systems, optimising settings via MERT cannot be done at all, given the lack of a standalone test set; rather, the system must be robust in the face of *any* user input. Considering all these factors, we believe that tuning one's system to a particular evaluation metric is very much a case of the tail wagging the dog, rather than the other way round. Automatic evaluation metrics continue to have their place, but in our view they have taken on rather too much significance, to the possible detriment of *real* improvements in translation quality.

3.2. What's *Good* about PB-SMT

While much of this paper is critical of a number of issues related to statistical models of translation, it would be altogether remiss of us if we were to avoid any mention of some of the benefits that PB-SMT has brought to the wider MT community. These include resources such as:

- *Sentence-aligned corpora*, e.g. Europarl (Koehn, 2005);
- *Tools* such as:
  - word and phrase alignment software (principally Giza++,[15] (Och & Ney, 2003));
  - language modelling toolkits (e.g. SRILM,[16] (Stolcke, 2002));
  - decoders (freely available, such as Pharaoh (Koehn, 2004), but more recently open-source, such as Moses[17] (Koehn et al., 2007));
  - evaluation software (e.g. BLEU (Papineni et al., 2002), NIST (Doddington, 2002), GTM (Turian et al., 2003), Meteor (Banerjee & Lavie, 2005).

In addition, as SMT is rooted in decision theory, it's absolutely clear why the system outputs a translation as the most probable, namely because that output string maximizes the product of the translation model $P(S \mid T)$ and the language model $P(T)$ in the noisy channel model (cf. (1)), or the joint probability of the target and source sentences in the log-linear equation (Och & Ney, 2002) (cf. (2), and section 3 above for more discussion).

It is also very clear that the evaluation campaigns (such as NIST, IWSLT, WMT etc.) have enabled systems to be compared against one another, as standard training, development and test data are made available for each campaign. As in other areas of language processing, this competitive edge has caused groups to try to improve their systems, and such campaigns have doubtlessly resulted in advances in the state of the art. However, Callison-Burch et al. (2006) demonstrate that using string-based evaluation metrics is decidedly unsuitable for comparing systems of quite different types (SMT vs. RBMT, say), which is why the ultimate arbiter of system performance in the WMT tasks remains human evaluation, although a host of automatic evaluation scores are provided for each competing system.

3.3. What's *Less* Good about PB-SMT

For all these reasons, newcomers to the field of MT can very quickly build a system which is competitive compared to those systems of much more experienced groups in the field. Given the enormous ramp up in terms of resources needed, these resources (especially now that Moses is open-source) have been a huge help to newcomers to MT, as well as to more established groups.

However, in our view it remains to be seen whether PB-SMT is the leading method because it's the *best* way of doing MT,or because the tools *exist* which facilitate the rapid prototyping of systems on new language pairs, and different data sets.

While the provision of parallel training corpora (not just of use in SMT, of course) and decoders is very much appreciated by the community, one wonders how much we are now reliant on Philipp Koehn[18] coming up with more data sources and (open-source) software in order for the field to make further advances. For instance, it's not clear that enough is being done (a) to fix things that need fixing; and (b) to make any fixes which *have* been made available to the wider community.

As an example, consider the case of alignment templates (Och & Ney, 2004), which is quite closely related to the use of generalized templates in EBMT. As many others have shown (e.g. Brown, 1999; Cicekli & Güvenir, 2003; Way & Gough, 2003), the use of generalized templates can improve the coverage and quality of EBMT systems. Furthermore, researchers such as Maruyama and Watanabe (1992) stated that "there is no essential difference between translation examples and translation rules - translation examples are special cases of translation rules" (cf. section 2.3 for an alternative view at the time).

Nonetheless, quite clearly the use of alignment templates has not caught on in PB-SMT anywhere near as much as templates/rules in EBMT and RBMT.[19] This is not because they are not useful; Och and Ney (2004) demonstrated their utility several years ago. Rather, in our view it is simply because the developers of PB-SMT decoders have not (yet) made provision for their use in the code-base.

This is just like the situation with the use of phrases (cf. section 5) and syntax (cf. section 4.1) in other paradigms. Years before phrases and syntax were shown to be of benefit in PB-SMT, practitioners in RBMT and EBMT had been incorporating them into their systems;[20] from its inception (Nagao, 1984), EBMT has sought to translate new texts by means of a range of sub-sentential data (both lexical *and* phrasal) stored in the system's memory. As regards syntax, EBMT systems have been built using dependency trees (e.g. Watanabe, 1992; Menezes & Richardson, 2003), annotated constituency tree pairs (e.g. Hearne, 2005;, Hearne & Way, 2006), and pairs of attribute-value matrices (e.g. Way, 2003), among other methods. In much the same way, we contend that alignment templates will become incorporated into mainstream PB-SMT in the near future (cf. Zhao & Al-Onaizan, 2008) in hierarchical phrase-based MT (Chiang, 2005), at which point *everyone* will use them.

Finally, while it's clear that statistical models of translation are modelled on a well-defined decision problem, there is undoubtedly a lack of perspicuity in PB-SMT when it comes to explaining the data. Back in the bad old days of MT, ten Hacken (2001, p. 2) observed that most researchers "take linguistic phenomena as discussed in theoretical linguistics as a basis for the identification of topics in MT". While we agree that we never want to go back to that way of doing things, today's preoccupation with the size of one's BLEU score has gone too far in the opposite direction, so that most PB-SMT researchers would be unable to tell you whether their systems were able to cope with particular cases of 'hard' translational phenomena (e.g. headswitching, relation-changing, etc. See Hearne et al. (2007) for a recent example of what's possible using this tried and tested terminology, and even if they could, they would find it difficult to tell you how such constructions were handled.[21]

On a related point, Galley et al. (2006) state (our italics): "the broad statistical MT program is aimed at a wider goal than the conventional rule-based program - it seeks to *understand and explain human translation data*, and automatically learn from it."

This seems to us to be so far from the truth that it would not be recognised at all by people from outside SMT. For starters, there's an entire body of research dedicated to this - namely, corpus-based translation studies - which Galley et al.(2006) seem to have missed completely. As we stated in Hearne and Way (2009b) (cf. section 3 above), we believe there to be no linguistic or cognitive plausibility in the statistical model of translation. What's more, in our view a statistical approach is almost the *least* appropriate way to go about understanding and explaining human translation data.

4. Extending the Basic Model

Until very recently, it proved difficult to incorporate syntactic knowledge in order to obtain better quality translation output from PB-SMT systems on large benchmark test suites. Worse still, Koehn et al. (2003) demonstrated that adding syntactic constraints harmed the quality of their PB-SMT system.

4.1. Adding Syntax Helps PB-SMT

However, as we stated in the previous section, researchers have recently shown that the basic model of PB-SMT can be improved by the integration of syntax. The first paper to demonstrate this on a large benchmark translation task was (Chiang, 2005). However, his derived transduction grammar does not rely on any linguistic annotations or assumptions, so that the formal syntax induced is not linguistically motivated and does not necessarily capture grammatical preferences in the output target sentences.

More recently, Galley et al. (2006) and Marcu et al. (2006) present two similar extensions of PB-SMT systems with syntactic structure on the target language side. Both employ tree-to-string (so-called xRS) transducers, but their methods of acquiring the xRS rules and training them are different (cf. Hassan et al., 2009, for discussion of these differences).

In a different strand of work, other researchers have demonstrated that lexical syntax in the form of 'supertags' can be used to improve translation quality on a range of language pairs (Hassan et al., 2009) (cf. (3) and resultant discussion above).

4.2. Some Observations

It is evident that given the importance of statistical linguistic processing in NLP in general, many researchers have crossed over from statistical parsing to SMT, and these individuals have contributed enormously to syntactic models of SMT. This is a good thing, as until recently the parsing and MT communities have largely been distinct.

However, such researchers are themselves more likely to come from mathematical, statistical or computer science backgrounds, with much of the linguistics surfacing as annotated data. One could argue that they have been able to enter the field, and contribute to improvements in the area, because current SMT discourse is more accessible to them.

Nonetheless, the fact that syntax has been shown to be of use in PB-SMT is in stark contrast to prominent members of the community - albeit those with no linguistic background to speak of - stating in invited talks at recent large MT gatherings that integrating syntax would not be beneficial, and that linguists and translators had no role to play in the development of today's state-of-the-art MT systems. You don't have to think long to see how ironic this is, when SMT (and other corpus-based) systems are entirely dependent on parallel text generated by human translators (see Ozdowska et al., 2009, for investigation of the effect on translation quality of training SMT systems with such more or less appropriate sets of training data).

One might, therefore, hope that these statements have proven themselves to be ill-founded and have since been largely put to bed. However, more recently Zollmann et al. (2008) demonstrated on a range of Arabic-English tasks that the hierarchical model of Chiang (2005) and the syntax-augmented model of Zollmann and Venugopal (2006) do not show consistent improvements over a baseline PB-SMT system which is allowed access to reorderings up to 12 words apart, so perhaps the debate will continue for a while yet.

5. PB-SMT and other Models of Translation

At the time of writing, statistical models of MT have been around for 20 years, but MT in general has been around for much longer.

In the previous sections, we noted that syntax had been integrated into models of RBMT and EBMT long before showing itself to be of use in PB-SMT, and even here, most of the breakthroughs have come about from those MT researchers with a broader NLP background.

Furthermore, we predicted that the use of templates/rules, long since useful in EBMT and RBMT, will, as Och and Ney (2004) demonstrated, but which has not led to widespread adoption in SMT so far, prove beneficial in phrase-based models of translation also (cf. Zhao & Al-Onaizan, 2008, for a first step in this direction for tree-based models).

Even here, though, if one consults the list of references in Och and Ney (2004), not *one* EBMT or RBMT citation is seen. Prior to Marcu and Wong (2002), the primary *modus operandi* in SMT was word-based (Brown et al., 1990; Brown et al., 1993). That graduating to phrase-based models led to improvements in quality is unsurprising given that from the very beginning (Nagao, 1984), EBMT has used both word and phrase alignments to translate new input strings. However, try to find *any* attributions in the SMT literature to EBMT and you'll (largely) be wasting your time.

The point is, of course, that the PB-SMT community is remarkably inward-looking. Again, this is due to its dominance in the field of MT; not only is it the case that many SMT people do not see the need to provide access to their work to non-specialists because they do not think they have anything to contribute, but also SMT practitioners feel that there is little to be gained from accessing the wider MT literature. Those of us not operating solely in the mainstream are forced to consult the primary SMT literature, as it constitutes by far the bulk of what is published in our field today. Accordingly, most EBMT and RBMT papers contain references from SMT. Regarding the situation pertaining at ACL-COLING 1998, already eleven years ago ten Hacken (2001, p. 15) stated that "(some) researchers still clinging to the old values [...] have included at least a token reference to the new (statistical) values in order to increase their chances of being accepted". In our view, rather than an act of 'tokenism', in most cases non-SMT practitioners need to relate their work to the mainstream statistical models of translation in order to have a reasonable chance of getting their papers published, given (a) the relative lack of published research in other areas, and (b) the preponderance of SMT-trained reviewers of conference and journal submissions.

There is much to be learned by the SMT community from the other paradigms. It should be noted that novelties are not so just because they've been 'discovered' in an SMT paradigm. One such example is Chang and Toutanova (2007), who discuss the difficulties associated with projecting dependency trees from source to target sentences, without mentioning in the text the term *transfer*, nor referring to any such works in the bibliography. More recently, Lopez (2008) finds that "Translation by Pattern Matching" avoids the problem of computing unfeasibly large statistical models in PB-SMT by extracting from the bilingual training corpus stored in memory only those source phrases and their aligned target equivalents suitable for translating the current input string. This is an *exact* description of pretty much any EBMT system. To be fair, Lopez (2008) does cite one EBMT paper, but the steps taken to avoid the term 'EBMT' are remarkable.
In Way (2009), we observed that

> There has undoubtedly been a colossal move away from RBMT to more statistical methods, but now the pendulum is swinging back (slowly) in the opposite direction . . . As a community we are moving up the "Vauquois Pyramid" (Vauquois, 1968) just like people were trying to do in the old rule-based times, but eventually, we will doubtless still need more than can be inferred from "just looking at annotated text pairs".

If this is true, then SMT practitioners will have to take these comments on board if they do not want to be left behind, in much the same way that the linguistic proponents of MT were left behind by the SMT movement.

6. Conclusion

In this paper, we have argued that today's predominant MT paradigm is largely incomprehensible to translators, and more surprisingly, to many experienced MT protagonists who are not statistically trained. This is largely an artefact, we claim, of how PB-SMT practitioners have chosen to present their work (cf. Hearne & Way, 2009a, for a somewhat more accessible description of SMT).

We showed that this was not always the case; when the original IBM research was presented, the language used was much more inclusive. However, as SMT became *the* principal way of doing MT, this conciliatory tone soon changed, to the point where today many people who *want* to understand have been left *so* far behind that they feel that it is impossible to ever catch up. We expressed the view that linguists and translators have to share the blame in allowing the field to move almost entirely in the statistical direction, especially when the seminal IBM papers very much left the door open for collaboration with the linguistic community.

However, in our view SMT researchers will soon have to alter their position, if the use of syntax (and later, once a further ceiling has been reached, semantics) *is* to become mainstream in today's models. These syntactic improvements have largely come about from those practitioners with a wider background than is the norm in SMT. Those without a linguistic background, then, appear to have two choices: (i) to attempt to include the linguists, so that they may be of help; or (ii) to continue to exclude linguists, while at the same time trying to make sense out of *their* writings.

We also discussed the overly important role nowadays of automatic evaluation metrics, to the exclusion of *actual* improvements in the translations output by our systems as measured by real users in real applications. The organisers of the WMT task, in particular, are to be applauded for maintaining human evaluation as the primary means by which translation quality is measured.

Finally, we have pointed out that there is much to be gained from consulting the research literature from the other MT paradigms. RBMT and EBMT practitioners have learnt much from SMT, and those communities will, we are certain, be very happy for SMT practitioners to learn from them also.

Acknowledgements

This work is partially funded by Science Foundation Ireland (http://www.sfi.ie) awards 05/IN/1732, 06/RF/CMS064 and 07/CE/I1142. Many thanks to Pierre Isabelle, Harold Somers and Walter Daelemans for providing their recollections regarding the early presentations of SMT, and to Makoto Nagao for his thoughts on the impact of EBMT on RBMT. We are especially grateful to Peter Brown for sharing with us the intentions of the IBM group when it came to clearly putting down their thoughts regarding the new paradigm, and for providing the first review of SMT for inclusion here. Finally, thanks to Mikel Forcada and Felipe Sánchez Martínez for comments on an earlier draft of this paper.

Bibliography

Arnold, D. & des Tombe, L. (1987). Basic theory and methodology in EUROTRA. In S. Nirenburg, (Ed.), *Machine translation: Theoretical and methodological issues* (pp. 114-135). Cambridge, UK: Cambridge University Press.

Banerjee, S. & Lavie, A. (2005). METEOR: An automatic metric for MT evaluation with improved correlation with human judgments. In Proceedings of the ACL 2005 Workshop on Intrinsic and Extrinsic Evaluation Measures for MT and/or Summarization (pp. 65-73); Ann Arbor, MI, USA..

Bangalore, S. & Joshi, A. (1999). Supertagging: An approach to almost parsing. *Computational Linguistics*, *25*(2), 237-265.

Bennett, W. & Slocum, J., (1985). The LRC machine translation system. *Computational Linguistics*, *11*, 111-121.

Brown, P., Cocke, J., Della Pietra, S., Della Pietra, V., Jelinek, F., Mercer, R., & Roossin, P. (1988). A statistical approach to French/English translation. In Second International Conference on Theoretical and Methodological Issues in Machine Translation of Natural Languages (TMI 1988) (pages not numbered); Pittsburgh, PA, USA.

Brown, P., Cocke, J., Della Pietra, S., Della Pietra, V., Jelinek, F., Mercer, R., & Roossin, P. (1988). A statistical approach to language translation. In Proceedings of the 12th International Conference on Computational Linguistics (Vol.1, pp. 71-76); Budapest, Hungary, August 22-27, 1988. Budapest: John von Neumann Society for Computing Sciences.

Brown, P., Cocke, J., Della Pietra, S., Della Pietra, V., Jelinek, F., Lafferty, J., Mercer, R., & Roossin, P. (1990). A statistical approach to Machine Translation. *Computational Linguistics*, *16*(2), 79-85.

Brown, P., Della Pietra, S., Della Pietra, V., Lafferty, J., & Mercer, R. (1992). Analysis, statistical transfer, and synthesis in Machine Translation. In Expanding MT Horizons: Proceedings of the Second Conference of the Association for Machine Translation in the Americas (pp. 83-10); Montreal, QC, Canada.

Brown, P., Della Pietra, S., Della Pietra, V., & Mercer, R. (1993). The mathematics of statistical machine translation: Parameter estimation. *Computational Linguistics*, *19*(2), 263-311.

Brown, R. (1999). Adding linguistic knowledge to a lexical example-based translation system. In Proceedings of the 8th International Conference on Theoretical and Methodological Issues in Machine Translation (pp. 22-32); Chester, England.

Callison-Burch, C., Fordyce, C., Koehn, P., Monz, C., & Schroeder, J.. (2007). (Meta-)evaluation of machine translation. In Proceedings of the Second Workshop on Statistical Machine Translation (pp. 136-158); Prague, Czech Republic.

Callison-Burch, C., Fordyce, C., Koehn, P., Monz, C., & Schroeder, J. (2008). Further (meta-)evaluation of Machine Translation (pp. 70-106). In Proceedings of the Third Workshop on Statistical Machine Translation; Columbus, OH, USA.

Callison-Burch, C., Koehn, P., Monz, C., & Schroeder, J. (2009). Findings of the 2009 workshop on statistical Machine Translation. In Proceedings of the Fourth Workshop on Statistical Machine Translation (pp. 1-28); Athens, Greece.

Callison-Burch, C., Osborne, M., & Koehn, P. (2006). Re-evaluating the role of BLEU in Machine Translation research. In EACL-2006, 11th Conference of the European Association of Computational Linguistics, Proceedings of the Conference (pp. 249-256); Trento, Italy.

Carbonell, J., Mitamura, T., & Nyberg, E., 3rd (1992). The KANT perspective: A critique of pure transfer (and pure interlingua, pure statistics,...). In 4th International Conference on Theoretical and Methodological Issues in Machine Translation (pp. 225-235); Montreal, QC, Canada.

Chang, P-C. & Toutanova K,. (2007). A discriminative syntactic word order model for machine translation. In Proceedings of the 45th Annual Meeting of the Association of Computational Linguistics (pp. 9-16); Prague, Czech Republic.

Chiang, D. (2005). A hierarchical phrase-based model for statistical machine translation (pp. 263-270). In 43rd Annual Meeting of the Association for Computational Linguistics; Ann Arbor, MI, USA.

Cicekli, I. & Güvenir, A.. (2003). Learning translation templates from bilingual translation examples. In M. Carl & A. Way (Eds.), *Recent advances in example-based machine translation* (pp. 255-286). Dordrecht, The Netherlands: Kluwer Academic Publishers.

Clark, S. & Curran, J. (2004). The importance of supertagging for wide-coverage CCG parsing. In Proceedings of the 20th International Conference on Computational Linguistics (COLING'04) (pp. 282-288); Geneva, Switzerland.

Doddington, G. (2002). Automatic evaluation of MT auality using n-gram co-occurrence statistics. In Proceedings of Human Language Technology Conference 2002 (pp. 138-145); San Diego, CA, USA.

Dorr, B., Pearl, L., Hwa, R., & Habash, N. (2002). DUSTer: A method for unravelling cross-language divergences for statistical word-level alignment. In Proceedings of the 5th Conference of the Association for Machine Translation in the Americas (AMTA-02) (pp. 31-43); Berlin/Heidelberg: Springer-Verlag.

Fordyce, C. (2007). Overview of the IWSLT07 evaluation campaign. In Proceedings of the International Workshop on Spoken Language Translation (pp. 1-12); Trento, Italy.

Galley, M., Graehl, J., Knight, K., Marcu D., DeNeefe, S., Wang, W.,& Thayer, I. (2006). Scalable inference and training of context-rich syntactic models. In Proceedings of the 21st International Conference on Computational Linguistics and 44th Annual Meeting of the Association for Computational Linguistics (pp. 961-968); Sydney, Australia.

Habash, N., B. Dorr & C. Monz. 2009. Symbolic-to-statistical hybridization: extending generation-heavy machine translation. Machine Translation 22(4) (in press).

Hassan, H., Ma, Y., & Way, A. (2007). MaTrEx: The DCU machine translation system for IWSLT 2007. In Proceedings of the International Workshop on Spoken Language Translation (pp. 69-75); Trento, Italy.

Hassan, H., Sima'an, K. & Way, A. (2009). Syntactically lexicalized phrase-based SMT. *IEEE Transactions on Audio, Speech and Language Processing, 16* (7), 1260-1273.

He, Y. & Way, A. (2009). Improving the objective function in minimum error rate training. In Proceedings of the Twelfth Machine Translation Summit (pp. 238-245); Ottawa, Canada.

Hearne, M. (2005). *Data-oriented models of parsing and translation.* Ph.D. thesis, Dublin City University, Dublin, Ireland.

Hearne, M., Tinsley, J., Zhechev, V., & Way. A. (2007). Capturing translational divergences with a statistical tree-to-tree aligner. In Proceedings of the 11th International Conference on Theoretical and Methodological Issues in Machine Translation (TMI 2007) (pp. 85-94); Skövde, Sweden.

Hearne, M. & Way, A. (2006). Disambiguation strategies for data-oriented translation. In Proceedings of the 11th Annual Conference of the European Association for Machine Translation (pp. 59-68); Oslo, Norway.

Hearne, M. & Way, A. (2009). Statistical machine translation: A guide for linguists and translators. COMPASS (in press).

Hearne, M. & Way, A. (2009). On the role of translations in state-of-the-art statistical machine translation. COMPASS (in press).

Hutchins, W. (1986). Machine Translation: past, present, future. Chichester, UK: Ellis Horwood. http://www.hutchinsweb.me.uk/PPF-2.pdf

Koehn, P. (2004). Pharaoh: A beam search decoder for phrase-based statistical machine translation models. In *Machine translation: From real users to research.* Proceedings of the 6th Conference of the Association for Machine Translation in the Americas (pp. 115-124). AMTA 2004, LNAI 3265. Berlin/Heidelberg: Springer-Verlag.

Koehn, P. (2005). Europarl: A parallel corpus for statistical machine translation. In Proceedings of Machine Translation Summit X (pp. 79-86); Phuket, Thailand.

Koehn, P. et al. (2007). Moses: Open source toolkit for statistical machine translation. In Proceedings of the ACL 2007 Demo and Poster Session (pp. 177-180); Prague, Czech Republic.

Koehn, P., Och, F., & Marcu, D. (2003). Statistical Phrase-Based Translation. In Proceedings of the Joint Human Language Technology Conference and the Annual Meeting of the North American Chapter of the Association for Computational Linguistics (HLT-NAACL) (pp. 127-133); Edmonton, AB, Canada.

Lehrberger, J. & Bourbeau, L. (1988). Machine Translation: Linguistic characteristics of MT systems and general methodology of evaluation. Amsterdam: John Benjamins.

Levenshtein, V. (1966). Binary codes capable of correcting deletions, insertions, and reversals. *Soviet Physics Doklady, 10*, 707-710.

Liu, D. & Gildea, D. (2005). Syntactic features for evaluation of machine translation. In Proceedings of the ACL 2005 Workshop on Intrinsic and Extrinsic Evaluation Measures for Machine Translation and/or Summarization (pp. 25-32); Ann Arbor, MI, USA.

Lopez, A. (2008). Tera-scale translation models via pattern matching. In Proceedings of the 22nd International Conference on Computational Linguistics (Coling 2008) (pp. 505-512); Manchester, UK.

Marcu, D., Wang, W., Echihabi, A., & Knight, K. (2006). SPMT: Statistical machine translation with syntactified target language phrases. In Proceedings of the 2006 Conference on Empirical Methods in Natural Language Processing (EMNLP 2006) (pp. 44-52); Sydney, Australia.

Marcu, D. & Wong, W. (2002). A phrase-based, joint probability model for statistical machine translation. In Proceedings of the Conference on Empirical Methods in Natural Language Processing (EMNLP-02) (pp. 133-139); Philadelphia, PA, USA.

Maruyama, H. & Watanabe, H. (1992). Tree cover search algorithm for example-based translation. In Proceedings of the Fourth International Conference on Theoretical and Methodological Issues in Machine Translation: Empiricist vs. Rationalist Methods in MT, TMI-92 (pp. 173-184); Montréal, QC, Canada.

Melby, A. (1995). The possibility of language: A discussion of the nature of language, with implications for human and machine translation. Amsterdam: John Benjamins.
Menezes, A. & Richardson, S. (2003). A best-first alignment algorithm for automatic extraction of transfer mappings from bilingual corpora. In M. Carl & A. Way (Eds.), *Recent advances in example-based machine translation* (pp. 421-442). Dordrecht: Kluwer Academic Publishers.
Nagao, M. (1984). A framework of a mechanical translation between Japanese and English by analogy principle. In A. Elithorn & R. Banerji (Eds.), *Artificial and human intelligence* (pp. 173-180. Amsterdam: North-Holland.
Nirenburg, S., Domashnev, C. & Grannes, D. (1993). Two approaches to matching in example-based machine translation. In Proceedings of the Fifth International Conference on Theoretical and Methodological Issues in Machine Translation TMI '93: MT in the Next Generation (pp. 47-57); Kyoto, Japan.
Och, F. (2003). Minimum error rate training in statistical machine translation. In Proceedings of the 41st Annual Meeting of the Association for Computational Linguistics (pp. 160-167); Sapporo, Japan.
Och, F. & Ney, H. (2002). Discriminative training and maximum entropy models for statistical machine translation. In Proceedings of the 40th Annual Meeting of the Association for Computational Linguistics (pp. 295-302); Philadelphia, PA, USA.
Och, F. & Ney, H. (2003). A systematic comparison of various statistical alignment models. *Computational Linguistics*, *29*(1), 19-51.
Och, F. & Ney, H. (2004). The alignment template approach to statistical machine translation. *Computational Linguistics*, *30*(4), 417-449.
Owczarzak, K., van Genabith J., & Way, A. (2008). Evaluating machine translation with LFG dependencies. *Machine Translation*, *21*(2), 95-119.
Ozdowska, S. & Way, A. (2009). Optimal bilingual data for French-English PB-SMT. In Proceedings of EAMT-09, the 13th Annual Meeting of the European Association for Machine Translation (pp. 96-103); Barcelona, Spain.
Papineni, K., Roukos, S., Ward, T., & Zhu, W-J. (2002). BLEU: A method for automatic evaluation of machine translation. In Proceedings of the 40th Annual Meeting of the Association for Computational Linguistics (ACL-02) (pp. 311-318); Philadelphia, PA, USA.
Paul, M. (2006). Overview of the IWSLT 2006 evaluation campaign. In Proceedings of the International Workshop on Spoken Language Translation (pp. 1-15); Kyoto, Japan.
Paul, M. (2008). Overview of the IWSLT 2008 evaluation campaign. In Proceedings of the International Workshop on Spoken Language Translation (pp. 1-17); Honolulu, HI, USA.
Rosetta, M. (1994). Compositional translation. Dordrecht: Kluwer Academic Publishers.
Sánchez Martínez, F. (2008). *Using unsupervised corpus-based methods to build rule-based machine translation systems*. Ph.D thesis, Universitat d'Alacant, Alacant, Spain.
Shannon, C., & Weaver, W. (1949). The mathematical theory of communication. Urbana, IL: University of Illinois Press.
Somers, H. (2003). Introduction to Part III: System Design. In S. Nirenburg, H. Somers & Y. Wilks (Eds.), *Readings in machine translation* (pp. 321-324). Cambridge, MA: The MIT Press.
Steedman, M. (2000). The syntactic process. Cambridge, MA: The MIT Press.
Stolcke, A. (2002). SRILM - An extensible language modeling toolkit. In Proceedings of the 7th International Conference on Spoken Language Processing (pp. 901-904); Denver, CO.
Sumita, E., & Iida, H. (1991). Experiments and prospects of example-based machine translation. In Proceedings of the 29th Annual Meeting of the Association for Computational Linguistics (ACL-91), (pp. 185-192); Berkeley, CA, USA.
Sumita, E., & Tsutsumi, Y. (1988). A translation aid system using flexible text retrieval based on syntax-matching. In Second International Conference on Theoretical and Methodological Issues in Machine Translation of Natural Languages (TMI 1988), Proceedings Supplement, (pages not numbered); Pittsburgh, PA, USA.
ten Hacken, P. (2001). Has there been a revolution in machine translation? *Machine Translation* *16*(1), 1-19.
Turian, J., Shen, L., & Melamed, D. (2003). Evaluation of machine translation and its evaluation. In Proceedings of Machine Translation Summit IX (pp. 386-393); New Orleans, LA, USA.
Vauquois, B. (1968). A survey of formal grammars and algorithms for recognition and transformation in machine translation. In IFIP Congress-68 (pp. 254-260); Edinburgh. Reprinted in C. Boitet (Ed.), *Bernard Vauquois et la TAO: Vingtcinq ans de traduction automatique – analectes* (pp. 201-213) (1988). Grenoble: Association Champollion.

Wahlster, W. (Ed.). (2000). Verbmobil: Foundations of speech-to-speech translation. Berlin: Springer-Verlag.

Watanabe, H. (1992). A similarity-driven transfer System. In Proceedings of the fifteenth (sic) International Conference on Computational Linguistics, COLING-92 (pp. 770-776); Nantes, France.

Way, A. (2003). Machine translation using LFG-DOP. In R. Bod, R. Scha & K. Sima'an (Eds.), *Data-Oriented Parsing* (pp. 359-384). Stanford, CA: Center for the Study of Language and Information.

Way, A. (2009.) Panning for EBMT gold, or "Remembering not to forget": The DCU Experience. *Machine Translation* (in press).

Way, A., & Gough, N. (2003). wEBMT: Developing and validating an EBMT system using the World Wide Web. *Computational Linguistics 29*(3), 421-457.

Zhao, B., & Al-Onaizan, Y. (2008). Generalizing local and non-local word-reordering patterns for syntax-based machine translation. In Proceedings of EMNLP 2008, Conference on Empirical Methods in Natural Language Processing, (pp. 572-581); Waikiki, HI, USA.

Zollmann, A., & Venugopal, A.. (2006). Syntax-augmented machine translation via chart parsing. In Proceedings of the Workshop on Statistical Machine Translation, HLT-NAACL (pp. 138-141); New York, NY, USA.

Zollmann, A., Venugopal, A., Och, F., & Ponte, J. (2008). A systematic comparison of phrase-based, hierarchical and syntax-augmented statistical MT. In Proceedings of the 22nd International Conference on Computational Linguistics (Coling 2008) (pp. 1145-1152); Manchester, UK.

---

[1] Although Nagao's paper dates from 1984, its contents were delivered in a presentation in 1981.

[2] Notable exceptions are Philipp Koehn and Kevin Knight, who have given many lucid tutorials on SMT at various conferences.

[3] This paper was followed ten weeks later by (Brown et al., 1988b). Note that (ten Hacken, 2001) incorrectly observes that (Brown et al., 1988b) was "probably the first presentation of the groundbreaking IBM project". Apart from the slightly different titles (cf. also the similarity of the title in (Brown et al., 1990)), the content of the papers barely differs. One (probably!) wouldn't get away with this nowadays.

[4] However, a portent of what was to come is the observation that "preliminary experiments... indicate that only a very crude grammar may be needed". See section 2.3 for more on this topic.

[5] If one consults (Hutchins, 1986), as the reviewer invites us to do, one notes, for example, that "Weaver's own favoured approach, the application of cryptanalytic techniques, was immediately recognised as mistaken" (section 2.4.1). However, Weaver also expounded the virtues of "the probabilistic foundations of communication theory" (as (Hutchins, 1986) puts it), so while it was right to say that the cryptanalytic approach was mistaken, it was far from correct to say that the ideas of (Shannon & Weaver, 1949) had no potential for application in MT.

[6] Interestingly, this is perhaps more true nowadays than it was 20 years ago! See section 4 for more discussion. Note that as has been made plain here, the dichotomy used by (ten Hacken, 2001) to explain the various approaches was not one shared by the IBM team. Rather, in their view, linguistic insight would be necessary once the model had been given an adequate mathematical description.

[7] This is confirmed by Peter Brown, who informed us that "Jelinek is famous for that statement and made it many times but with regard to speech recognition not translation." See http://en.wikiquote.org/wiki/Fred\Jelinek, where one particular source is given as a Workshop on Evaluation of NLP Systems, Wayne, PA, USA, December, 1988. Note that (ten Hacken, 2001) erroneously attributes this quote to Peter Brown (p.10).

[8] As a brief aside, around 1996 the IBM SMT team broke up, and went to work for Renaissance Technologies applying their statistical models to predict stock market fluctuations. Fortunately, around the same time, Hermann Ney took on four PhD students in Aachen—Franz Och, Stephan Vogel, Cristoph Tillmann, and Sonja Nießen—and Alex Waibel also took on YeYi Wang as an SMT student in Karlsruhe/CMU, both as a result of their participation in the Verbmobil project (Wahlster, 2000). It is interesting to speculate about what would have happened to SMT if this fresh (and clearly significant) input had not come onstream at that time; it is possible that SMT would have disappeared from view, for a while at least.

[9] Furthermore, while the latter point regarding the void between the statistical and linguistic camps is largely true even today, we address it in more detail in section 4.

[10] As stated, most developers of PB-SMT systems, including this author, refer to the model in equation (2) somewhat loosely as the 'log-linear' model. This is, of course, not entirely accurate; rather, it is a method whereby linear combinations of logarithms of probabilities may be combined. Of course, when things like word and phrase penalties are used as feature functions, one can quickly see that not even this is strictly true.

[11] National Institute of Standards and Technology: http://www.nist.gov/speech/tests/mt/

[12] Workshop on Statistical Machine Translation. For the 2009 edition see http://www.statmt.org/wmt09/.

[13] International Workshop on Spoken Language Translation. For the 2008 edition see http://www.slc.atr.jp/IWSLT2008/.

[14] Without going into unnecessary detail, a supertag essentially describes lexical information such as the Part-of-Speech tag and subcategorisation information of a word.

[15] http://www.fjoch.com/GIZA++.html

[16] http://www.speech.sri.com/projects/srilm/

[17] http://www.statmt.org/moses/

[18] Philipp maintains a rich source of information on SMT at http://www.statmt.org.

[19] For a novel application, see (Sánchez Martínez, 2008) who uses PB-SMT alignment templates to bootstrap the acquisition of transfer rules in the open-source Apertium RBMT platform (http://www.apertium. org). If our comments in section 5 are accurate, given the title of this work, these interesting findings will remain largely undiscovered by the SMT community.

[20] For the uninitiated, many people have criticised the use of the term "phrase" to describe the basic units of translation in PB-SMT. We will not add to this here, but will merely note that the term as used in PB-SMT has a quite different meaning to that used in traditional linguistics.

[21] Note that in one particular corpus, (Dorr et al., 2002) report that 10.5% of Spanish sentences and 12.4% of Arabic sentences have at least one such translation divergence, while in another, divergences relative to English occurred in around one third of Spanish sentences. (Habash et al., 2009) observe that "there is often overlap among the divergence types... with the categorial divergence occurring almost every time that there is any other type of divergence".

The FEMTI guidelines for contextual MT evaluation: Principles and resources

Paula Estrella*
FaMAF, National University of Córdoba, Argentina

Andrei Popescu-Belis
Idiap Research Institute, Martigny, Switzerland

Maghi King
ISSCO/TIM/ETI, University of Geneva, Switzerland

A large number of evaluation metrics exist for machine translation (MT) systems, but depending on the intended context of use of such a system, not all metrics are equally relevant. Based on the ISO/IEC 9126 and 14598 standards for software evaluation, the Framework for the Evaluation of Machine Translation in ISLE (FEMTI) provides guidelines for the selection of quality characteristics to be evaluated depending on the expected task, users, and input characteristics of an MT system. This approach to contextual evaluation was implemented as a web-based application which helps its users design evaluation plans. In addition, FEMTI offers experts in evaluation the possibility to enter and share their knowledge using a dedicated web-based tool, tested in several evaluation exercises.

1. Introduction

A variety of approaches have been proposed for the evaluation of machine translation systems, and numerous metrics have been proposed as well. Researchers typically focus on output quality, which is generally the most important aspect of research-oriented systems. Output quality can be measured using human-based as well as automatic metrics designed to capture the quality of machine translation (MT). A system can also be assessed indirectly through its operational use, in a task-based evaluation approach. In either approach, MT systems can be compared against each other during an evaluation campaign. However, end-users of MT tend to include other factors in an evaluation, not only those related to output quality. The methodology that takes into account the intended context of use of a system when designing its evaluation has become known as *context-based evaluation*. This paper describes the application of this approach to the evaluation of MT systems, which has resulted in the Framework for the Evaluation of Machine Translation in ISLE (International Standards for Language Engineering), abbreviated FEMTI. This framework aims at standardizing the

MT evaluation process and provides support tools that help users define contextual evaluation plans. The goal of FEMTI is to organize the different characteristics of an MT system into a coherent taxonomy and to help evaluators select the right subset of characteristics to be assessed given the specific purpose of the evaluation and the factors related to the environment where the system will be deployed.

This paper is structured as follows: Section 2 gives an overview of the context-based evaluation paradigm; Section 3 introduces the quality model used by FEMTI, a notion inspired from ISO/IEC standards; Section 4 presents the different components that constitute the FEMTI framework, while Section 5 presents the activities that were carried out to disseminate the framework and collect feedback from experts. Finally, Section 6 presents conclusions and possible extensions of FEMTI.

2. Methods for the evaluation of MT systems

To measure the quality of an MT system by evaluating its output, automatic metrics, task-based ones, and the subjective rating of certain aspects of translation quality have all been used. Some practitioners have also taken into account the intended context of use of an MT system, in what is called *context-based evaluation*. One of the first initiatives considering other factors than simply MT output quality was a report by the Japan Electronic Industries Development Association (JEIDA), which advocated a framework for the evaluation of MT systems from a user's and developer's point of view (Nomura, 1992). Two sets of criteria were proposed: evaluators (users or developers) are required to answer one questionnaire about their present work situation and another one about their specific needs. After that, radar charts are created with the results of both questionnaires and finally, the evaluator chooses the type of system that appears to be the most suitable based on the overlap of the two radar charts.

The Evaluation Working Group of the EAGLES EU project (Expert Advisory Group on Language Engineering Standards) also adopted a user-oriented point of view on the evaluation of human language technology products. The general framework for evaluation proposed by this group was partly inspired by the ISO/IEC 9126 standard for the evaluation of software (ISO/IEC, 1991) which was used to relate potentially important attributes of a product to a class of users. The framework also covered the implied needs of users in what was called the *consumer report paradigm* (EAGLES Evaluation Working Group, 1996), where users identify the class of users that better represents their needs (among a predefined set of user classes) and select the characteristics of the product believed to be relevant for that class of users. Subsequent projects using the EAGLES framework have contributed to its validation and to testing its usefulness for evaluation design (Canelli, Grasso, & King, 2000; Rocca, Spampinato, Zarri, & Black, 1994; TEMAA, 1996).

Hovy (1999) proposed an intermediate solution between the JEIDA and EAGLES methodologies, consisting of a hierarchy or taxonomy of both user needs and quality characteristics of systems, originally called *user purpose* and *user process*, dealing with the reason for translation and the translation method, respectively. Each level of the hierarchy had a set of associated metrics and was decomposed into finer detail. Although this solution was formally very close to that of EAGLES or JEIDA, Hovy's work was more flexible, as it allowed the evaluator to decide the level of detail and other features to include in the evaluation – as opposed to the other solutions that had a fixed predefined set of features for user types and systems.

The continuation of EAGLES into the (ISLE) EU project focused on the evaluation of MT systems and on how to relate user needs to system quality characteristics. The ISLE Evaluation Working Group applied the ISO/IEC 9126 and 14598 standards to MT software and extended existing methodologies, building up the FEMTI framework (Hovy, King, & Popescu-Belis, 2002). After the ISLE project, work on FEMTI continued with the goal of converting these guidelines into a more interactive tool that would guide the evaluator through the generation of customized evaluation plans (Estrella, Popescu-Belis, & Underwood, 2005). The FEMTI framework is now a web-based application publicly available at http://www.issco.unige.ch/femti and will be presented in detail in Section 4.

3. ISO/IEC standards applied to context-based evaluation

The FEMTI framework took as a starting point the ISO/IEC 9126 (ISO/IEC, 2001) and ISO/IEC 14598 (ISO/IEC, 1999) standards, which are domain independent guidelines for the evaluation of software products and are, therefore, intended to be applicable to all kinds of software.

Quality characteristic	Quality sub-characteristics
Functionality	Suitability, Accuracy, Interoperability, Security, Functionality compliance
Reliability	Maturity, Fault tolerance, Recoverability, Reliability compliance
Usability	Understandability, Learnability, Operability, Attractiveness, Usability compliance
Efficiency	Time behavior, Resource utilization, Efficiency compliance
Maintainability	Analysability, Changeability, Stability, Testability, Maintainability compliance
Portability	Adaptability, Installability, Co-existence, Replaceability, Portability compliance

Figure 1. Generic quality model proposed by ISO/IEC 9126.

The 14598 series provides guidelines and examples to support different stakeholders during the evaluation process, while the 9126 series defines the components of a generic quality model. These series complement each other, since the specification of a quality model is part of the evaluation process and this process could be different, depending on the stakeholders involved (evaluators, developers, acquirers, etc).

In the ISO/IEC 9126 view, quality is defined as "the totality of characteristics of an entity that bear on its ability to satisfy stated and implied needs" (ISO/IEC, 2003a). The ISO/IEC quality model aims at representing the different aspects of a product that together will make its overall quality, resulting from the six top-level quality characteristics: *functionality*, *reliability*, *usability*, *efficiency*, *maintainability*, *portability*. These quality characteristics are decomposed as shown in Figure 1, and the attributes of the quality model (i.e. the terminal nodes in such a hierarchy) are measurable features of the software product. In all cases, metrics are required to measure these attributes and, therefore, a set of metrics should be associated to each attribute of a quality model. The ISO/IEC 9126 series offers specific parts devoted to external metrics (ISO/IEC, 2003a) and internal metrics (ISO/IEC, 2003b).

- 2.1 Functionality
  - 2.1.1 Accuracy
    - 2.1.1.1 Terminology
    - 2.1.1.2 Fidelity – precision
    - 2.1.1.3 Consistency
  - 2.1.2 Suitability
    - 2.1.2.1 Target-language suitability
      - 2.1.2.1.1 Readability
        - ⇒ Metric 1: Cloze Tests
        - ⇒ Metric 2: Subjective rating of intelligibility
        - ⇒ Metric 3: Reading time
      - 2.1.2.1.2 Comprehensibility
      - 2.1.2.1.3 Coherence
      - 2.1.2.1.4 Cohesion
    - 2.1.2.2 Cross-language - Contrastive suitability
    - 2.1.2.3 Translation process models
    - 2.1.2.4 Linguistic resources and utilities
  - 2.1.3 Well-formedness
    - 2.1.3.1 Morphology
    - 2.1.3.2 Punctuation errors
    - 2.1.3.3 Lexis - Lexical choice
    - 2.1.3.4 Grammar – Syntax
      - ⇒ Metric 1: Percentage of phenomena correctly treated
      - ⇒ Metric 2: List of error types

Figure 2. Partial decomposition of the *Functionality* quality characteristic in the FEMTI quality model for MT software. Metrics are exemplified for two quality attributes, *Readability* and *Grammar/syntax*.

If the generic model proposed in ISO/IEC 9126 is to be applied to software in a particular domain, it needs to be specialized through the definition of attributes and metrics which fit that particular domain. In FEMTI, the ISO/IEC generic quality model was tailored to the MT domain, maintaining its top-level structure and extending it with an additional top-level quality characteristic, namely *Cost*, and with sub-characteristics specific to MT systems. An example of instantiating the model for the MT domain is shown in Figure 2, which illustrates the resulting decomposition of *Functionality*. From the figure, it appears that some characteristics were added at the same level as the ISO/IEC ones (e.g. *Well-formedness*), while others were further decomposed (e.g. *Suitability* → *Target-language suitability* → *Readability*). This figure also shows the place of metrics in the quality model, for example under *2.1.2.1.1 Readability*, and *2.1.3.4 Grammar – syntax*. Numbering of the taxons was added to facilitate cross-referencing in all subsequent work using FEMTI. Besides offering a broader view of a system's overall quality, this ISO-inspired quality model for MT systems allows evaluators to integrate many other aspects of quality beyond the generic characteristic *output quality*, usually assessed with the popular *adequacy* and *fluency* metrics.

4. Making the FEMTI guidelines operational

The first version of the FEMTI framework was developed until 2003 with support from the ISLE EU project. This version focused on the integration of the existing quality and context characteristics for MT into classifications that organize them hierarchically. The main limitation of the initial interface that was designed to access FEMTI's content was that it demanded a significant effort from the users who wanted to build an entire evaluation plan using it: they had to manually construct the plan by keeping track of their selection (context and quality characteristics plus metrics) while navigating back-and-forth the hierarchies. Another limitation was that its web pages had to be re-generated each time a change was made to the contents of FEMTI, due to its implementation as a set of separate, static web pages. Therefore, the goal of the new version of FEMTI was to increase its usability by creating a set of complementary tools that help users browse the framework when creating quality models and to reduce the maintenance needed by using a dynamic document server for the implementation.

This section outlines the support tools developed as part of FEMTI; Section 4.1 describes the tool for evaluators, then Section 4.2 describes the mechanism in FEMTI that implements the context-based approach to evaluation and Section 4.3 describes the mechanism that allows knowledge from the MT community, to be entered into FEMTI.

4.1. Generating customized evaluation plans

The target audience of FEMTI is the evaluators (end-users, developers, acquirers, etc.) who want to specify an evaluation plan for one or more MT systems intended to be used in a particular environment. This can be achieved using the *evaluators' interface* of FEMTI, which contains the following parts:

- A classification of possible contexts of use (*Part I*): a hierarchy of features describing the intended environment of use for the MT system.
- A classification of quality characteristics (*Part II*): a hierarchy of desirable system characteristics, whose top level nodes match the generic quality model proposed by the ISO/IEC 9126-1 standard, and a set of metrics associated to most quality characteristics.
- A *context-to-quality relation*: an automatic mechanism that retrieves the relevant quality characteristics according to the specified context of use.

Figure 3 shows the workflow that evaluators must follow in order to generate a quality model using FEMTI. Evaluators start by defining the intended environment of use of the MT system by selecting characteristics related to the *translation task* to be performed by the system, the *author* and *text* characteristics and the *type of user* of the system (as well as a preliminary reflection on the *purpose* of the evaluation). When this is done, evaluators work with Part II, where they select the quality characteristics and metrics of interest, starting with a blueprint that is automatically suggested by FEMTI based on the selected environment of use.

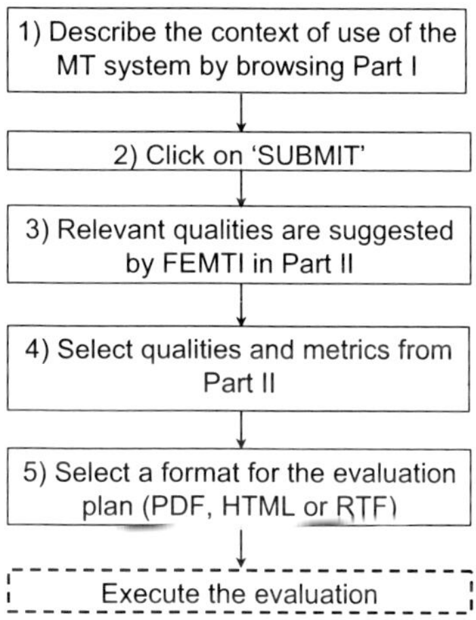

Figure 3. Workflow for the evaluators' interface of FEMTI.

Quality characteristics can be aspects directly related to translation quality (such as adequacy, readability, style, etc) or related to the desired features of the MT system (such as file formats handled, portability to different operating systems, user-friendliness of the interfaces, etc). Consequently, the metrics used to measure the selected quality characteristics include human-based or automatic metrics for translation quality, such as, for adequacy, the rating of sentences on a 5-point scale by humans (White & O'-Connell, 1994), or the BLEU metric for fluency (Papineni, Roukos, Ward & Zhu, 2001). Checklists could be used to measure other features, for instance to make a list of the operating systems, languages and formats supported.

The result of using FEMTI is a document containing the context and quality characteristics chosen by the user plus the metrics. The set of items contained in this report is thus called a *customized quality model.* Users indicate to the FEMTI interface the actual format in which the document can be saved, currently HTML, RTF or PDF.

The execution of the evaluation requires further steps that are outside the scope of FEMTI and focus on the practical details of the evaluation, for example, to prepare the necessary test material, to state acceptance levels for each metric, to interpret the results the result of applying the metrics and so on. Therefore, the report generated with FEMTI serves as a basis during the preparation and execution of an evaluation, for example, to choose a the test set representative of the text domain and genre specified with characteristics from Part I or to gather relevant toolkits to apply the metrics selected in Part II.

4.1.1. Using the evaluators' interface

The following screen captures illustrate the use of the evaluators' interface. Figure 4 shows the initial state of the tool, where Part I is displayed on the left frame of the screen and Part II is displayed on the right frame. The labels for each characteristic in Part I and II are hyperlinked to the relevant content, which is displayed in a separate window when clicked on.

In the first example displayed here, suppose that an evaluator has to buy an MT system in order to monitor a large volume of texts produced outside the evaluator's organization. Initially, the evaluator defines a context of use by selecting a type of evaluation, in this case *Operational evaluation* (node 1.1.4) is suitable as he wants to address the question of whether the MT system he will buy will actually serve its purpose; he further specifies the context selecting the type of task the system is supposed to perform (*Assimilation* (node 1.2.1)) and the type of users of the system (*Machine translation user* (node 1.4.1)). These steps of the workflow are illustrated in Figure 5.

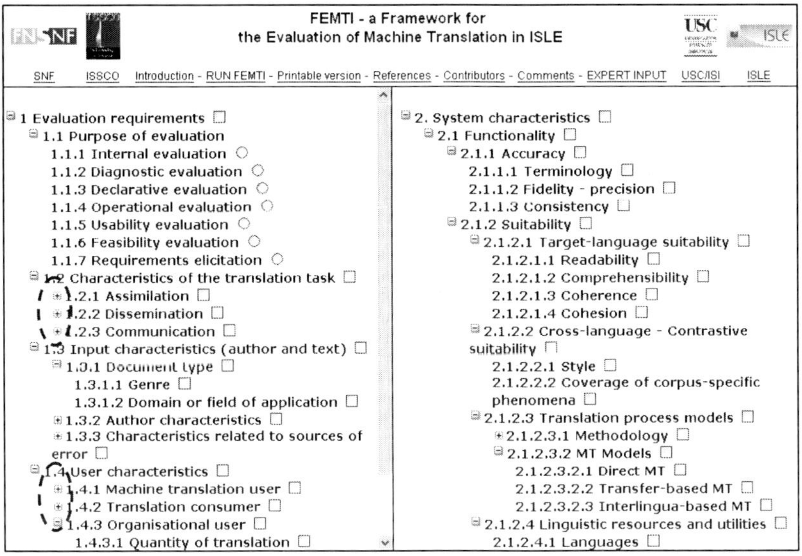

Figure 4. Home page for the evaluators' interface; classifications can be expanded or collapsed using the +/– buttons exemplified with dashed circles.

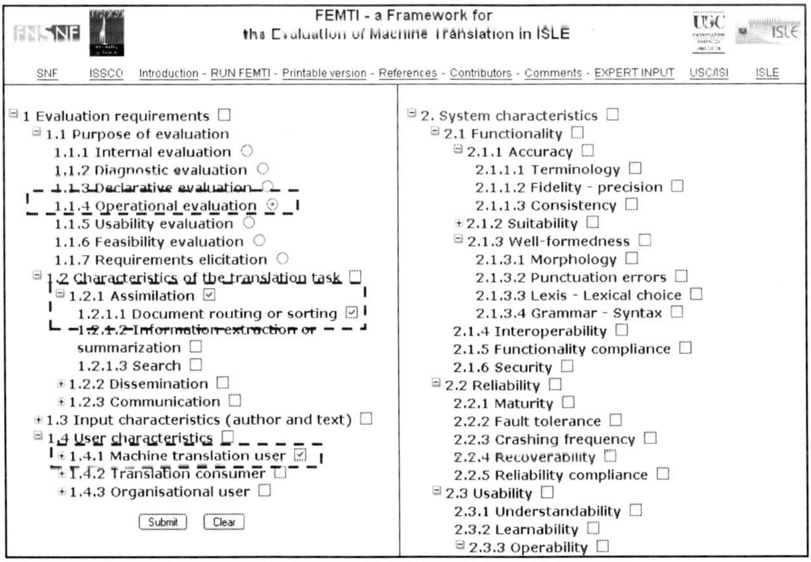

Figure 5. Part I: sample definition of the context of use for an MT system intended to monitor a large volume of texts.

The linking mechanism that implements the context-to-quality relation is activated when the evaluator confirms his selection from Part I by pressing the 'Submit' button at the bottom of the left frame. The result of its operation (fully transparent to the evaluator) is shown in Figure 6: the quality characteristics relevant to the context defined previously are highlighted in Part II, so that the evaluator selects one or more quality characteristics and metrics.

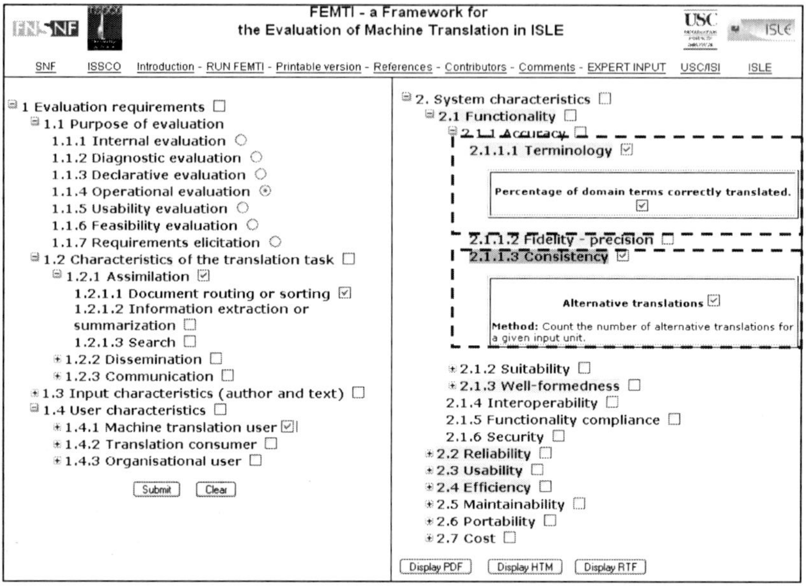

Figure 6. Part II: sample selection of quality characteristics and metrics for an MT system intended to monitor a large volume of texts.

Evaluation type

- Operational evaluation:
Operational evaluations generally address the question of whether an MT system will actually serve its purpose in the context of its operational use. The primary factors include the cost-benefit of bringing the system into the overall process (costs).

Context Characteristics

- Machine translation user:
This refers to the person who interacts with the machine translation system and with the output produced by it.
- Operational evaluation:
Operational evaluations generally address the question of whether an MT system will actually serve its purpose in the context of its operational use. The primary factors include the cost-benefit of bringing the system into the overall process (costs).
- Assimilation:
The ultimate purpose of the assimilation task (of which translation forms a part) is to monitor a (relatively) large volume of texts produced by people outside the organization, in (usually) several languages.
- Characteristics of the translation task:
Characteristics of the translation task refers to the information flow intended for the output, from the point of view of the agent (human or otherwise) who receives the translation.

Additional Quality Characteristics (not suggested by FEMTI)

- Consistency:
Capability of the system to produce from a given input, and at a given point in time, the same output
Metrics:
- *Alternative translations*
- Method: Count the number of alternative translations for a given input unit.

- Terminology:
Correct translation of technical (domain-specific) terms.

Figure 7. Excerpt of evaluation plan generated with FEMTI.

Corresponding to step 4 of the workflow, Figure 6 shows the state of the interface when the evaluator selects one quality characteristic proposed by the linking mechanism (node 2.1.1.1 *Terminology*) and one additional characteristic (node 2.1.1.3 *Consistency*), along with the metric available under each characteristic. Regardless of the automatic result of relating a particular context to a set of quality characteristics, evaluators are free to add or remove any other quality (sub-)characteristics and metrics.

When the selection of the quality characteristics and metrics is complete, the evaluator saves the plan by clicking on 'Display', as illustrated in Figure 7. This document displays the selected context characteristics first, followed by the quality characteristics separated in two sections: a section for the characteristics *suggested by FEMTI* (i.e. resulting from the operations performed by the linking mechanism), which are ranked according to their importance assigned by the linking mechanism, and a section for characteristics *not suggested by FEMTI*, ordered by their index number in Part II.

In this example, the evaluator could have selected other quality characteristics related to the portability of the system (e.g. node 2.6.2 *Installability*), to the efficiency of the system if there is a large volume of texts to translate (e.g. node 2.4.1.3 *Input to Output Translation Speed*) and related to the cost (node 2.7) given that he is supposed to buy an MT system. However, in a different context, some of these aspects might be less important.

Suppose now that the same person must evaluate an MT system that is already available in his organization, and is used daily to translate manuals of a product to be sent to potential customers. In this case, the context of use could be minimally described with the following items from Part I: *Usability evaluation* (node 1.1.5), *External dissemination* (node 1.2.2.2), *Advanced proficiency in source language* (node 1.3.2.1.3 about the author's characteristics) and *Computer literate* (node 1.4.1.4 about the person interacting with the MT system). Given that the chosen task demands high quality translations, many of the characteristics from Part II that are chosen by the evaluator will be related to this aspect of the system, for example *Fidelity* (node 2.1.1.2), *Consistency* (node 2.1.1.3), *Readability* (node 2.1.2.1.1) and *Punctuation errors* (node 2.1.3.2). Other quality characteristics could be related to general features of the system, for example to the language pairs handled (*Languages*, node 2.1.2.4.1) and the *Reliability* of the system (node 2.2), which should have a high tolerance to faults so that it is online most of the time.

It can be noted from these examples that the quality models generated in each case are quite different even if they are created by the same evaluator and for the same organization. To summarize the examples discussed in this section, Table 1 compares the contexts of use and quality models corresponding to the two previous examples. As these examples suggest, the most original aspect of FEMTI's new version is the linking mechanism from Part I to Part II storing knowledge about MT evaluation, which is used to formalize the context-to-quality relation and which is explained in more detail in the next section.

Table 1: Sample quality models created with FEMTI for two different contexts of use

Context of use	Example 1	Example 2
Evaluation type	Operational	Usability
Translation task	Assimilation	Dissemination
MT user	Computer literate	Computer literate
Author's linguistic proficiency	Advanced in SL	Advanced in SL and TL
Quality model	**Example 1**	**Example 2**
Quality characteristics	Consistency Terminology Installability Translation speed Cost	Fidelity Consistency Readability Punctuation errors Reliability Languages

4.2. Relating context to quality characteristics

In order to convert FEMTI into a context-based evaluation tool, it is necessary to account for the influence of the context of use on the desired features of the system. Once this relation is identified, it is possible to link each context characteristic to a set of quality characteristics indicating the importance of the connection as weighted links. In FEMTI this relation is now implemented through a core structure called a *Generic Contextual Quality Model* (GCQM), which embodies the knowledge necessary to create customized quality models.

In the GCQM an item in Part I is related to a given item in Part II only if the weight connecting them is not null; in this case, the weight indicates the strength of this connection. The weights on the links to the same quality characteristic are added during the operation of the linking mechanism (step 3 of the workflow shown in Figure 3, so that the higher the number of context characteristics related to one quality characteristic, the higher that quality characteristic's final weight in the resulting quality model. Intuitively, this means that quality characteristics with higher weights are more important with respect to other characteristics in the model. This result of the linking mechanism is used when the quality model is generated (step 5 of the workflow shown in Figure 3 and serves to rank the quality characteristics by decreasing order of importance: the most important ones according to this mechanism appear first. These weights are included in the resulting quality model, in case evaluators are willing to use them, for example, to compute final scores.

Assuming a quality model for a given domain is a hierarchy of characteristics, sub-characteristics and attributes, as in the case of ISO-based models, it can be flattened (e.g. by traversing it depth-first or breadth-first) to be transformed into a list of items (or equivalently into vectors), which are needed to interact with the GCQM. Once a hierarchy is flattened, its *vector representation* is straightforward: each node becomes a component of the vector. Thus, FEMTI's linking mechanism is general enough to be ported to any other domain where a taxonomy of contexts of use and a taxonomy of quality characteristics exist: the hierarchies are flattened as vectors and the corresponding GCQM is a table, where the rows represent context features and columns represent quality features.

The procedure proposed here to suggest to evaluators a list of relevant quality characteristics starts by converting Part I into a *context vector*, where non-zero components indicate the context characteristics selected by the evaluator. Then, the matrix product of this vector with the GCQM is computed, 'filtering' thus only the relevant quality characteristics, and resulting in a customized *quality vector*, i.e. a set of quality characteristics. This procedure to create quality vectors captures the contribution of every component of the context vector to each component of the quality vector. Therefore, the higher the number of non-zero terms in the computation of a quality vector's component the higher its importance in the specific quality model. Conversely, the higher the number of zero terms, the lower the importance of the component.

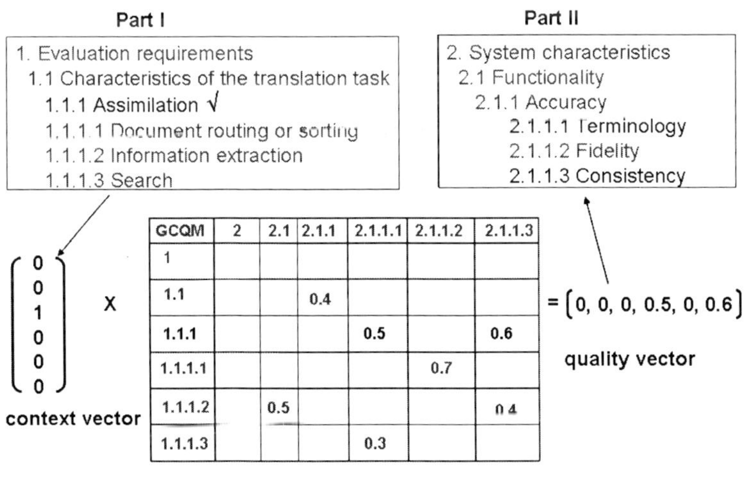

Figure 8. Illustration of the algorithm to obtain a customized quality model (represented as a vector) from a context vector.

The use of the GCQM by the linking mechanism is illustrated in Figure 8. Parts I and II were simplified to consist only of the characteristics depicted in the figure and the relation between them is represented with the weights in the GCQM of the same figure. In this example, the user has selected

Assimilation as the translation task, and the result of filtering the GCQM with that particular context vector is a quality vector with two non-zero components corresponding to *Terminology* and *Consistency*. In practice, when using the evaluators' interface, this would result in *Terminology* and *Consistency* being highlighted in Part II and included in the final evaluation plan if the user selects them.

4.3. Input of expertise into FEMTI's GCQM

A major challenge of the model proposed here to relate context and quality characteristics is to fill in the values of the GCQM. FEMTI's GCQM was initially filled in with the information that was already present in the previous version – more specifically in the section on *Relevant qualities from Part II* in some of the descriptions of context characteristics – but many links are still missing. Additionally, to validate the links created, the GCQM should be populated by several experts. This implies that experts willing to create links for FEMTI, would have to work on a GCQM whose size is currently around 100 by 100, which is particularly unpractical. Therefore, to collect feedback from the MT community, a support tool called the *experts' interface* was developed as part of the FEMTI framework, aiming at simplifying this task.

The goal of the experts' interface is to help experts create and populate as many individual GCQMs as needed, which could be merged to create one 'averaged GCQM' representing the consensus of experts about the relation between Parts I and II of FEMTI. Such an averaged GCQM can be used by the linking mechanism, thus contributing to improve the evaluators' interface as well, by increasing the number of relevant quality characteristics that are suggested automatically.

To construct a GCQM for a given domain, in this case MT, experts proceed as shown in Figure 9. Once logged in, experts select one context characteristic from which the links to quality characteristics will be created (step 1) and make this selection effective by pressing a 'Select' button (step 2). Then experts browse Part II to find the quality characteristics that, according to their experience and knowledge of the domain, are relevant to the selected context characteristic (step 3). The links are created by selecting one or more quality characteristics with a weight and saving them to one's own GCQM (step 4). After one cycle of work, experts can log out (step 5) or continue working on a different context characteristic (step 6).

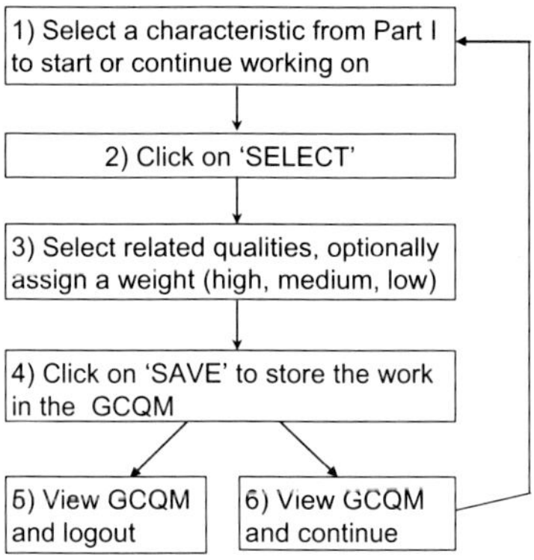

Figure 9. Workflow for the experts' interface of FEMTI.

The use of this tool will be explained using the first example discussed in Section 4.1.1. In order for an evaluator selecting *Assimilation* to get suggestions for the quality characteristics *Terminology* and *Consistency* as above, an expert must have created those relations first. In that case, the expert proceeds as follows: after accessing the framework, he selects the context characteristic *Assimilation* to work on, as shown in Figure 10.

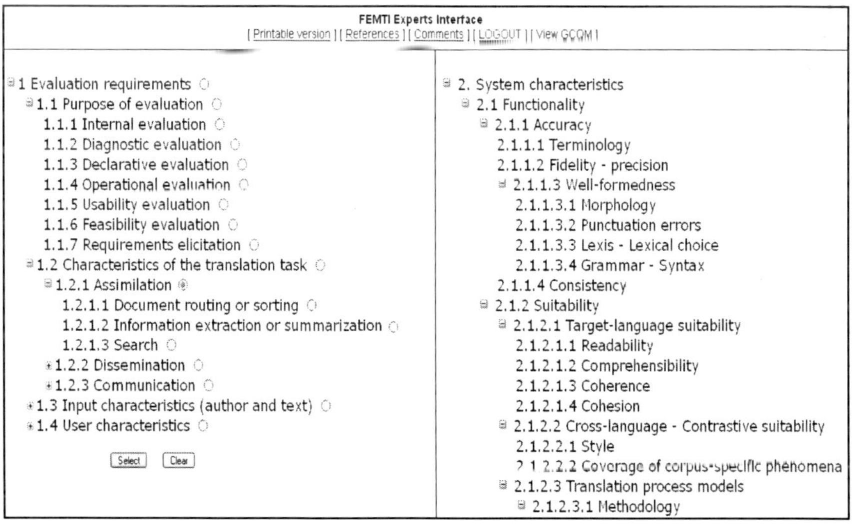

Figure 10. Example of using the experts' interface, where an expert will create links from the context characteristic *Assimilation*.

At this point Part II is expanded with a set of labels that indicate the possible weights for the links to be created, coded for the time being as *high*, *medium*, *low* and *n/a*, the latter indicating that the link exists but the weight is unspecified (numbers are avoided as they would make this task overly complex). Figure 11 shows that the expert has selected two quality characteristics that will be important to the translation task *Assimilation*; in this case, the expert chooses to assign different weights to these characteristics, namely *medium* for *Terminology* and *low* for *Consistency*. Figure 12 shows the result of the expert saving the work and viewing the resulting GCQM.

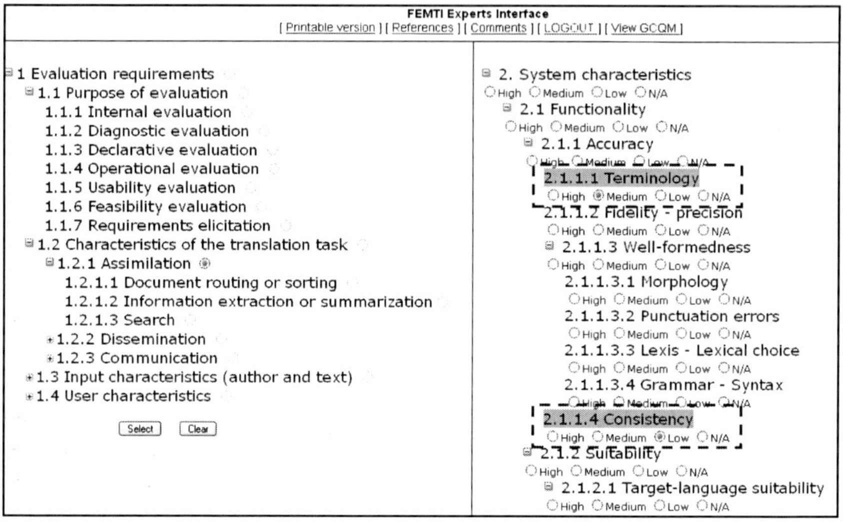

Figure 11. Example of expert selecting quality characteristics *Terminology* and *Consistency* to be linked to *Assimilation.*

FEMTI GCQM	**Assimilation**	Search	Dissemination	Internal dissemination
System characteristics	Low			
Functionality	Low			
Accuracy			High	
Terminology	Medium			
Fidelity - precision			High	
Well-formedness				
Morphology				
Punctuation errors			Low	
Lexis - Lexical choice				
Grammar - Syntax				
Consistency	Low		N/A	
Suitability				
Target-language suitability				
Readability			Medium	
Comprehensibility				

Figure 12. Excerpt of an expert's GCQM showing the relations created from *Assimilation* to *Terminology* and *Consistency.*

As already mentioned, the primary goal of this support tool is to collect knowledge from experts, which will be integrated into the evaluators' interface of FEMTI to improve the suggestion of quality characteristics. A possible way to achieve this is to merge several GCQMs by averaging or accumulating the weights for the same links of the different GCQMs. However, this will be of practical interest only once the experts' interface has been used extensively and enough valid and rich GCQMs are available.

5. Refinement and assessment of FEMTI

This section describes and discusses two activities carried out to collect feedback from the MT community and bring input to FEMTI's GCQM. Two tutorials were set up in 2007 and 2008, using the new version of FEMTI, in order to introduce the framework to potential users and to explain how it can be applied. In addition, the goal was also to encourage the use of the evaluators' interface and to transfer knowledge from the MT community into FEMTI. Following the EAGLES and ISLE series of workshops, these tutorials have been organized in conjunction with major international conferences: the MT Summit in 2007 and the Language Resources and Evaluation Conference in 2008.

The structure of the tutorials was similar in both cases: after introducing the tools, a practical session led participants to specify a quality model for a given scenario of MT use; the quality models were then summarized and discussed during the final slot. Most of the participants used a printed compilation of FEMTI's content while a few accessed the online version. The scenarios proposed to participants were defined as a compromise between specificity and generality: participants needed a reasonably clear scenario to be able to describe it in terms of the context characteristics in FEMTI, but it had to be general enough to avoid biasing the participants too directly towards any specific characteristic. For the exercise participants were arranged in groups of about four persons and were asked to perform the following tasks:

- Identify the context characteristics from FEMTI Part I that would best characterize the given scenario of MT use.
- Indicate the quality characteristics from FEMTI Part II that are believed relevant to each of the selected context characteristic.
- If possible, indicate the importance of each quality characteristic for each context characteristic on a 3-point scale.

For the first tutorial, the proposed scenario featured an MT system that would help select articles from the Chinese press about the preparation for the Beijing 2008 Olympic Games, before handing the articles for proper translation into English by humans. All the four groups of participants agreed on the top-level context characteristic that defined the translation task (namely, *Assimilation*), but when further specifying it in terms of sub-characteristics, the groups chose different sub-tasks: *Search* vs. *Information extraction* vs. *Document routing*. Other context characteristics that were considered as describing the scenario were: the *Domain or field of application* of the input text, the author's *Superior proficiency in source language*, and the user's *Novice proficiency in source language* and their S*uperior or Distinguished proficiency in target language*. Similarly, a common set of quality characteristics appeared to be important for the given scenario: *Fidelity*, *Terminology*, *Dictionaries*, *Input to output translation speed* and *Cost* – exact answers varied from group to group. From this hands-on exercise, around 40 new links between characteristics from Part I and Part II were created and then added to FEMTI's GCQM by the organizers. Most of them concerned context characteristics that were recently added and had no connections yet to Part II, such as nodes under *Author's proficiency in source* or *target language*.

At the second tutorial, a scenario inspired from a real world use case was proposed. The scenario featured an MT system used for the Global Public Health Intelligence Network (GPHIN) – a web-based early warning system, permanently monitoring several sources of information, in several languages, for disease outbreaks and other public health events, and disseminating the information selected as relevant nearly in real time (Blench, 2007). With the authorization of the GPHIN's contributors, the requirements for the MT system used in their network were presented in detail to the participants, including information about the workflow, type of users, type of texts handled and the evaluation of the overall system and of each MT component.

In the second tutorial the answers of the groups were more detailed than for the first one and showed more overlap across groups, most likely due to the more detailed specification of the scenario. Several relations between Part I and Part II were shared among several groups, thus validating both the description of the scenario and the links themselves; the shared links are:

- Information extraction/summarization → Fidelity; Comprehensibility
- Domain or field of application → Terminology; Word lists or glossaries
- Number of personnel → Cost
- Time allowed for translation → Overall production time; Input to output translation speed
- Quantity of translation → Input to output translation speed
- Multi-client external dissemination → Readability

The particularities of the given scenario are reflected in some context characteristics chosen by several groups, namely *Characteristics related to the sources of error*, *Document type*, *Genre*, *Domain or field of application* and

Communication. In this second tutorial, 115 distinct links were produced, from which 87 were new to FEMTI and were added to the GCQM; the rest of the links will be first validated and then integrated to FEMTI in the near future.

In addition to dissemination of FEMTI and knowledge collection, these tutorials served as an additional validation of the framework, given that participants helped the developers identify areas of Parts I and II to be improved. For instance, the context characteristics regarding *Genre* and *Domain or field of application* are important aspects of the environment of use and should be further decomposed into sub-characteristics to increase their specificity and make them a selectable item in Part I. Similarly, some quality characteristics, such as *Cost* or those related to *Resource utilization,* should be augmented with relevant metrics.

Furthermore, the feedback obtained indicates that, in the current state, FEMTI still requires prior knowledge or experience about MT evaluation in order to be effectively used. As FEMTI users would benefit from more guidance, it is planned to integrate the results of these tutorials into templates or use cases for FEMTI that will be available to the general public. Similarly to EAGLES, increasingly extensive use of the FEMTI framework will help to asses and to validate it, both by experts and evaluators. Ongoing work includes using FEMTI to design the evaluation of speech-to-speech translation systems and one of the expected results of this work is a new list of possible updates to FEMTI.

6. Conclusions and future work

This paper argued that the methodologies taking into account the context of use of a system, for example the JEIDA criteria or the EAGLES consumer report paradigm or FEMTI, are very useful in practice to design informative evaluations that help users get a clear picture of a system's qualities with respect to its intended use. However, context-based evaluation might also seem limited to specific cases, thus reducing the evaluation's reusability, moreover, it demands more effort from an evaluator to design and execute a contextual evaluation plan. This paper presented an interactive version of the FEMTI guidelines, whose primary goal is to overcome some of the drawbacks of context-based evaluation, especially by offering a set of user-friendly web-based tools to help evaluators generate their plans and to help experts contribute to the field with their knowledge by creating relations between contexts and quality characteristics. In addition to these new functionalities, the current FEMTI provides a simple way to browse through the content, which is an important aspect given the large amount of information available. The most innovative component of FEMTI is the implementation of an automatic linking mechanism, which uses a GCQM to suggest relevant quality characteristics given a particular context of use. These improvements greatly simplify the evaluators' task when designing an evaluation. FEMTI is thus the first context-based evaluation tool available for MT, and its principles and software infrastructure can be extended to other domains. Combined to particularized ISO/IEC 9126 quality models, the FEMTI tool can contribute to the standardization of evaluation in other domains, as illustrated by (Miller, 2008).

Given that new metrics for MT evaluation appear very often, the contributors and developers of FEMTI are well aware that their work might never be completed. Therefore, future work should keep focusing on FEMTI's content and on providing more practical details about how to design an evaluation with FEMTI. As part of this work, it would be useful to attach an additional section with practical guidelines about the resources that might be needed to execute an evaluation plan, as well as with additional information about the use of automatic and human-based MT metrics for non-experts in the field.

Although the first steps were undertaken to disseminate the framework, to obtain feedback from the MT community and to identify directions for improvement, a more thorough assessment of FEMTI should be performed. For example, This could be done, for example, by organizing workshops or expert meetings where the interfaces would be used intensively or, alternatively, these actions could be performed remotely if the organization of such meetings is not logistically possible. Moreover, during such meetings, participants could work on any context characteristic instead of being constrained to a given scenario or they could provide their own context of use, for which a quality model could be created.

Several extensions of FEMTI should also be explored. The current version does not allow evaluators to set the weights in the context or quality vectors, given that the interface only allows them to select or unselect characteristics. In the future, this constraint could be suppressed to let evaluators enter the importance of each selected context characteristic, using a nominal or ordinal scale that provides the weights for both context and quality vectors. Another way of allowing evaluators to tune the weights in their quality models could be to let them load into the evaluators' interface their own GCQM previously created with the experts' interface or to merge the two interfaces into a more sophisticated one, where there is no radical difference between evaluators and experts.

Acknowledgments

The authors would like to acknowledge the steady support of the Swiss National Science Foundation (SNSF), through grants n. 200021-103318 and 200020-113604 for the first author, and through the IM2 National Center of Competence in Research for the second author.

Bibliography

Blench, M. (2007). Global Public Health Intelligence Network (GPHIN*)*. Paper presented at the MT Summit XI, Copenhagen, Denmark.

Canelli, M., Grasso, D. , & King, M.(2000). Methods and Metrics for the Evaluation of Dictation Systems: A Case Study. Paper presented at the Proceedings of the 2nd LREC, Athens Greece.

EAGLES Evaluation Working Group. (1996). EAGLES Evaluation of Natural Language Processing Systems (Final Report No. EAG-EWG-PR.2 (ISBN 87-90708-00-8)). Copenhagen, Danmark: Center for Sprogteknologi.

Estrella, P., Popescu-Belis, A.& Underwood, N. (2005).. Finding the System that Suits you Best: Towards the Normalization of MT Evaluation. Paper presented at the 27th ASLIB International Conference on Translating and the Computer, 24-25 November 2005, London, UK.

Hovy, E. H. (1999). Toward Finely Differentiated Evaluation Metrics for Machine Translation. Paper presented at the EAGLES Workshop on Standards and Evaluation, Pisa, Italy.

Hovy, E.H., King, M.& Popescu-Belis, A. (2002). Principles of Context-Based Machine Translation Evaluation. *Machine Translation, 17*(1), 1-33.

ISO/IEC. (1991). *ISO/IEC 9126 – Information Technology – Software Product Evaluation / Quality Characteristics and Guidelines for Their Use*. Geneva: International Organization for Standardization / International Electrotechnical Commission.

ISO/IEC. (1999). *ISO/IEC 14598-1:1999 (E) – Information Technology – Software Product Evaluation – Part 1: General Overview*. Geneva: International Organization for Standardization / International Electrotechnical Commission.

ISO/IEC. (2001). *ISO/IEC 9126-1:2001 (E) – Software Engineering – Product Quality – Part 1:Quality Model*. Geneva: International Organization for Standardization / International Electrotechnical Commission.

ISO/IEC. (2003a). *ISO/IEC TR 9126-2:2003 (E) – Software Engineering – Product Quality – Part 2:External Metrics*. Geneva: International Organization for Standardization / International Electrotechnical Commission.

ISO/IEC. (2003b) *ISO/IEC TR 9126-3:2003 (E) – Software Engineering –Product Quality – Part 3:Internal Metrics*. Geneva: International Organization for Standardization / International Electrotechnical Commission.

Miller, K. (2008). *FEIRI:* Extending ISLE's FEMTI for the Evaluation of a Specialized Application in Information Retrieval. Paper presented at the ELRA Workshop on Evaluation "Looking into the Future of Evaluation" at LREC, Marrakech, Morroco.

Nomura, H. (1992). *JEIDA Methodology and Criteria on Machine Translation Evaluation*: Japan Electronic Industry Development Association (JEIDA).

Papineni, K., Roukos, S., Ward, ., & Zhu, Wei-Jing. (2001). *BLEU: a Method for Automatic Evaluation of Machine Translation* (Research Report, Computer Science No. RC22176 (W0109-022)). Yorktown Heights, NY: IBM Research Division, T.J.Watson Research Center.

Rocca, G, Spampinato, L, Zarri, G.P. & Black, W. (1994). COBALT: Construction, Augmentation and Use of Knowledge bases from Natural Language Documents. Paper presented at the Proceedings of the Artificial Intelligence Conference.

TEMAA. (1996). *TEMAA Final Report* (No. LRE-62-070 (March 1996)): Center fo Sprogteknologi, Copenhagen, Danemark.

White, J. S., & O'Connell, T. A. (1994). The ARPA MT Evaluation Methodologies: Evolution, Lessons, and Future Approach*es*. Paper presented at the AMTA Conference, 5-8 October 1994, Columbia, MD, USA.

---

* Work performed while at ISSCO, University of Geneva.

Scaling up a hybrid MT system: From low to full resources

Vincent Vandeghinste
K.U.Leuven

This article describes a hybrid approach to machine translation (MT) that is inspired by the rule-based, statistical, example-based, and other hybrid machine translation approaches currently used or described in academic literature. It describes how the approach was implemented for language pairs using only limited monolingual resources and hardly any parallel resources (the METIS-II system), and how it is currently implemented with rich resources on both the source and target side as well as rich parallel data (the PaCo-MT system). We aim to illustrate that a similar paradigm can be used, irrespectively of the resources available, but of course with an impact on translation quality.

1. Introduction

There are myriad approaches to machine translation, but none have shown acceptable levels of translation quality from an end-user's perspective. MT systems that exist today reach at best a level of translation quality that might speed up the work of a human translator. The most widespread use of MT systems are *online translation services*, which are available through many Web sites and provide a gist translation of the source language text. MT systems in limited domains are occasionally sufficiently accurate to be useful for *real* translation tasks.

In *rule-based machine translation*, the development of a new language pair, especially with so-called 'smaller' languages, is rather rare due to high costs and long development times. In *statistical machine translation*, these expenses depend on the availability of parallel corpora containing aligned sentences in both the source and target language.

In order to develop MT systems for new language pairs more efficiently, we developed a new methodology which allows reuse of existing tools and corpora for both the source and target language. Since deep syntactic parsers and parallel corpora are unavailable for many language pairs, we implemented this new methodology with low resource source and target languages in the METIS-II system (Carl et al., 2008), limiting ourselves to using only the kind of very basic resources that are available for many languages or that can be built relatively easily. When more tools and resources are available, we can still apply similar methodology. We are now scaling up to more sophisticated tools and large parallel corpora: Parse and Corpus-based Machine Translation (PaCo-MT).

This article will first describe the used approach in general (Section 2), then the METIS-II approach using low resources (Section 3), and then the PaCo-MT approach using full resources (Section 4).

2. A Hybrid Approach toward MT reusing existing resources

This section describes the common ideas behind both the METIS-II system, for which the implementation of a Dutch-English translation system is described in Vandeghinste (2008), and the PaCo-MT system, which is currently implemented and which is partially described in Vandeghinste (2007; 2009). Figure 1 shows where both the METIS and PaCo approach can be situated on the Vauquois triangle (1968) and this paper aims to illustrate how to climb the Vauquois triangle within the presented approach.

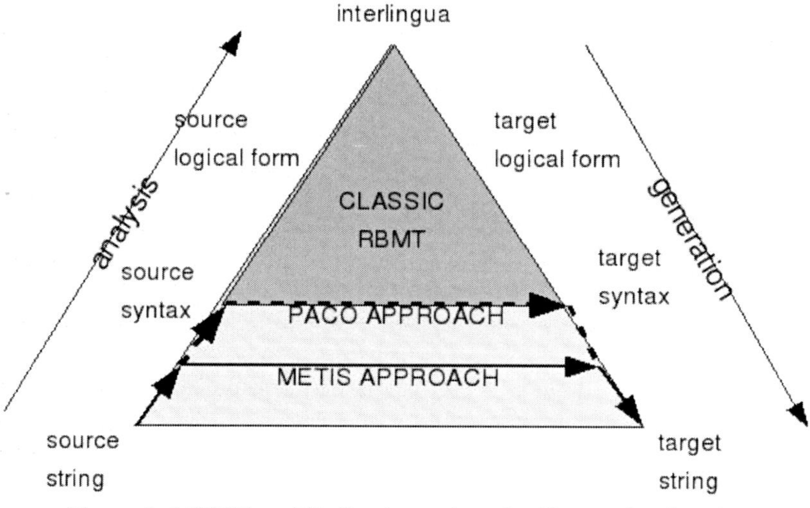

Figure 1. METIS and PaCo situated on the Vauquois triangle.

We describe how both approaches borrow from different MT paradigms, including rule-based MT, statistical MT, and example-based MT.

2.1. Rule-based Machine Translation (RBMT)

RBMT is characterised by use of linguistic rules in translation. It consists of source language syntactic and semantic analysis, a series of structural conversions, and target language generation. There are two approaches toward RBMT: the interlingua approach and the transfer approach.

In the *interlingua* approach, the source language analysis leads to an interlingual representation of the sentence. This is an abstract (in principle *language independent*) representation from which a target language string is generated. For the interlingual treatment, abstraction is applied by the monolingual modules so that the content or function of all lexical items is recoded in terms of semantic universals. An example interlingua system is described by Rosetta (1994). Some disadvantages of interlingua systems are described in Van Eynde (1993).

In *transfer* systems, the source sentence is analysed, most often by a rule-based parser; and transfer rules convert the source sentence structure into the target sentence structure, from which the target sentence is generated by a language generator, using target language generation rules.

Although in academia most current approaches are no longer rule-based, many of the industrial MT engines still are. For instance, most of the translation pairs available at free online MT engines, including Babelfish and Microsoft, are transfer systems.

2.2. Statistical Machine Translation (SMT)

SMT systems implement a theory of probability distribution and probability estimation. They learn a *translation model* from a parallel corpus, which contains aligned source and target language information, and a *language model* from a target language corpus. The best translation is searched for by maximising the probability according to these models. Using statistics in MT has had a major impact on translation accuracy (Ney, 2005).

One *advantage* of statistics and probability distributions is that they offer a formalism for expressing and combining scores for each translation hypothesis: The probabilities can be used as scores, and it is obvious how to combine scores. Nuances and shades of difference can best be expressed in values between 0 and 1. There are ways to estimate these probabilities without human intervention (Ney, 2005).

There are also *disadvantages* to SMT. One major disadvantage is the need for a large parallel corpus. This is often unavailable, and when available is often limited to specific domains. Another disadvantage is that SMT systems are often like a *black-box*: it is very hard to improve results after a basic system has been built (except by enlarging the corpora). Due to the models that are used, SMT systems are known to have, among other things, problems with capturing information about long-distance dependencies, and hence produce incorrect translations in such cases. SMT also seems to suffer from *ceiling* effects in performance (Lønning et al., 2004). To break through these ceilings, we see increasing use of linguistic features within the SMT paradigm.

Another approach to improve SMT is to move from the word level to the *phrase* level, using a set of heuristics to determine phrase boundaries (Koehn, et al., 2003). The term *phrase* is not used in the linguistic sense, but denotes *any sequence of words*. This seems to be the most used approach in current SMT systems.

2.3. Example-based Machine Translation (EBMT)

EBMT can be located somewhere between RBMT and SMT, as many EBMT approaches integrate both rule-based and data-driven techniques (Carl and Way, 2003).

EBMT is sometimes confused with the related technique of *translation memory* (TM). Although both have the idea of reusing already existing translations, they differ in the sense that a TM is an interactive tool for the *human* translator, whereas EBMT is an *automatic* translation technique (Somers, 2003).

The idea for EBMT dates back to Nagao (1984). He identified the three main components of EBMT as matching fragments of text against a database of real examples, identifying the corresponding translation fragments, and recombining these to give the target text.

An EBMT system is developed on the basis of a parallel, aligned corpus. These corpora, however, are often only available for limited domains and a limited set of languages, but for general translation purposes they are not as easy to acquire. In this respect, EBMT suffers from the same drawback as SMT. A related issue is the required size of the database of translated text fragments. Although Mima et al. (1998) reported that the MT improvement was more or less linear with the number of examples, it is assumed (Somers, 2003) that there is some limit after which adding more examples no longer improves (and even worsens) the quality of the output, as examples might contradict each other.

Other problematic issues in EBMT are how examples are stored and which information is stored with them; how source language strings are matched with the corpus; extraction of appropriate fragments from the translation; and recombination of these fragments into a grammatical target language output (Somers, 2003).

2.4. A hybrid approach

The general approach behind the METIS-II and PaCo-MT systems draws on these three paradigms and seeks to combine their strengths and avoid their weaknesses. Figure 2 presents the general architecture of our approach.

The first processing step consists of *source language analysis*, which results in one or more parse trees representing the syntactic structure of the sentence. This parse tree can be very shallow or it can be a full parse tree, depending on the tools and resources available for the source language. It can be a phrase structure tree or a dependency tree, or it can simply contain chunked data, with a depth of only 1. The use of a (full) parser for linguistic analysis is common in RBMT systems, as well as performing a source language analysis independently of the target language.

The second processing step consists of *converting the source language tree into one or more target language bags of bags*. A bag is an unordered list of words or phrases, so a bag of bags is a tree-like structure but the daughters of each node in the bag of bags are unordered. All terminal nodes in the source language analysis tree can be converted to target language equivalents by looking up the node's *lemma* or *word form* and *part-of-speech* in the dictionary.

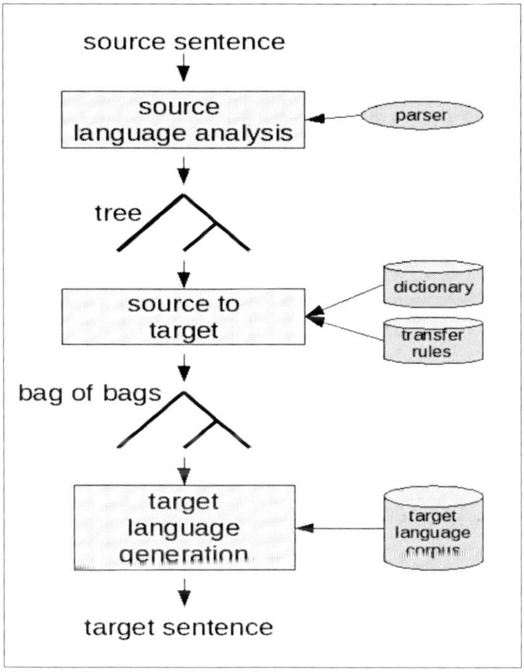

Figure 2. General Architecture

Using dictionaries consisting of lemmas or stems has the advantage of greatly improving its coverage over using a dictionary containing all surface word forms as they appear in text. Terminal nodes (lemma/word form + part-of-speech) which are not in the dictionary are left untranslated by default. As shown in figure 3, apart from single words, the dictionary can also contain more complex, structured items, both on the source and the target language side, covering more complex cases than simple word-by-word translations. This means that:

- the part-of-speech tag sets for source and target language need not be the same, as the tags are *translated* via dictionary look-up;
- the syntactic structure for source and target language can be different, as the structure is also *translated* via dictionary look-up;
- non-terminal nodes can be found in the dictionary, and can lead to translations which are fragments of syntactic trees in the target language. For these nodes, the order of the daughters in the target language can already be fixed.

There are often structural changes between source and target language which are not word-specific but more general and are thus not covered in the dictionary. Therefore, we introduce *transfer rules* which model these structural differences, and bring the bag of bags closer to the desired target language structure.

Figure 3. Examples of dictionary entries

An example transfer rule is, when translating from Dutch to English, *Verb Group Treatment* (Vandeghinste, 2008): In Dutch, the auxiliary and past participle can be separated, but in English they tend to stay together, except in certain cases, which we ignore for now. We detect if, within the same clause, we find an auxiliary and a past participle. If so, we put them under the same mother node, so they stay close together in target language modelling, as words belonging to the same mother node will not be separated by the target language model. This is illustrated in figure 4.

The use of a dictionary combined with a set of transfer rules is similar to what is done in transfer-based RBMT. The difference with our approach is that, depending on the available parallel resources, we can both use manual dictionary entries and automatically derived entries, each with a weight representing its confidence.

The final step in the core MT engine is the *generation of target language strings* from the bags of bags, using a target language corpus. Therefore, the target language corpus needs to be *pre-processed* similarly to how the source language is analysed. The daughters of each of the bags and sub-bags are looked up in the target language corpus in order to retrieve the frequency of occurrence for each permutation of the order of the daughters, and to determine the most probable target language string. For instance, if we have the target language noun-phrase bag containing the words *big, the, black* and *dog,* what is the most likely permutation of these four words? Two permutations yield a grammatical surface string: *the big black dog* and *the black big dog,* but the former is most likely to appear in real English text. Using a target language model to order the bags of bags allows for a very light transfer model, as it defers a great part of the reordering modelisation onto the target language model.

The target language corpus is also used to perform *lexical selection* between several translation alternatives by looking at which translation alternatives are most likely to co-occur in the target language corpus. For instance, the Dutch word *zwart* can have the English translations *black* and *gloomy*. When we want to translate the phrase *de zwarte hond,* the target language corpus tells us that the word *black* is far more likely to co-occur with *dog* than the word *gloomy*.

This is somewhat similar to what is done in traditional EBMT, albeit EBMT tries to find these nodes in a parallel corpus, whereas we try to find them in a pre-processed target language corpus. The use of probabilities and weights at every step in the translation process is borrowed from statistical NLP and SMT.

3. Using only low resources

In this section we first give a system description of METIS-II for Dutch to English, and end with a description of how the evaluation of this system was performed at several stages in its development. With low resources we essentially mean that neither full parsers nor parallel corpora were used.

3.1. System description

In the METIS-II project (Carl et al, 2008; Vandeghinste et al., 2008) this approach was tested using only limited resources on different language pairs: Greek to English, German to English, Spanish to English and Dutch to English. We briefly describe the approach, which is used for the latter language pair (Vandeghinste, 2008). figure 4 presents an example sentence.

Source language analysis is performed using a tokeniser, a part-of-speech tagger (Brants, 2000), a lemmatiser, a shallow parser (NP and PP detection, head detection) and a clause detector (relative phrases and subordinate clauses). The system does *not* use a full syntactic parser.

To *translate nodes* in the shallow parse tree, a manually compiled *dictionary* (gathered from several internet sources plus further manual editing) is used together with a limited set (<20) of manually defined transfer rules. *Part-of-Speech Tag mapping rules* which convert the source language tags (Van Eynde, 2005) into target language tags[1] are used to *translate* the non-lemma features of the source language tags (*singular* vs. *plural*, *present* vs. *past*, etc) into features of the target language tag (for instance, the Dutch tag the Dutch tag WW(pv,tgw,ev) is converted into VVB).

As described in the previous section, every node is looked up in the dictionary, and the structure of the bag of bags is converted by the transfer rules in a structure more similar to English sentence structure. These rules can concern word and chunk ordering information. For instance, as shown in figure 4, there is a rule in English (see also Huddleston & Pullum, 2002) that puts auxiliaries and past participles together under one node except in the case of inversion, frequency adverbs and some other adjuncts. In Dutch, however, they are separated. Other rules concern mappings of tense and aspect.

Note that *not* using a parallel corpus is one of the key properties of METIS-II, as parallel corpora are not available, not large enough or too domain specific for most language pairs. It is what makes METIS-II different from most data-driven approaches of MT.

From all the previous processing steps, we have a ranked set of bags of bags each representing a translation alternative. They are ranked according to their weight, which is a combination of the weight generated by the different statistical source language analysis modules. These weights estimate the probability of an analysis, and the lower the weight, the less trustworthy the analysis.

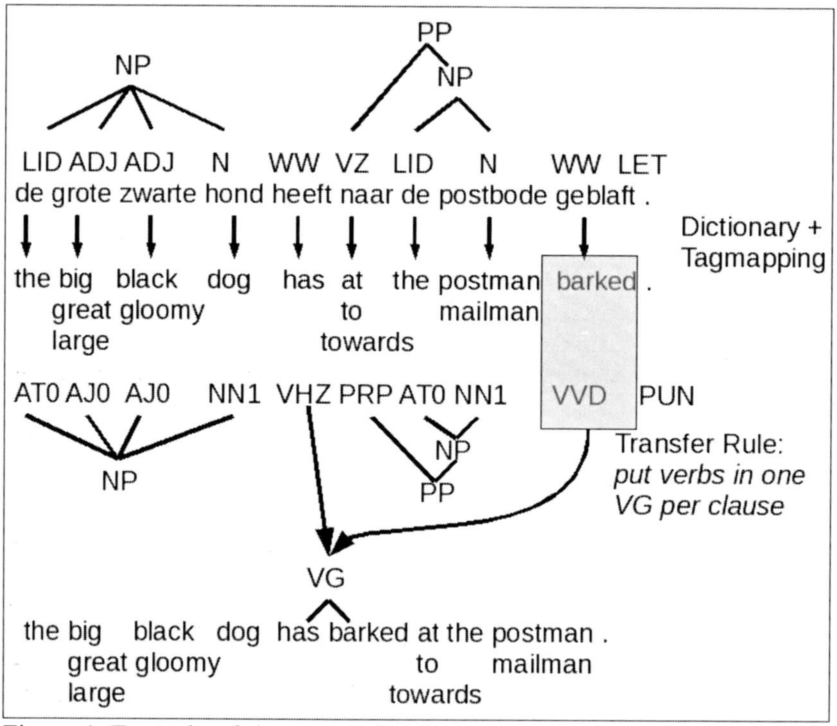

Figure 4. Example of the conversion from source to target language in the METIS-II engine.

For each of these bags of bags, the order of the daughters of each of the bags and daughter-bags needs to be determined, so the bags of bags are converted into conventional tree representations of the target language sentence, each with a weight. This is done by looking up each bag (and daughter-bag) in the pre-processed *target language corpus*.

The target language corpus in this case is the British National Corpus (BNC), a balanced collection of samples of written and spoken language from a wide range of sources, which is already tagged. Pre-processing consisted of lemmatisation (done by the *Reversible Lemmatiser* (Carl et al., 2005)), chunking, and clause detection.

Matching a bag with the BNC results in a number of permutations of the bag elements each receiving a matching score, because they match with corpus chunks. The closer they match with what is found in the corpus, the higher they score. Since not all elements of each bag are leaf nodes, the lemmas of the heads of the translation candidates are used to perform matching. A bag element is matching a corpus element when the lemma (or the lemma of the head daughter) matches. The accuracy of matching (a_m) is calculated according to this formula:

$$a_m = m / (n + p^2)$$

where m is the number of matching bag elements, n is the total number of bag elements, and p is the number of elements in the corpus chunk which are not in the bag, and which cannot be replaced by one of the elements in the bag. We take the square of p to make it a more important factor. Experiments showed that this improved translation accuracy.

This matching process allows us to retrieve word order information from the target language corpus, by using word order information from the matching corpus fragment. In addition, this process performs lexical selection because not every bag alternative matches with the same accuracy, leading to translation candidate selection when a certain combination of words occurs in the corpus.

Apart from the matching accuracy we also take into account the relative frequency of the corpus chunk with respect to the total frequency of all corpus chunks in which the same or a higher number of elements match (m).

Permutations which do not match with any corpus fragments are no longer considered, allowing us to move from a *bag* representation to several conventional tree representations. For a more detailed description of this system and some examples, we refer to Vandeghinste (2008).

After lexical selection and word order have been determined, a final step remains: the target language tree contains lemmas and part-of-speech tags, and these need to be converted into the appropriate tokens. For this purpose we again use the *Reversible Lemmatiser* (Carl et al., 2005) in reverse mode.

3.2. Evaluation

When building a prototype, it is of utmost importance to test and evaluate the prototype at different stages in its implementation. In Vandeghinste et al. (2005), we described an experiment on the first version of the prototype, in which we validate the general idea behind the approach, viz. noun phrase translation. For this evaluation, we translated 685 NPs, which resulted in a number of translation alternatives, ranked by their weight. Humans judged whether the first translation alternative was correct (57.7%), or amongst any of the translation alternatives (13.6%). This implies that, by only changing the weighing mechanism, we were able get a maximum of 71% correct NPs. The moderate results can be explained by the limited coverage of the lexicon (80% word coverage) and bugs in this early version (no output for 12%).

Another partial evaluation, described by Dirix et al. (2006) was a source language independent evaluation. For this evaluation, a set of 150 bags of bags was generated, having chunk structures derived from original Dutch, Greek or Spanish sentences. All words were manually translated into English. An average BLEU score (Papinemi et al., 2002) of 21.17% was reached and the error analysis led to the observation that the dictionary was clearly not sufficient to bridge the gap between source and target language. This led to the introduction of a transfer mechanism in the next version of the system.

In Vandeghinste et al. (2007) we tested the effect of adding a limited set of transfer rules, leading to a clear improvement in both BLEU and NIST scores (Doddington, 2002). The evaluation of this final METIS using automatic MT metrics showed that the BLEU score was not that different from a standard unoptimised statistical MT system trained on the Europarl corpus (Zwarts & Dras, 2007), as shown in table 1.

Table 1. Evaluation Results

	METIS-II	**Zwarts&Dras**
BLEU	19.79%	20.70%
NIST	6.06	
TER	59.33%	

In other words, the performance of the METIS-II system, without using parallel data other than a dictionary, reaches a performance level almost similar to that of an (unoptimised) SMT system, but without using a parallel corpus.

4. Scaling up to full resources

In the PaCo-MT system, we scale up this approach, using far more tools and resources. We implement the translation pairs Dutch-English and Dutch-French in both directions. In this section, we describe the approach for translation from Dutch to English, and compare it with the low resources approach from the previous section.

Instead of a shallow source language analysis, we now use *full parsers*, giving us a detailed analysis of the source language sentence. For Dutch, we use the Alpino parser (Van Noord, 2006), resulting in a dependency tree representation combined with a phrase structure tree of the source sentence, as shown in figure 5. Not only do we know the NPs and PPs, we also know for instance what the *subject* or *direct object* of a sentence or any of its clauses is.

Instead of using only a hand-made dictionary, we derive dictionary entries from publicly available parallel corpora. As described in Vandeghinste (2007) we parse the Dutch side of Europarl (Koehn, 2005) (and other parallel data) with Alpino and the aligned English side with the Stanford parser (Klein & Manning, 2003). This is a stochastic parser, trained on the Penn treebank[2] and yielding a phrase structure tree and a dependency tree as output.

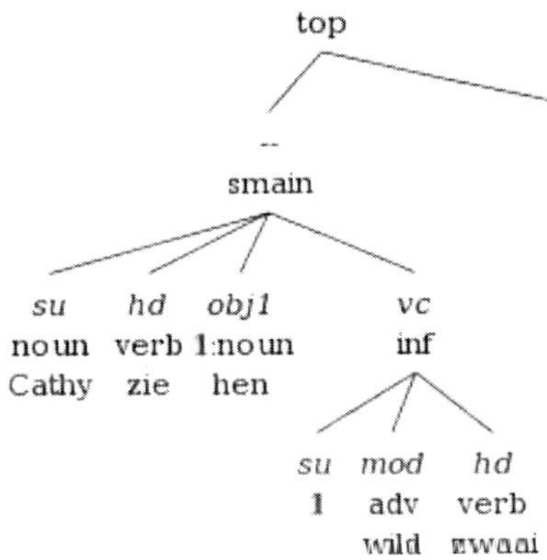

Figure 5. Alpino parse tree for the sentence "*Cathy zag hen wild zwaaien.*" *(Cathy saw them wave wildly.)* [3]

Parsing both sides results in a parallel Treebank, in which all sentences are aligned. We also align at the word level, using GIZA++ (Och & Ney, 2003), a tool designed for SMT. Word and sentence alignments are put in the dictionary, together with their alignment frequency in order to obtain a dictionary containing full sentences and single words, each with a weight.

In addition to this, we align at the sub-sentential level, meaning that we align non-terminal non-root nodes in both source and target language trees, so that for instance subject noun phrases are aligned. This is similar to what is done by Hearne (2005) in what is called Data-oriented Translation (DOT), but she applies it on a small parallel corpus only.

We put the resulting alignments in our *dictionary*, together with weights based on the alignment and parser confidence and the frequency of occurrence, leading to a dictionary that contains all sorts of entries: single words, phrases and constituents, clauses, and full sentences. Note that deriving dictionary entries from a large parallel corpus is one of the major differences (together with the use of full linguistic parsers) between this approach and the low resources approach used in the METIS-II project.

Returning to the translation processing chain of PaCo-MT, we try to match every node of the input parse tree with the source language side of the dictionary entries, retrieving, when possible, the full sentence (and in this way functioning like a translation memory). If the full sentence cannot be retrieved, we seek for lower level matches, recursively descending down the input parse tree, resulting in target language fragments that need to be recombined into one target language sentence, much like in EBMT. This dictionary matching process leads to a number of bags of bags, each representing an alternative translation hypothesis for the target sentence.

The structure of these bags of bags can be altered by the automatically derived *transfer rules*. When nodes in the parallel treebank are aligned, we do not only extract dictionary entries from these alignments, butalso transfer rules, making abstraction of the concrete words and tokens which align, and only taking into account categories (constituents) and relations (dependency labels). Using the relative frequencies of occurrence of these alignments gives us weighting information, which allows us to prefer one transfer rule over the others.

Using automatically derived transfer rules is another difference with the low resource approach, in which we used manually edited transfer rules. Of course, transfer rules in PaCo-MT can also be manually edited.

The final step, before outputting a target language sentence, consists of generating a string from the bag of bags. For each unresolved bag (and recursively for the whole tree), we try to find the most probable order and combination for the daughter nodes. All permutations of the daughter nodes are looked up in the pre-processed target language corpus in order to retrieve their frequency of occurrence. This is done at different levels of abstraction, beginning with the most concrete level in which we try to find the exact same words in the exact same functions. When we do not find these, we abstract over the words and so on, until we find some information allowing us to prefer one ordering over the others (for more details we refer to Vandeghinste , 2009). Our approach is somewhat similar to the *feature templates* approach used by Velldal (2007), although we only derive *context free* information, by only linking the node with its immediate daughters, whereas Velldal's extracted information expands over several levels in the tree.

Apart from the order of the daughter nodes we need to select which of the translation alternatives will be used in the output. The alternatives that co-occur within linguistically motivated corpus fragments in the target language corpus are identified , and the resulting relative frequencies are used to estimate the weights of the translation alternatives.

As the PaCo-MT system is currently under development no results for the full MT processing chain are available yet, but first results for the target language generation, both for Dutch and for English are promising. As described in Vandeghinste (2009), we set up an experiment in which we compare our tree-based target language modeling with a standard trigram model. We performed a source language independent evaluation, in which we used the parse trees of the test sentences as input, but with all surface order information removed. It is then up to the target language generator to generate a surface sentence from this bag of bags. Figure 6 compares tree-based language modeling with a standard backoff trigram model with a branch and bound approach.[4] Results were consistent for a set of different MT metrics (WER, NIST, TER (Snover et al., 2006).

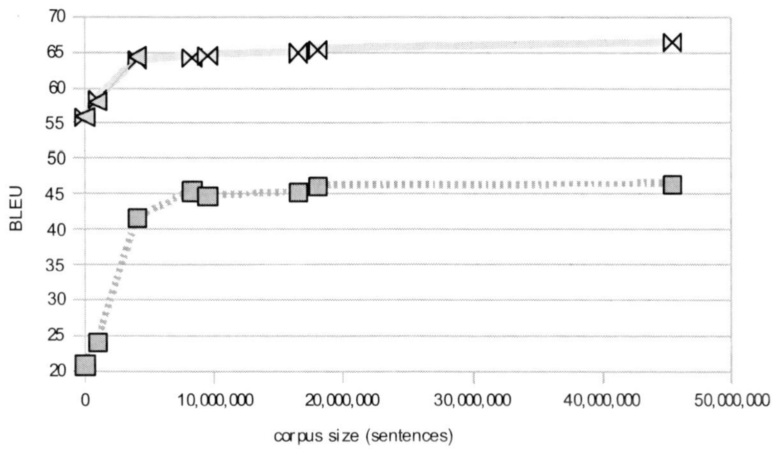

Figure 6. BLEU scores for target language generation for Dutch. Comparing tree-based language modeling (continuous line) with trigram language modeling (dotted line).

5. Conclusions

In this paper we described a hybrid approach towards machine translation, seeking to combine the strengths and avoid the weaknesses of the classic approaches towards MT.

The difficulty in developing an RBMT system resides in the huge cost and effort of rule design; especially for the transfer rules, which are language pair dependent. This becomes unfeasible when the commercial potential of the language pair is low. However, even when language pairs have a high commercial potential, and rules have been designed and improved for more than 30 years, the results are often disappointing. Therefore, most commercial RBMT systems are starting to use corpora in order to give weights to their rule-sets and to allow for rule ranking when more than one rule applies.

The difficulty in developing an SMT system (and an EBMT system) resides in the need for large parallel and monolingual corpora to feed the translation and target language model. In SMT systems, the use of *n-grams* with a low *n* leads to weak models in the case of long distance dependencies and other long distance phenomena. For languages such as Dutch the subject and verb can be very far apart in sub-ordinate clauses, which is problematic for subject-verb agreement in SMT systems. Apart from using even larger corpora, there is a tendency in SMT to extend the models used to include more and more syntactic features.

Consequently, the RBMT and SMT worlds are moving closer to each other. The linguists of the RBMT world are starting to use statistics, while the engineers of the SMT world are starting to use linguistic features.

The hybrid approach described here currently has two instantiations. The first one is the METIS-II system, a system designed to minimise the use of tools and resources, especially language pair specific resources, by avoiding the use of parallel corpora. The only parallel data required for this system is its dictionary. Other tools used in METIS-II are monolingual analysis tools, which are available for many more languages or which can be easily built or trained. While translation quality of this system is not very good, it is not much worse than translation quality of an SMT system, which does require a parallel corpus, but does not require any language specific tools.

The second system is the PaCo-MT system. Although it is hard to draw firm conclusions about a system which is still in an early development stage, we can focus on the design of the system and why certain design choices have been made in order to overcome weaknesses of other approaches toward MT.

In the PaCo-MT project we use a rule-based architecture, but avoid the high development time for the rules by automatically deriving them from parallel treebanks. The parsers we use can be rule-based (like Alpino) with a stochastic component for disambiguation and speed, or they can be purely stochastic (like the Stanford parser), trained on a linguistically annotated treebank like the Penn treebank. We use already existing parsers so that we do not need to develop monolingual grammars. From the alignment between fragments we want to derive language pair specific translation grammars. For alignment we primarily look at techniques coming from the SMT world, but these might be improved using some linguistic features.

Acknowledgements

This research is made possible by the STEVIN-programme of the Dutch Language Union, Project PaCo-MT (STE-07007), which is sponsored by the Flemish and Dutch Governments, and by the SBO-programme of the Flemish IWT, Project AMASS++, Project Nr. 060051.

The PaCo-MT system is built in cooperation with the University of Groningen, which provides us with the treebanks and the alignments, and with the translation company Oneliner, which provides us with translation memories and test sets.

Bibliography

Brants, T. (2000). TnT - a statistical part-of-speech tagger. In Proceedings of 6th Applied Natural Language Processing Conference (ANLP) (pp.224-231). Seattle, Washington.

Carl, M. „Melero, Badia,T., Vandeghinste,V., Dirix,P. Schuurman,I., Markantonatou,S. Sofianopoulos, S.,Vassiliou, M. & Yannoutsou, O. (2008). METIS-II: Low Resources Machine Translation. *Machine Translation 22 (1),* 67-99.

Carl, M. & Way, A. (2003). *Recent advances in Example-based Translation.* Mechelen: Kluwer Academic Publishers.

Carl, M.,. Schmidt, P.& Schütz, J. (2005). Reversible Template-based Shake & Bake Generation. In M.Carl & A. Way (Eds) Proceedings of the 2nd workshop on Example-based Machine Translation at the Tenth MT Summit (pp.17-25). Phuket, Thailand.

Dirix, P., Vandeghinste, V.& Schuurman, I. (2006). A new hybrid approach enabling MT for languages with little resources. In. K.S. de Rijke, R. Scha, & R. van Son (Eds.), *Proceedings of the Sixteenth Computational Linguistics in the Netherlands (CLIN)* (pp.117-132). Universiteit van Amsterdam. Amsterdam, The Netherlands.

Doddington, G. (2002). Automatic Evaluation of Machine Translation Quality using N-gram Co-occurrence statistics. In Proceedings of HLT-2 (pp.138-145). San Diego, California.

Hearne, M. (2005). Data-Oriented Models of Parsing and Translation. PhD Thesis. Dublin City University.

Huddleston, R. & Pullum, G. (2002). *The Cambridge Grammar of the English Language.* Cambridge: Cambridge University Press.

Klein, D. & Manning, C.. (2003). Fast Exact Inference with a Factored Model for Natural Language Parsing. In *Advances in Neural Information Processing Systems 15* (NIPS 2002), Cambridge, MA: MIT Press, 3-10.

Koehn, P., Och, F. & Marcu, D. (2003). Statistical Phrase-Based Translation. In Proceedings of HLT-2003 (pp127-133). Edmonton, Canada.

Koehn, P. (2005). Europarl: a parallel corpus for statistical machine translation. In Proceedings of the Tenth Machine Translation Summit. (pp.79-87).Phuket, Thailand.

Lønning, J. T., Oepen,S. Beermann, D. Hellan, L. Carroll, J., Dyvik, H. Flickinger, D. Johannsen, J B , Meurer, P. Nordgård, T., Rosén, V. & Velldal, E. (2004). LOGON. A Norwegian MT effort. In Proceedings of the Workshop in Recent Advances in Scandinavian Machine Translation. Uppsala, Sweden.

Mima, H. Iida, H. & Furuse, O. (1998). Simultaneous Interpretation Utilizing Example-based Incremental Transfer. In Proceedings of COLING/ACL-1998 (pp.855-861).Montreal, Canada.

Nagao, M. (1984). A Framework of a Mechanical Translation between Japanese and English by Analogy Principle. In A. Elithorn, A. and R. Banerji, R. (Eds) *Artificial and Human Intelligence* (pp.173-180). Amsterdam. The Netherlands.

Ney, H. (2005). One Decade of Statistical Machine Translation: 1996-2005. In Proceedings of MT Summit X. (pp.i-12-17).Phuket, Thailand. .

Och, F.& Hermann N. (2003). A Systematic Comparison of Various Statistical Alignment Models, *Computational Linguistics 29*(1). 19-51.

Papinemi, K., Roukos, S., Ward, T., Henderson, J., & Reeder, F. (2002). BLEU: a method for automatic evaluation of Machine Translation. In Proceedings of ACL2002 (pp.311-318).Philadelphia, USA.

Rosetta, M.T. (1994). *Compositional Translation.* Kluwer International Series in Engineering and Computer Science, Volume 273, Dordrecht: Kluwer.

Snover, M., Dorr, B., Schwartz, R., Micciula, L., & Makhoul, J. (2006). A study of translation edit rate with targeted human annotation. In Proceedings of AMTA-7. (pp.223-231). Cambridge, Mass..

Somers, H. (2003). An overview of EBMT. In M.Carl and A.Way (Eds) *Recent advances in Example-Based Machine Translation.* Mechelen: Kluwer Academic Publishers.

Vandeghinste, V., Dirix, P., Schuurman, I. Markantonatou, S., Sofianopoulos, S.,Vassiliou, M., Yannoutsou, O., Badia, T., Melero, M., Boleda,G., Carl, M. & Schmidt, P. (2008).

Evaluation of a Machine Translation System for Low Resource Languages: METIS-II. In *Proceedings of LREC-2008*. Marakesh, Morocco.

Vandeghinste, V., Dirix, P. & Schuurman, I. (2005). Example-based Translation without Parallel Corpora: First experiments on a prototype. Proceedings of the Workshop on Example-Based Machine Translation. Hosted by MT SUMMIT X. Phuket, Thailand.

Vandeghinste, V., Dirix, P. & Schuurman, I. (2005). The effect of a feq rules on a data-driven MT system. In F. Van Eynde, I. Schuurman, & V. Vandeghinste (Eds.), *New Approaches to Machine Translation*. Proceedings of the METIS-II Workshop *(pp.27-34).*Centre for Computational Linguistics. KULeuven. Leuven, Belgium..

Vandeghinste, V.(2007). Removing the distinction between a translation memory, a bilingual dictionary and a parallel corpus. In *Proceedings of Translation and the Computer* (29). London, UK.

Vandeghinste, V. (2008). A Hybrid Modular Machine Translation System. PhD Thesis. LOT. Utrecht. The Netherlands.

Vandeghinste, V.(2009). Tree-based Target Language Modeling. In Proceedings of the 13th Annual Meeting of the European Association for Machine Translation *(pp.125-159).*Barcelona.

Van Eynde, F. (1993). Machine Translation and linguistic motivation. In F. Van Eynde (Ed.), *Linguistic Issues in Machine Translation.*. Communication in Artificial Intelligence Series. London: Pinter Publishers.

Van Eynde, F.(2005). P*art of Speech Tagging en Lemmatisering van het D-Coi Corpus* . Annotation Protocol. Centrum voor Computerlinguïstiek. Leuven. Belgium.

Van Noord, G. (2006). At Last Parsing Is Now Operational. In *Proceedings of TALN06* (pp.20-42). Leuven,.

Vauquois, B.(1968). Structues profondes et traduction automatique. Le système du CETA. In *Revue Roumaine de Linguistique, 13(2),* 105-130.

Velldal, E. (2007). Empirical Realisation Ranking. PhD Thesis. University of Oslo. Norway

Zwarts, S. &Dras, M. (2007). Syntax-based Word Reordering in Phrase-Based Statistical Machine Translation: Why Does it Work? In B.Maegaard (Ed.), *Proceedings of the Eleventh Machine Translation Summit* (pp.559-566).Copenhagen, Denmark.

---

[1] CLAWS 5 tag set at http://www.comp.lancs.ac.uk/ucrel/claws5tags.html

[2] http://www.cis.upenn.edu/~treebank/

[3] Taken from http://www.let.rug.nl/~vannoord/bin/alpinods_act2svg?lot_test_suite1/1

[4] Note that we achieved higher BLEU scores than in Vandeghinste (2009) because of a bug that was found, which led to reduced quality.

Automated error analysis for multiword expressions: Using BLEU-type scores for automatic discovery of potential translation errors

Bogdan Babych
University of Leeds

Anthony Hartley
University of Leeds

We describe the results of a research project aimed at automatic detection of MT errors using state-of-the-art MT evaluation metrics, such as BLEU. Currently, these automated metrics give only a general indication of translation quality at the corpus level and cannot be used directly for identifying gaps in the coverage of MT systems. Our methodology uses automatic detection of frequent multiword expressions (MWEs) in sentence-aligned parallel corpora and computes an automated evaluation score for concordances generated for such MWEs which indicates whether a particular expression is systematically mistranslated in the corpus. The method can be applied both to source and target MWEs to indicate, respectively, whether MT can successfully deal with source expressions, or whether certain frequent target expressions can be successfully generated. The results can be useful for systematically checking the coverage of MT systems in order to speed up the development cycle of rule-based MT. This approach can also enhance current techniques for finding translation equivalents by distributional similarity and for automatically identifying features of MT-tractable language.

1. Introduction

Automated MT evaluation methods such as BLEU, NIST and Meteor have been shown to be useful for monitoring progress in MT development, for parameter optimisation of statistical systems and, in some controlled circumstances, for comparing the performance of different MT systems. All such MT evaluation experiments rely on a corpus of human translations which are used as a reference for the MT output. Automated evaluation scores correlate with human scores and correctly establish the ranking of systems only if this corpus is relatively large, i.e. more than 6,000-7,000 words (Estrella et al., 2007; Babych et al., 2007b). Smaller samples of data are too noisy for reliably predicting a system's performance, since individual lexical mismatches between MT output and human reference are not informative on their own: they may be attributable either to errors of translation or to choices of different legitimate translation variants. While human judgements are meaningful at any granularity for which they are generated (the levels of syntactic constituent, sentence, paragraph, text and corpus as a whole), automated scores are generally not meaningful at any level below that of the corpus. As a result, automated evaluation scores are currently uninformative for error analysis tasks—specifically, for discovering typical translation errors and prioritising them for the purposes of MT development—since they give only a very general, 'birds-eye' view of MT performance.

Moreover, MT developers are often less interested in such non-specific performance figures than in a more detailed analysis and ranking of typical problems for their MT system whose resolution will improve the system's performance generally. As a result, developers of industry-standard (especially rule-based) systems consider these core automated evaluation metrics to be of little help in the MT development cycle (Thurmair, 2007), noting that they are not designed to provide direction to R&D (Miller & Vanni, 2005). Although human evaluation scores can be much more useful in this respect, they are expensive to obtain and are not available for significantly large corpora. Thus it is not feasible to rely on them for determining the range, frequency and seriousness of errors and, especially, for monitoring the progress of an MT system over time.

From this perspective, the challenge for automatic MT evaluation research is to develop methodology suitable for differentiated and fine-grained error analysis along the lexical, grammatical and stylistic dimensions. Our paper reports on a project for automatically discovering and ranking errors in translating multiword expressions (MWEs). We use the term in the sense of 'phraseological units' proposed by Vinogradov, as discussed in Cowie (1998). MWEs are defined as *repeated (continuous or discontinuous) combinations of words which are* ***re-constructed*** *(rather than* ***constructed)*** *in speech and are part of the 'mental lexicon'*. This definition includes both 'compositional MWEs' (e.g. *washing machine*) and 'non-compositional MWEs', or idioms in the broad sense (e.g. *meet the demand*, etc.).

While at this stage our methodology targets only the lexical dimension, we argue that it is a useful step towards more informative MT evaluation for developers and users of state-of-the-art MT systems.

2. Methodology

Our method is based on automatic evaluation of the translation of concordances for frequent MWEs extracted from aligned corpora. The methodology follows the following five stages.

Firstly, we generate automatically frequency-ranked lists of MWEs, using the approach described by Babych et al. (2007a), which relies on a combination of part-of-speech and frequency filters. The idea behind this approach is to collect all possible multiword candidates found inside a sliding window of a certain length (usually up to five words) and to compute the frequency of every candidate. Larger windows can also be used, but these result in smaller sets of MWEs passing the frequency threshold, since N-gram frequency quickly drops with longer N-grams.

Candidates which are above a specified frequency threshold and conform to certain part-of-speech patterns are typically found to be meaningful MWEs. Part-of-speech patterns can be specified either as a list of permitted configurations, or as a set of restrictions on them.

We modified this approach in order not to depend on morphological annotation, thereby making it knowledge-light and language-independent. The idea came from an observation that part-of-speech filters typically prevent the appearance of function words at one or both edges of MWEs. For example, the sequences *visual processing to, visual processing in, visual processing and* are filtered out, leaving only *visual processing* as a candidate MWE, which is selected if it passes a certain frequency threshold in a corpus. But rather than using a filter that relies on prior knowledge of parts-of-speech, we filter instead by log IDF scores, which distinguish content words from function words:

$$logIDF = \log\left(\frac{N}{df_i}\right)$$

where *N* is the number of texts in the corpus and df_i is the number of texts in which $word_i$ is found. The value of *logIDF* which best distinguishes content words from function words must be established experimentally for each corpus. It depends on the size of the texts and the total number of documents in the collection. For a corpus which contains 100 texts, each of about 350 words, the threshold *logIDF > 1* yields a relatively good distinction between content and function words.

Function words can be included inside candidate continuous MWEs (a productive pattern in Romance languages especially, e.g. *Fr: discrimination fondée* ***sur la*** *race – 'racial discrimination'*), but normally do not appear at the edges.

Thus, in our experiment we used a simple frequency filter and a statistical differentiation between content and function words for extracting MWEs. Other researchers have used different word association measures: mutual information, Dice's coefficient, t-score, chi-square and log likelihood (Baldwin, 2006). However, according to Evert and Krenn (2001), simple frequency can be as good as a wide range of such association measures for this task.

For continuous MWEs, a lower frequency filter can also yield good results, e.g. *Freq(MWE) >1* (Sharoff et al., 2006). However, since our methodology uses MWEs to generate concordances for which BLEU scores will be computed, a higher threshold was chosen in order to enhance the reliability of the automated scores by using a larger concordance sample.

Other methods of identifying MWEs may use linguistic annotation (e.g. part-of-speech tags) and apply different settings to the selection parameters, which will yield different types of expressions: discontinuous MWEs, expressions underspecified for certain lexical or morphological features, certain types of linguistic constructions, such as light verb constructions (*make decision, take into account, put pressure*) or phrasal verbs (*look after, come along*). The choice of setting is determined by the aspect of MT performance the research is intended to address.

In the second stage, and for the most frequent MWEs in a sentence-aligned parallel corpus, we automatically generate concordances that contain the MWEs themselves and several words in their local context. Thus the concordances can be viewed as sub-corpora selected by a specific MWE, intended to characterise the successfulness of their translation by MT. Moreover, concordances can be generated either for the source language (SL) or for the target language (TL): SL concordances are generated from original source texts while TL concordances are generated from human reference translations. Both are used for evaluating the quality of MT output sentences aligned with them.

In the third stage, the SL concordances are translated by the MT systems which are under evaluation. Interestingly, TL concordances can be used even if there is no access to the MT engine itself, that is, if only its MT-generated corpus is available. This is the case for some old systems which are no longer maintained, and for some in-house systems for which the developers choose not to give the evaluators direct access to their engine. In practical MT-evaluation scenarios, the users of MT systems often have no access to the working MT engine, and can use only an MT-translated corpus. Such scenarios typically occur when the evaluations of a system that is no longer maintained are intended to serve as an 'historic baseline', or when the MT system to be evaluated does not offer remote access and cannot be installed on the evaluators' local machines.

The reason that such use of the TL corpus is nonetheless possible is that the dynamic data (MWE concordances) is generated from human reference translations and not from texts translated by MT. Thus it is possible to use a 'frozen' corpus of previously translated MT output. This property of TL concordances proved useful for normalising the proposed methodology using human scores associated with the DARPA-94 MT evaluation corpus (White et al., 1994), even though the MT engines which translated the source texts are no longer available.

In the fourth stage, we compute BLEU scores (Papineni et al., 2002) based on both types of concordance. The scores for the translations of each SL concordance indicate how well a particular SL expression and its immediate context are translated, while the scores for the MT-generated versions of each TL concordance show whether a particular TL expression can be successfully generated by MT.

There are two important technical issues with using BLEU as a metric for this type of concordance-based MT evaluation. In the case of SL concordances, since word alignment may be too noisy we take the whole sentences (or even paragraphs) aligned with the concordance segments as the reference. As a result, the reference texts may be much longer than the tested concordances. This, however, is not a problem for BLEU, which is an asymmetric, precision-based metric and which therefore characterises the ability of MT to avoid generation of redundant N-grams. With the brevity penalty switched off, BLEU is only interested in whether a test file contains any spurious items which are not found in the reference. Therefore, the reference text can be arbitrarily large.

In the case of TL concordances, the MT output may be longer: it contains complete sentences rather than the immediate context of specific MWEs. In this case, we either use a recall-oriented metric – e.g. WNM (Babych and Hartley 2004) – or, if we prefer to use a precision-oriented metric, we swap the test and the reference files such that the MT output becomes a reference.

In the final stage, we generate the evaluation results in the form of tables, where particular MWEs are ranked by BLEU or other automated scores. MT developers can use the resulting tables similarly to how they use traditional risk-analysis tables: they can focus on highly-probable (i.e. most frequent) lexical errors with the greatest impact on quality (i.e. lowest BLEU for the concordance).

3. Experiments

We extracted MWEs from two aligned parallel corpora – a section of about 700k words from the Europarl corpus (Koehn, 2005) and the French/English section of the DARPA-94 corpus (35k words). The DARPA-94 data contains two human translations of the SL texts, named 'reference' and 'expert'. Despite the DARPA-94 corpus being much smaller, it is useful for normalising the proposed evaluation method because it offers two independent professional translations of the same text and human scores for *adequacy, fluency* and *informativeness*.

Our first group of experiments characterises the performance of the state-of-the-art rule-based system Systran 6.0 in translating between English and French/German/Spanish. The second group of experiments focuses on translations between English and French produced by several MT systems, (both rule-based and statistical) and on a meta-evaluation of the proposed methodology.

3.1. Extracting MWEs

From both corpora we extracted continuous MWEs with a high *logIDF* threshold, which produced lists of terminological or near-terminological expressions and proper names.

The selected part of the Europarl corpus was divided into 20 sections, each containing up to 1,500 segments, corresponding to approximately half a day of a plenary session of the Parliament. The sessions took place on different days between February 2000 and July 2001, and so the extracted terms and named entities reflect the topics discussed over this period. Since the sections were relatively large (up to 50k words), and the number of sections (treated as 'documents' in the collection) was small, we set a threshold of *logIDF>0.4* and applied a frequency filter of *Freq>4*. For the DARPA-94 corpus, which includes 100 relatively short news stories, we set *logIDF>1.0* and kept the same frequency threshold of *Freq>4*. Since MWEs were extracted only from original SL texts and from human reference translations, not from MT output, the set of MWEs was the same for all evaluated MT systems. Table 1 shows the number of MWEs extracted for each translation direction under these settings.

Table 1: Size of corpora and number of extracted MWEs

Corpora		French		*German*		*Spanish*	
		en>fr	fr>en	en>de	de>en	en>es	es>en
Europarl section	Words (tokens)	675k	706k	670k	625k	661k	683k
	MWEs (types)	279	333	249	283	287	273
DARPA94 (en transl.: 'expert'/ 'reference'	Words (tokens)	39k	39k	-	-	-	-
	MWEs (types)	58/68	54	-	-	-	-

For the Europarl, 154 English MWEs were found in all three sets aligned with French, German and Spanish (with different frequencies), and 106 other English MWEs occurred in two of the three sets. We used these common MWEs to investigate the quality of the translation of MWEs out of English into different target languages.

The majority of discovered MWEs consist of two words, but some have up to five. Frequencies of MWEs are in the range of 42-5 for the DARPA corpus and in the range of 86-5 for the Europarl corpus, and have the usual Zipfian distribution with a steeper hyperbolic curve typical for MWEs. Figure 1 illustrates the frequency distributions of MWEs, here in the DARPA-94 corpus.

Our selection settings (relatively high *logIDF* and frequency thresholds) in the experiments described here yielded primarily named entities and terminology or near-terminological expressions, and these provide the material for illustrating our error-analysis methodology. However, as we noted earlier, the range of evaluated constructions can potentially be much wider.

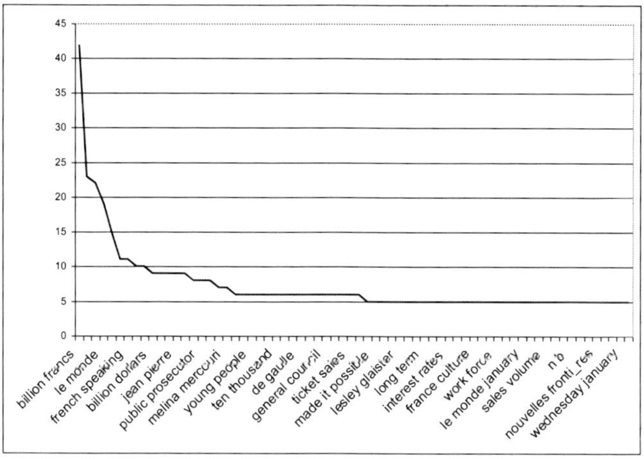

Figure 1: Frequency distribution of MWEs in DARPA-94

3.2. Generating aligned concordances, MT output and BLEU scores

For each extracted MWE, we generated aligned concordances. The concordances included the MWE itself and up to four words to the left and to the right. Each of these lines was aligned with a full segment (typically a sentence in the Europarl corpus, or a paragraph in the DARPA-94 corpus).

In our methodology, the use of both Source and Target Language concordances is designed to characterise two different aspects of MT quality. SL concordances identify problems mainly on the *analysis* side and highlight SL MWEs that are not translated properly. TL concordances identify problems on the *generation* side, listing TL MWEs that should be used in translation, but are not produced by the MT systems.

3.2.1. Source Language concordances

We use SL concordances to check the quality of MT for the immediate contexts of source MWEs. The concordances generated on the SL side are translated by MT and then aligned with the corresponding segments in the human reference translation (by their segment IDs). Table 2 illustrates these original concordances, their translation generated by the Systran 6.0 MT system ('Syst'), and the aligned human reference translations of the corresponding segments.

The rationale for our approach is that BLEU penalises disfluencies in MT output like *Minister **for the** European **businesses** (20-2), Minister **for the interior matters** (28-4), minister **for the** social affairs (35-2).* Since these contexts are selected systematically and in a controlled way, if an SL expression is systematically mistranslated, this has a measurable effect on the BLEU score for the concordance. Despite the evaluated concordance being much smaller than the texts normally evaluated by BLEU, the scores prove meaningful in that they allow MT evaluators to prioritise errors in the contexts of individual MWEs using the 'risk-analysis' framework, which we propose in Section 4

Table 2: Fr>En: SL concordance: French MWE *ministre des affaires*

seg	Aligned concordance	
12-2	ori.:	t il feint d'être **ministre des affaires** culturelles auprès du général
	Syst.:	it pretends to be a Minister for the cultural affairs near the general
	hum.:	[...] Malraux pretended to be minister of cultural affairs under General de Gaulle [...]
3-3	ori.:	et un représentant du **ministre des affaires** étrangères de même que
	Syst.:	and a representative of the Foreign Minister just as
	hum.:	[...] and a representative of the Ministry of Foreign Affairs," as well as with General Rahimi [...]
20-2	ori.:	théodore pangalos **ministre des affaires** européennes du gouvernement papandréou
	Syst.:	Theodore pangalos Minister for the European businesses of the government papandréou
	hum.:	[...] Theodore Pangalos, Minister of European Affairs in the Papandreou government [...]
28-4	ori.:	mathot (également du ps) **ministre des affaires** intérieures du même gouvernement
	Syst.:	mathot also of the PS Minister for the interior matters of the same government
	hum.:	[...] Guy Mathot (also a SP member), the minister of internal affairs of the same regional government.
35-2	ori.:	de vote. simone veil **ministre des affaires** sociales, de la santé
	Syst.:	of vote. Simone Veil, Minister for the social affairs, of health
	hum.:	[...] the right to vote. Simone Veil, Minister of Social Affairs, Health, and Cities [...]

As noted previously, in the case of SL concordances, the human reference segments are longer than their corresponding concordance segments and MT-generated translations (the table shows only part of these segments, which are one paragraph long and typically contain several sentences). To account for this, we switch off the brevity penalty when computing BLEU scores for each concordance. With these settings, the scores become meaningful thanks to the asymmetric nature of BLEU, which calculates only the *precision* of the N-gram matches, such that the scores are affected only by spurious items in MT output but not by missing items.

For the example in Table 2, the raw BLEU precision score (without brevity penalty) is 0.2563; the brevity penalty value is 0.0010 (an unusually low value for the standard text-level evaluation) and the final BLEUr1n4 score (the score with a single reference and N-gram size = 4, which takes into account the brevity penalty) is 0.0003. In our experiments we use the raw BLEU *PrecScore* alone as the only meaningful score under these settings.

Since the SL concordance lines are short and do not form complete sentences, the MT output may not be exactly the same for a particular concordance line as for the whole sentence from which it was extracted. However, MT systems usually take into account only local context of words and expressions, and normally the output is close to the sentence-level MT. It is not possible to use full sentences instead of concordances on the source side, because there will also be full sentences on the target side, and therefore BLEU scores will be influenced by errors in other parts of the sentence and will not characterise the quality of translation of particular individual MWEs.

3.2.2. Target Language concordances

We use TL concordances to check whether particular TL MWEs and their immediate contexts are accurately generated by the evaluated MT systems. The concordances generated on the TL side are aligned with the segments in the MT output produced by different MT systems. Table 3 illustrates the aligned concordance for the target English MWE *once again*, aligned with MT output from Systran 6.0 RBMT system ('Syst.') and the Google on-line SMT system ('gSMT'). The French original is given for explanatory purposes only and plays no part in the evaluation.

The rationale for evaluating TL concordances is that MT should be able to generate idiomatic TL expressions used by human translators, even if they come from a variety of different contexts in the source language. As can be seen from Table 3, for Systran and for Google SMT, the English MWE *once again* is only generated if it comes from the French source *une fois encore*, but not from the expressions *à nouveau, de nouveau,* nor from the lexical sources of this meaning like *redevenir ('to become once again'), revenir ('to come back').*

The table also shows that while Systran usually preserves a trace of all SL lexical items, the SMT system sometimes drops 'awkward' expressions which do not fit the target fluency model (segments 22-7, 73-5). In the standard BLEU evaluation scenario, only the brevity penalty accounts for these omissions, and at the text level they can pass practically unnoticed. However, our approach of using TL concordances reveals and penalises such omissions. To account for the fact that, in the case of TL concordances, the MT output is longer than the human reference, we again compute BLEU without the brevity penalty. In addition, we submit the TL concordances (i.e. the human reference translations) as *test* files and the aligned MT output segments as *reference* files. This may seem counter-intuitive (usually the MT output is the *test),* but it is done because BLEU, as a precision-based metric, basically counts how many N-grams from the *test* file are not in the *reference* and penalises these omissions. Since in our experiments we want to know whether TL expressions like *once again* have been omitted or mistranslated by MT, these TL expressions need to be in the *test* file when they are processed by the BLEU script.

Table 3: Fr>En: TL concordance: English MWE *once again*

seg	Aligned concordance	
22-7	hum.:	united states hopes to **once again** dominate the communications satellite
	Syst.:	Thanks to this experimental apparatus of 363 million dollars, the United States hopes to *again* dominate the market of the communications satellites [...]
	gSMT:	With this experimental device of 363 million dollars, the U.S. hopes to dominate the market for communications satellites [...]
	fr.ori.:	Grâce à cet appareil expérimental de 363 millions de dollars, les Etats-Unis espèrent dominer *à nouveau* le marché des satellites de communication. [...]
73-5	hum.:	hostile posture and become **once again** that affable champion the
	Syst.:	[...] Johann Koss could get rid of its quarrelsome airs. And to become *again* this gracious champion, [...]
	gSMT:	[...] Johann Koss could get rid of its air war. And become the champion affable, [...]
	fr.ori.:	[...] Johann Koss pouvait se débarrasser de ses airs belliqueux. Et redevenir ce champion affable, [...]
81-3	hum.:	also by declining prices. once again gains were realized by
	Syst.:	[...] but also by a fall of the prices. The profits *once again* came from the branch health [...]
	gSMT:	[...] but also by lower prices. Gains *once again* came from the health branch [...]
	fr.ori.:	[...] mais aussi par une baisse des prix. Les gains *une fois encore* sont venus de la branche santé [...]

Table 3: Fr>En: TL concordance: English MWE *once again* (continued)

81-4	hum.:	its available self-financing. **once again** stable in 1992, it now
	Syst.:	[...] the group which chairs Jean-Rene Fourtou improved its self-financing available. *Returned* with balance in 1992, it is from now on surplus of 2,15 billion. [...]
	gSMT:	[...] the group chaired by Jean-Rene Fourtou has improved its cash available. *Income* balance in 1992, it is now surplus of 2.15 billion. [...]
	fr.ori.:	[...] le groupe que préside Jean-René Fourtou a amélioré son autofinancement disponible. Revenu à l'équilibre en 1992, il est désormais excédentaire de 2,15 milliards. [...]
83-2	hum.:	the rail line, connecting **once again** with the casa dei
	Syst.:	He was always among those which, twenty-two years later, on the same way, inaugurated at the summer 1993 the rebirth of the way, rejoining *again* put it dei Puy-de-Dôme,
	gSMT:	He was always those who, twenty-two years later on the same route, inaugurated in the summer of 1993 the revival of the road, rallying *again* casa dei du Puy de Dome[...]
	fr.ori.:	Il était toujours de ceux qui, vingt-deux ans plus tard, sur le même trajet, inaugurèrent à l'été 1993 la renaissance de la voie, ralliant *de nouveau* la casa dei du Puy-de-Dôme [...]

Furthermore, TL concordances use MT output generated from complete sentences and texts (not just from very short concordance lines), so the result is not influenced by missing or inadequate contexts (a potential problem for the evaluation of SL concordances that we acknowledged above).

Finally, in the case of SL concordances mistranslated MWEs can usually be corrected by extending dictionary coverage, e.g. adding entries for *ministre des affaires culturelles, ministre des affaires étrangères, ministre des affaires européennes, ministre des affaires intérieures*. In contrast, the evaluation of TL concordances usually reveals more subtle translation problems, which may not be easy to rectify directly, e.g. that of generating the phrase *once again* from implicit semantic components of the verbs *redevenir* and *revenir*, while restricting this to appropriate contexts only.

4. Evaluation results

In this section we describe the results of SL and TL concordance-based evaluation for different MT systems before presenting the results of normalising the automated scores using human evaluation scores. The distribution of BLEU scores for the 260 MWEs identified in the Europarl corpus is shown Figure 2. BLEU scores are shown on the vertical axis, and ranks of MWEs on the horizontal axis. In this distribution there are fewer MWEs (39%) with scores below the average value of BLEU=0.11.

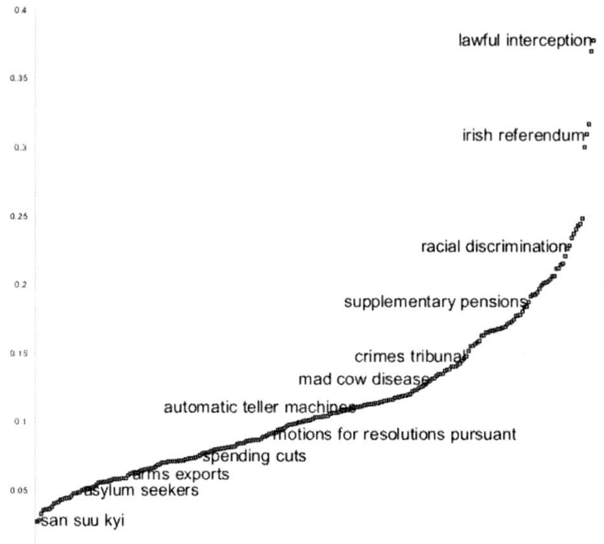

Figure 2. Distribution of BLEU scores for MWEs in the Europarl corpus

4.1. Evaluation of SL concordances of MWEs

We summarise the evaluation results for the contexts of all the identified MWEs within the framework of risk analysis. Traditionally, this framework is used to prioritise 'risks' for a particular project using two dimensions: the likelihood that some unfortunate event will occur, and the magnitude of its impact on the project. Thus the most likely events with the highest detrimental impact can be addressed first. In our approach we interpret frequencies of particular MWEs as the likelihood of events, and BLEU scores for their concordances as the magnitude of their impact. Our framework prioritises MWEs for MT developers, who can in the first instance deal with the most frequent MWEs with the lowest BLEU scores. For presentation purposes we plot *log(Frequency)* against *exp(BLEU)*, which scatters the evaluated MWEs more evenly across the risk analysis chart.

One direction for future research is developing an experimental meta-evaluation procedure for the proposed MT evaluation method, which will enable us to determine different scaling and weighting factors for the risk analysis framework.

Figure 3 shows a risk analysis plot for SL concordances of English MWEs from the DARPA-94 corpus translated by Systran 6.0 into French.

To simplify the presentation we show only selected MWEs; *exp(BLEU)* is on the vertical axis and *log(Frequency)* on the horizontal axis. Items in the bottom right quadrant are the most 'risky', since they have the highest frequency and the lowest BLEU score.

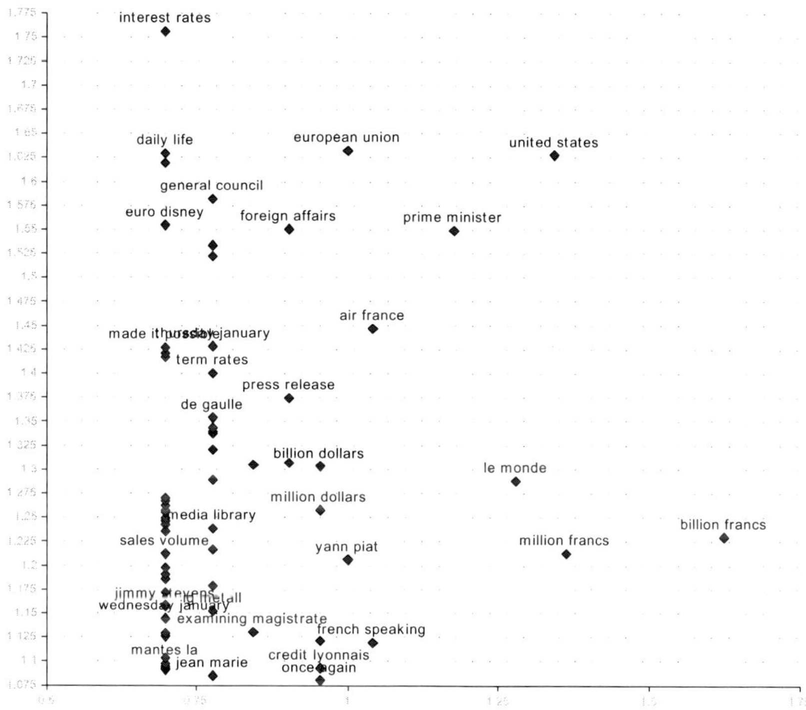

Figure 3. DARPA-94 MWE risk analysis chart: *x=log(Freq), y=exp(BLEU)*

Priority lists of MWEs can be generated by combining the two plotted parameters in different ways, e.g. *log(Freq)/exp(BLEU)=Priority* (possibly with different weights for Frequency and inverse BLEU scores). Table 4 shows the top of one such priority list.

Error analysis of these items identifies the following problems (we focus solely on the linguistically most interesting examples):

- MWE *billion francs* in the context of numerals is often translated as *milliard de francs*, while the reference contains *milliard**s** de francs*.
- MWE *french speaking* is consistently translated as *de langue française* by Systran, instead of *francophone(s)* or *francophonie*.
- MWE *once again* is always translated as *de nouveau* by Systran, while in the reference translation it is variously rendered as: *les Etats-Unis espèrent dominer **à nouveau** le marché des satellites de communication; ... ils s'étaient glissés **sous le nouveau** record du monde; Les gains **une fois encore** sont venus de la branche santé...;*

Revenu *à l'équilibre en 1992, il est désormais excédentaire de 2,15 milliards*. This expression displays greater variation in the ways it is translated in different contexts.

Table 4: Priority list of English MWEs in the DARPA-94 corpus

MWE	*FRQ*	*log(frq)*	*exp(BLEU)*	*BLEU*	*Priority*
billion francs	42	1.62	1.23	0.21	1.32
million francs	23	1.36	1.21	0.19	1.12
le monde	19	1.28	1.29	0.25	0.99
french speaking	11	1.04	1.12	0.11	0.93
once again	9	0.95	1.08	0.08	0.88
...					

Figure 4 and Table 5 show a risk analysis chart and the top of a priority list for English MWEs from the Europarl corpus, translated by Systran 6.0 into French, German and Spanish (using the average of BLEU across all three target languages).

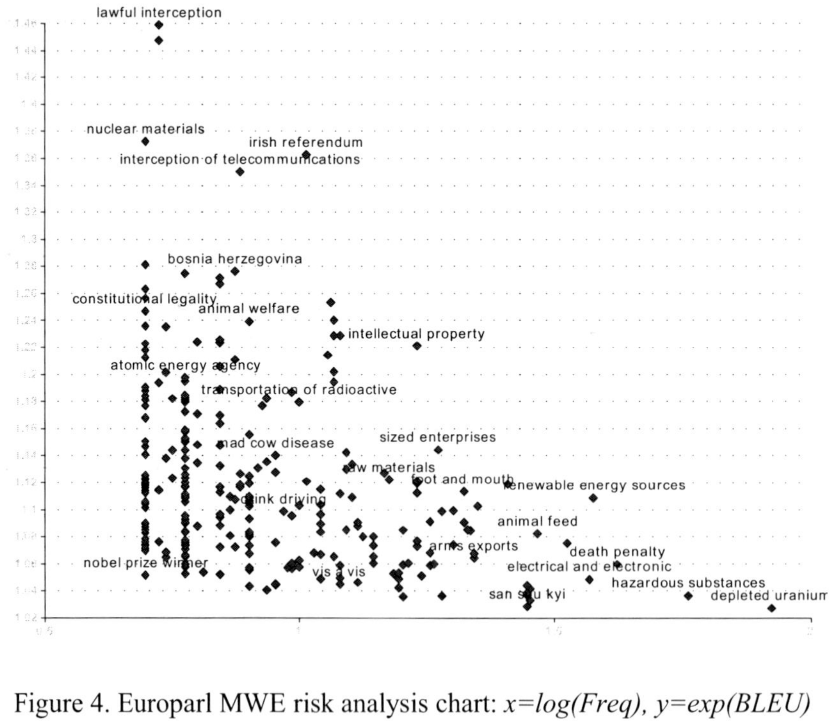

Figure 4. Europarl MWE risk analysis chart: *x=log(Freq), y=exp(BLEU)*

Table 5: Priority list of English MWEs in the Europarl corpus

MWEs	*frqAVE*	*log(FRQ)*	*exp(BLEU)*	*Priority*
depleted uranium	83.67	1.92	1.03	1.87
hazardous substances	57.5	1.76	1.04	1.7
death penalty	42	1.62	1.06	1.53
electrical and electronic	37	1.57	1.05	1.5
renewable energy sources	37.67	1.58	1.11	1.42
...				

These data identify the following problems with MWE translation:

- MWE *depleted uranium* is translated into German by Systran as *verbrauchtes Uran*, while the human reference translation uses *abgereichertes Uran* or in some contexts integrates the meaning into nominal compounds: *die Affäre um die Urangeschosse; uranhaltiger Munition*. This MWE is translated by Systran into French as *uranium épuisé,* while human translators always use *uranium appauvri*. The Spanish translation produced by Systran is always *uranio agotado,* while human translators use *uranio empobrecido*.
- MWE *death penalty* is translated by Systran into French as *pénalité de mort*, while human translators always use *peine de mort*.

4.2. Evaluation of TL concordances MWEs

To evaluate the TL concordances, we used four MT systems and the human 'expert' translation from the DARPA-94 MT evaluation corpus. For all five, we computed BLEU scores for each of our 68 concordances, using the (single) 'reference' translation and N-gram size up to 4. Table 6 presents the scores for some interesting MWEs for each MT system and for the 'expert' translation. The MWEs are sorted by the BLEU score for Systran. The headings in the table show the names of evaluated MT systems in DARPA-94 corpus: Human Expert translation, Candide SMT system, and Globalink, Metal, Reverso, Systran RBMT systems.

For MT output, low scores for the concordance of an MWE mean that it is not generated properly by the particular MT system. So we suggest that the highlighted MWEs are problematic for Systran and require the developers' attention. The threshold is set at the system's average BLEU score of 2.7, which also coincides with a jump in the series of values.

Table 6: BLEU scores for MWEs

	Hum (exp)	cand	glbl	ms	rev	syst
credit lyonnais	0.33	0.16	0.16	0.10	0.12	0.10
work force	0.37	0.35	0.10	0.10	0.12	0.11
ticket sales	0.26	0.24	0.09	0.11	0.2	0.11
once again	0.12	0.09	0.09	0.15	0.09	0.11
french speaking	0.48	0.11	0.15	0.23	0.26	0.12
sales volume	0.18	0.13	0.10	0.11	0.11	0.12
public prosecutor	0.21	0.17	0.16	0.12	0.30	0.18
take place	0.32	0.17	0.14	0.15	0.34	0.18
term rates	0.37	0.25	0.12	0.2	0.35	0.19
press release	0.23	0.22	0.19	0.15	0.17	0.19
daily life	0.39	0.17	0.23	0.17	0.45	0.20
so-called	0.38	0.20	0.15	0.19	0.16	0.21
young people	0.32	0.10	0.10	0.18	0.16	0.28
managing director	0.42	0.22	0.19	0.42	0.21	0.31
minister of foreign affairs	0.63	0.59	0.29	0.54	0.18	0.33
examining magistrate	0.36	0.13	0.14	0.29	0.25	0.34
media library	0.50	0.17	0.11	0.16	0.32	0.34
other hand	0.37	0.16	0.66	0.46	0.63	0.39
prime minister	0.54	0.33	0.44	0.24	0.44	0.39
interest rates	0.70	0.39	0.20	0.44	0.52	0.41
made it possible	0.23	0.21	0.10	0.11	0.18	0.41
european union	0.44	0.33	0.45	0.5	0.46	0.45
general council	0.43	0.21	0.49	0.45	0.48	0.48
united states	0.56	0.28	0.41	0.35	0.53	0.62

…

	Hum (exp)	cand	glbl	ms	rev	syst
Average	0.38	0.22	0.22	0.25	0.29	0.27

Note that average scores can characterise the general performance of any translation system, e.g. scores for human translation are higher than for MT output. Remember, however, that these scores are computed very differently than standard BLEU scores. The correlation of the average with human judgements is lower than the figures reported for BLEU, which are in the region of 0.98 (Babych & Hartley, 2004). Nevertheless, these concordance-based scores show a high positive correlation with adequacy, and a slightly lower correlation with fluency, despite the corpus size being much smaller. Table 7 shows these correlation figures.

Table 7: Correlation of average for all MWEs

	r correl
Adequacy	0.883
Fluency	0.620
Informativeness	0.380

We checked contexts for some expressions in Table 6 in order to determine whether lower BLEU scores are due to sporadic mismatches (since the size of the evaluation sub-corpus in this case is much smaller than for a standard BLEU evaluation), or whether lower scores indeed correspond to translation problems for these particular MWEs. In the majority of cases, lower BLEU scores correspond to consistently less fluent translations or mistranslations. Tables 8 and 9 illustrate such cases by comparing concordances for the human reference translation and MT output.

As can be seen from the tables, the MWEs were consistently translated less adequately than in the case of human translation. However, for MWEs with higher BLEU scores this was not the case: their translation was still adequate. Table 10 illustrates this fact for the MWE *minister of foreign affairs*, which is above the threshold of BLEU – 0.27.

Table 8: MWE *work force*

*Fr:... Depuis le début du siècle, ses **effectifs** sont passés de 15000 à 2500 emplois...*	
Human Ref	Systran
its **work force** has fallen from	its **manpower** passed from
believes that reducing the **work force** would	estimates that to touch **manpower** would
continues to reduce its **work force** in Europe	continues the reduction of its **manpower** in Europe
reducing its **work force** from	bringing back its **manpower** in

These results are surprising, given that BLEU is generally used only at 'higher' levels of evaluation: it offers high correlation with human judgments only at the level of an entire corpus, but not for individual texts or sentences. Yet it appears from our experiments that these scores present an additional 'island of stability' at the level of individual lexicogrammatic constructions. Concordance-based evaluation appears to provide an approach to these constructions that is sufficiently focused for BLEU scores to become meaningful also at the micro-level. A possible explanation for this is that the sub-corpus used for evaluating MWEs is collected in a very controlled way, which limits the noise factor.

Table 9: MWE *ticket sales*

*Fr:... Soit 53 % des **entrées** avec 40 % des écrans... La famille-fantôme fait mieux que la famille saint-bernard avec, respectivement, 75 000 (près de 160 000 en quinze jours) et 67 000 **entrées** (200 000 en trois semaines).*	
Human Ref	Systran
this would be 53% of **ticket sales** with 40% of the screens	That is to say 53% of the **entries** with 40% of the screens
and 67 000 **ticket sales** (200 000 in three weeks	and 67 000 **entries** (200 000 in three weeks
with another 43,000 **ticket sales** during its fifth week	with 43 more 000 **entries** in fifth week

Table 10: MWE *minister of foreign affairs*

*Fr:... Les négociations actuelles, patronnées par les Etats-Unis, sont menées par le **ministre** croate **des affaires étrangères**, Mate Granic, et le premier ministre bosniaque, Haris Silajdzic*	
Human Ref	Systran
in paris the **minister of foreign** affairs stated friday	In Paris, the **Foreign Minister** declared, Friday
the israeli **minister of foreign** affairs Shimon Peres thought	The Israeli **Foreign Minister** Shimon Peres estimated
led by the **croat minister of foreign affairs** Mate Granic	carried out by the Croatian **Minister for the Foreign Affairs**, Mate Granic
the nigerian **minister of foreign affairs** babangana kingibe left	**The minister** Nigerian **of the Foreign Affairs**, Babangana Kingibe, flied away

To conclude, we can define our risk analysis measure for MWE expressions as a (possibly weighted) combination of MT evaluation score for an MWE concordance and its frequency.

4.3. Normalisation for translation variation

As noted earlier, in the case of MT output, low BLEU scores for the concordance of an MWE mean that the MWE is not generated properly.

However, we included in our evaluation set the second human translation provided by DARPA-94 (the 'expert' translation) and for this human translation the meaning of lower BLEU scores is very different. If we suppose that professional human translators cannot frequently be wrong, then lower scores for a given MWE mean that there are other legitimate ways to express the intended meaning. Therefore, generating that specific MWE is not essential for the content. Such expressions typically belong to the general lexicon and can be freely re-phrased in the same context.

On the other hand, if a given MWE has a high BLEU score, then it was consistently inserted into the text by both human translators. Thus, it is more stable and possibly even obligatory for such contexts. Such expressions are usually terms or other stable constructions which require specific and invariable translation equivalents.

Table 11 presents MWEs sorted by the BLEU scores for the 'expert' human translation. The table shows that general language expressions with greater contextual variability are at the top, while more stable terminological units are at the bottom. (Highlighting of problematic expressions for Systran is preserved from Table 6.)

This finding suggests that MT systems should be rewarded for having higher BLEU scores for more stable constructions but allowed greater freedom to deviate from less stable equivalents. Accordingly, we should take into account not only absolute values of BLEU for a given construction, but also how different the score for an MT system is from the corresponding BLEU score for a human translation. In the general case, BLEU for MT and for human translations are independent, but the measure of MT quality is precisely how close they are: in other words, whether we can reliably predict the difference between the MT and human scores given the raw MT score.

Figure 5 illustrates this point. The horizontal axis shows values for human translation, and the vertical axis shows values for Systran.

Table 11: MWEs sorted by 'expert' human BLEU

	Hum (exp)	cand	glbl	ms	rev	syst
once again	0.12	0.09	0.09	0.15	0.09	0.11
sales volume	0.18	0.13	0.1	0.11	0.11	0.12
public prosecutor	0.21	0.17	0.16	0.12	0.30	0.18
press release	0.23	0.22	0.19	0.15	0.17	0.19
made it possible	0.23	0.21	0.10	0.11	0.18	0.41
ticket sales	0.26	0.24	0.09	0.11	0.20	0.11
take place	0.32	0.17	0.14	0.15	0.34	0.18
young people	0.32	0.1	0.10	0.18	0.16	0.28
credit lyonnais	0.33	0.16	0.16	0.10	0.12	0.10
examining magistrate	0.36	0.13	0.14	0.29	0.25	0.34
work force	0.37	0.35	0.1	0.10	0.12	0.11
term rates	0.37	0.25	0.12	0.20	0.35	0.19
other hand	0.37	0.16	0.66	0.46	0.63	0.39
so-called	0.38	0.20	0.15	0.19	0.16	0.21
daily life	0.39	0.17	0.23	0.17	0.45	0.20
managing director	0.42	0.22	0.19	0.42	0.21	0.31
general council	0.43	0.21	0.49	0.45	0.48	0.48
european union	0.44	0.33	0.45	0.50	0.46	0.45
french speaking	0.48	0.11	0.15	0.23	0.26	0.12
media library	0.50	0.17	0.11	0.16	0.32	0.34
prime minister	0.54	0.33	0.44	0.24	0.44	0.39
united states	0.56	0.28	0.41	0.35	0.53	0.62
minister of foreign affairs	0.63	0.59	0.29	0.54	0.18	0.33
interest rates	0.70	0.39	0.20	0.44	0.52	0.41

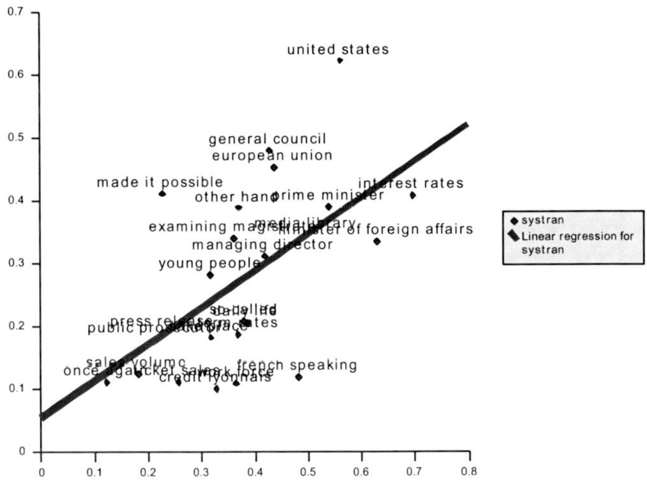

Figure 5: BLEU for human translation vs Systran MT

MWEs in this chart are located along two dimensions: MWEs closer to the right are more stable (more terminological), while those closer to the left belong to the general lexicon and can be more frequently rephrased. On the other hand, MWEs at the top are less problematic for Systran MT, while those at the bottom are more difficult. In an ideal case, the points of the chart should be close to the diagonal line. Deviations from this line mean either that an MT output matches the human translation of a variable term (e.g. MWE *made it possible* in the top-left corner of Figure 5), or that it does not cover specific stable terms (e.g. MWE *French-speaking* in the bottom-right corner of Figure 5 – there is a gap in Systran's dictionary: *...of the Flemish francophonie...* instead of ... *of the Flemish French-speaking community...*).

We suggest that we can measure certain aspects of MT quality by the degree of agreement between BLEU scores for human translation and for MT. Such agreement can be captured by the correlation coefficient *r*. We compute it between two arrays of scores: the array of raw BLEU figures for an MT system, and the array of differences between these scores and BLEU for the human translation (for corresponding MWEs):

$$N = r\frac{BLEU_{MT}^{MWE}}{BLEU_{MT}^{MWE} - BLEU_{HumanTr}^{MWE}}$$

We found that there is a high correlation between human judgments for informativeness and the N (normalised variation) score. Table 12 illustrates the correlation between N and each of the human evaluation parameters available for the DARPA corpus.

Table 12: Correlation: N-score vs human scores

	cand	glbl	ms	rev	syst	**r corr with N**
N-score	0.13	0.38	0.25	0.45	0.38	
[ade]	0.68	0.71	0.71		0.79	0.72
[flu]	0.45	0.38	0.38		0.50	-0.02
[inf]	0.64	0.75	0.66		0.76	**0.97**

The table suggests that for better, more informative MT systems there is better agreement between BLEU scores for MT and the difference {MT vs human}: if BLEU is low, then the difference should also be low, which means that the human score is low as well. Thus MT is allowed to have low scores only for re-phrasable, highly variable expressions from the general lexicon.

To summarise, the proposed N-score is the measure of how well MT translates stable (e.g. terminological or idiomatic) expressions, which are repeatable and highly recognisable by human users of MT, especially for particular subject domains, genres or types of texts. Normalisation for legitimate translation variation for N-scores comes at a cost, as it is essential to have more than one human translation for MT evaluation.

5. Applications

The proposed approach can be useful in two main ways, without the need for human scores. Firstly, it can discover MWEs on the SL side or on the TL side which are, respectively, poorly translated by one or several MT systems, or not properly generated. Along these lines, our method is useful for MT developers in their efforts to discover the most typical lexical errors and improve the quality of their systems. It is equally useful for MT users who wish to extend their dictionaries before launching production in a new subject domain.

Secondly, our approach can also highlight MWEs which are usually translated correctly by MT systems. This information can be useful in the specification of features of MT-tractability (Bernth et al., 2001) using large-scale corpus data, and based on the performance of a particular state-of-the-art MT system.

Finally, we have shown that the N-score, which is a correlation coefficient between standard and normalised BLEU scores for individual MWEs, is a good predictor of human judgements about informativeness at the corpus level. Previously, no automated metrics could approximate this particular quality parameter.

6. Future work

Future work will involve determining an optimal size of immediate context for the concordances, selecting the most revealing automatic metrics, the (meta-)evaluation of the approach using, for example, corpus-level human scores, and determining those classes of MT error which most influence human evaluation scores.

Acknowledgements

The work is supported by the Leverhulme Trust.

Bibliography

Babych, B. & Hartley, A. (2004). Extending the BLEU MT evaluation method with frequency weightings. In ACL 2004: Proceedings of the 42nd Annual Meeting of the Association for Computational Linguistics (pp. 621-628); Barcelona, Spain, July 21-26, 2004.

Babych, B., Sharoff, S., Hartley, A., & Mudraya, O. (2007a). Assisting Translators in Indirect Lexical Transfer. In ACL 2007: Proceedings of 45th Annual Meeting of the Association for Computational Linguistics (pp. 136-143); Prague, Czech Republic, June 23-30 2007.

Babych, B., Hartley, A., & Sharoff, S. (2007b). Translating from under-resourced languages: comparing direct transfer against pivot translation. In Proceedings of Machine Translation Summit XI (pp. 412-418); Copenhagen, Denmark, September 10-14, 2007.

Baldwin, T. (2006, July). *Compositionality and multiword expressions: Six of one, half a dozen of the other?* Invited talk given at the COLING/ACL'06 Workshop on Multiword Expressions: Identifying and Exploiting Underlying Properties, Sydney, Australia.

Bernth, A., & Gdaniec, C. (2001). MTranslatability. *Machine Translation, 16*, 175-218.

Cowie, A.P. (1998). Introduction. In A.P. Cowie, (Ed.), *Phraseology: Theory, analysis, and applications* (pp. 1-20). Oxford: Oxford University Press.

Estrella, P., Hamon, O., & Popescu-Belis, A. (2007). How much data is needed for reliable MT evaluation? Using bootstrapping to study human and automatic metrics. In Proceedings of Machine Translation Summit XI (pp. 167-174); Copenhagen, Denmark September 10-14, 2007.

Evert, S., & Brigitte K. (2001). Methods for the qualitative evaluation of lexical association measures. In Proceedings of the 39th Annual Meeting of the Association for Computational Linguistics and 10th Conference of the European Chapter (ACL-EACL 2001) (pp. 188–195); Toulouse, France, July 7, 2001.

Koehn P. (2005) Europarl: A parallel corpus for statistical machine translation. In Proceedings of Machine Translation Summit X (pp. 79-86); Phuket, Thailand, September 13-15, 2005.

Miller, K.J. & Vanni, M. (2005). Inter-rater agreement measures, and the refinement of metrics in the PLATO MT evaluation paradigm. In Proceedings of Machine Translation Summit X (pp. 125-132); Phuket, Thailand, September 13-15, 2005.

Papineni, K., Roukos, S., Ward, T., & Zhu, W-J. (2002). Bleu: A method for automatic evaluation of machine translation. In Proceedings of the 40th Annual Meeting of the Association for Computational Linguistics (pp. 311-318); Philadelphia, PA, July 6-12, 2002.

Sharoff, S., Babych, B., & Hartley, A. (2006). Using comparable corpora to solve problems difficult for human translators. In Proceedings of COLING/ACL 2006 Conference (pp. 739-746);, Sydney, Australia, July 17-21, 2006.

Thurmair, G. (2007, September). *Automatic evaluation in MT system production*. Invited talk given at Machine Translation Summit XI workshop: Automatic Procedures in MT Evaluation, Copenhagen, Denmark.

White, J.S., O'Connell, T., & O'Mara, F. (1994). The ARPA MT evaluation methodologies: evolution lessons and future approaches. In Technology partnerships for crossing the language barrier: Proceedings of the First Conference of the Association for Machine Translation in the Americas (pp. 193-205); Columbia, MD, USA, October 5-8, 1994.

Evaluating RBMT output for -ing forms: A study of four target languages

Nora Aranberri-Monasterio
Dublin City University

Sharon O'Brien
Dublin City University

-ing forms in English are reported to be problematic for Machine Translation and are often the focus of rules in Controlled Language rule sets. We investigated how problematic -ing forms are for an RBMT system, translating into four target languages in the IT domain. Constituent-based human evaluation was used and the results showed that, in general, -ing forms do not deserve their bad reputation. A comparison with the results of five automated MT evaluation metrics showed promising correlations. Some issues prevail, however, and can vary from target language to target language. We propose different strategies for dealing with these problems, such as Controlled Language rules, semi-automatic post-editing, source text tagging and "post-editing" the source text.

1. Introduction

The focus of this paper is on evaluating the Machine Translation (MT) output for one linguistic feature, -ing forms, into four target languages (French, Spanish, German and Japanese). Our interest in -ing forms stems from our study of Controlled Language (CL). Controlled Language is defined as "an explicitly defined restriction of a natural language that specifies constraints on lexicon, grammar, and style" (Huijsen, 1998, p. 2). CL rules can be implemented to reduce ambiguities in the source text in order to improve the machine translated output (Bernth and Gdaniec, 2001; O'Brien, 2003).

CL rule sets often include one or more rules on -ing forms in English. O'Brien (2003) found that six of the eight CLs she analysed shared a rule which recommended avoiding "gerunds". According to Dervišević and Steensland (2005), AECMA Simplified English does not allow the use of either gerunds or present participles, with the exception of certain technical terms. The Microsoft Manual of Style for Technical Publications (MSTP) (Microsoft Corporation, 1998) cautions against the use of gerunds. There is at least some consensus, then, that -ing forms can be problematic for RBMT. The following example, taken from our research corpus, illustrates the problem:

ST: *Viewing and changing active jobs*
DE: **Anzeigende und ändernde in Arbeit befindliche Programmteile*
ES: **Viendo y modificando tareas activas*
FR: **Les JOBs actifs de visionnement et changeants*
JA: *実行中のジョブを表示し、変更します

Rules controlling the use of -ing forms are often formulated in very general terms (e.g. "Avoid the use of -ings") and, consequently, technical writers find them difficult to implement. -ing forms can be categorised into different functional linguistic categories and sometimes the CL rule seeks only to govern "gerunds" (e.g. "Avoid the use of gerunds").[1] There are two problems with this. First, previous research has not made it clear why gerunds, and not other categories of -ing forms, are specifically targeted. Second, technical writers typically do not have a background in grammar or linguistics and the term "gerund" is therefore difficult for them to comprehend.[2] Given that there is general consensus that -ing forms, or at least gerunds, can create problems in RBMT output, coupled with the vagueness of rules governing this phenomenon, we felt that there was a need for more detailed research on this topic.

Our research was co-funded by Enterprise Ireland and Symantec under the Innovation Partnerships Programme. Symantec implemented the MT system, Systran, in 2006 to meet their increasing translation volumes for security alert information. They also implemented customised Controlled Language checking rules using the acrocheck™ tool.[3] Both Systran (version 5.05) and acrocheck™ were used in this research and the corpus was compiled from Symantec technical documentation.

Our primary research questions were: How problematic for RBMT are -ing forms, and what processes can we implement to reduce those problems for at least four target languages? To answer these questions it was necessary to evaluate the MT output for -ing forms. Automatic evaluation metrics such as BLEU (Papineni et al., 2002) and NIST (NIST report 2002) are commonly used for MT evaluation. Human evaluation of output is also used either in conjunction with automatic metrics or on its own. Much has been written about how these metrics work and on how human evaluation results correlate (or not) with automated metrics (cf. Callison-Burch et al., 2006). However, little has been written specifically on the evaluation of MT output for the -ing form and, to the best of our knowledge, no detailed, contrastive analysis has been published to date on -ing forms and their MT output into multiple target languages.

Section 2 of this paper discusses the methodology used for compiling the corpus, classifying the -ing forms and evaluating them. Section 3 gives details of our results and Section 4 provides the conclusions and an outline of future work.

2. Methodology

2.1. Classifying -ing forms

In order to analyse what effect -ing forms have on MT output in different languages, we needed a useful classification system. Traditionally, words ending in -ing have been divided into two categories: gerunds and participles (Quirk et al., 1985). Huddleston and Pullum (2002) claim that the current usage of the English language shows no systematic correlation of differences in form, function and aspect between the traditional gerund and present participle. They propose that words with a verb base and the -ing suffix be classified as gerundial nouns (genuine nouns); gerund-participles (forms with a strong verbal flavour); and participial adjectives (genuine adjectives).

In grammar books, -ing forms are described under the sections of different types of word classes, phrases or clauses in which they can appear, that is, a syntactic description of the -ing form is spread throughout the grammar description. However, no classification has focused on -ing forms as a main topic or in a detailed manner. Izquierdo (2006) faced this deficiency when carrying out a contrastive study of the -ing form and its translation into Spanish. She compiled a general language parallel English-Spanish corpus, mainly consisting of texts extracted from fiction, and analysed the -ing forms, comparing the theoretical framework set out in grammar books and the actual uses found in her corpus. She established a functional classification of -ing forms (see Table 1).

Table 1: Izquierdo's (2006) functional classification of -ing forms

Functions	**Adverbial**	**Progressive**	**Characterisation**		**Referential**
Grammatical Structures	time	past	Pre-modifiers	Post-modifiers	catenative
	process	present	participial adjective	reduced relative clause	prepositional clause
	purpose	future		nominal adjunct	subject
	contrast	conditional		adjectival adjunct	direct object
	place	etc.			attribute complement
	condition				comparative subordinate
	etc.				

Izquierdo's classification was considered suitable for our study for several reasons. Firstly, we focus on RBMT systems, that is, the analysis, transfer and generation modules are built upon grammatical rules. Therefore, a classification that could describe fixed grammatical patterns was considered appropriate.

Secondly, by using the syntax-based tagger of our CL checker (acrocheck™) during a search of our corpus, the behaviour of the checker for these particular forms would be better understood.

Thirdly, -ing forms cannot be classified in isolation; contextual information must be considered in order to distinguish a gerundial noun from a participial adjective or a gerund-participle. The functional classification would provide boundaries for this context.

Additionally, it would allow us to test whether the same classification used for general language would be suitable for a specialised domain such as IT.

2.2. Corpus Compilation

One of the first questions we had to answer regarding the design of our research was whether to use a test suite or a corpus in order to study the -ing form. Test suites allow the researcher to isolate the linguistic structures under study and to perform an exhaustive analysis of all the possible combinations of a specific linguistic phenomenon, with the certainty that each variation will only appear once (Balkan et al., 1994). On the other hand, a corpus allows the researcher to focus on authentic and real texts, on language as it is used (McEnnery et al., 2006, pp. 6-7). Given that this research focuses on text produced and machine-translated in an industrial context, we felt it was important to use a corpus that represented -ing forms as they are produced by technical writers. However, the corpus approach is not without its problems, which we discuss below.

It is essential to ensure the validity of a corpus, i.e. its suitability for studying the selected linguistic phenomenon. Literature on corpus design highlights the difficulties in guaranteeing ecological and sample validity. Yet, authors concur that the decisions made must depend on the purpose of each study (Bowker & Pearson, 2002, pp. 45-57; Kennedy, 1998, pp. 60-85; Olohan, 2004, pp. 45-61).

Kennedy (1998, pp. 60-70) highlights three design issues to be taken into consideration when building a corpus: stasis and dynamism; representativeness and balance; and size. A dynamic corpus is one that is constantly upgraded whereas a static corpus includes a fixed set of texts gathered in a specific moment in time. The aim of the present research is to study the current performance of our RBMT system when dealing with -ing forms given the current level of MT system development and source text quality. Dynamic corpora are mainly used when trying to capture the latest uses of language or when studying linguistic changes over time. Since we did not expect the use of -ing forms to change, we opted for a static corpus.

Representativeness is the second design issue highlighted by Kennedy (ibid, pp. 62-65). He points out that it is difficult to ensure that the conclusions drawn from the analysis of a particular corpus can be extrapolated to the language or genre studied (ibid, pp. 60). We focus on the -ing words which appear in IT manuals (user guides, installation guides, administrator's guides, etc.). These documents have in common that they are made up of descriptive and procedural text-types. Text-types are "groupings of texts that are similar with respect to their linguistic form" (Biber, 1988, pp. 70), which means that the syntactic patterns tend to be stable. This increases the representativeness of our data. Yet, additional controls suggested by Bowker and Pearson (2002, pp. 49-52) were taken into account in selecting the texts: text length, number, medium, subject, type, authorship, language and publication date. Complete texts were used so as to ensure that any variation in -ing form use from one text section to the next would be represented. Bowker and Pearson also recommend that studies of linguistic features include a series of texts written by a series of authors so as to avoid idiosyncratic uses affecting the results. In order to address this issue, texts describing different products and written by different writing teams were included. It was decided to use texts which had not undergone any language control, that is, the selected texts should not have been written following the Controlled Language rules. This would make it possible to measure the extent to which -ing forms cause problems prior to implementation of CL rules and also allow us to develop procedures for fixing any problems encountered (see "Conclusions").

Bowker and Pearson (2002, p. 48) state that in studies related to language for specialized purposes (LSP), corpus sizes ranging from between ten thousand to several hundred thousand words have proven "exceptionally useful". Following this, the initial corpus created for this project amounted to 494,618 words.

We feel that the ecological validity of the corpus was ensured by using real texts that meet both the relevant number, authorship and date variation, and stability in subject, type and medium as required for the population for which we intend to draw conclusions.

With the classification system in place and the corpus compiled, we then had to extract all occurrences of -ing forms in the corpus and classify them before sending them to the RBMT system and having their translations evaluated. Using acrocheck™ to extract as many instances as possible of -ing forms, 8,316 instances were classified from a total of 10,417 in the corpus, i.e. 79.83%.[4] Such high correlation with a classification presented from general language further reflects the suitability and coverage of our corpus. The classification of the 8,316 instances is shown in the appendix. One modification was made to Izquierdo's classification, i.e. we introduced the category of "Titles" starting with -ing forms. Titles have a high level of occurrence in instruction manuals and they are not always handled correctly by RBMT systems. Titles which start with -ing forms often require a different translation from identical -ing forms in running text. For example:

ST [Title]: *Using default su or query credentials*
ES [Title]: *Usar configuración predeterminada su o credenciales de consulta*
Vs.
ST: *Creating a policy for true image restore by using the Policy Wizard*
ES: *Crear una política para el establecimiento de la imagen verdadera usando el asistente de políticas*

This difference causes difficulties for RBMT systems, which are not yet designed to distinguish between running text and titles. It was therefore considered essential to study the performance of the MT system when dealing with this particular structure, especially given their frequency of occurrence (25% of -ing forms in the corpus).

2.3. Human Evaluation

Since our research focuses on evaluating the RBMT output for -ing forms and little work has to date been done using automated metrics for specific sub-sentential linguistic constituents (with the exception of constituents such as subjects, NPs and CNPs evaluated by Callison-Burch et al. (2007)), we opted for a human evaluation. While large-scale machine translation evaluation initiatives such as the NIST Open Evaluation or the Shared Translation Task in the ACL Workshop on Statistical MT use unlimited numbers of human judges to evaluate as many examples as they choose, smaller experiments report results based on 3 to 7 judges and this is expected to allow for enough variation, particularly if the evaluation is performed by experts (Pierce, 1966; Elliott et al., 2004; Estrella et al., 2007). In keeping with this trend, we hired four professional translators per target language to judge whether the translations of the -ing forms were "correct" or "incorrect". By "correct" we mean grammatical and accurate. MT evaluation experiments have recently converged into reporting the parameters "fluency" and "adequacy" (or "accuracy") (Cieri et al., 2007; etc). Whereas the meaning of adequacy seems generally agreed upon, the meaning of fluency is less clear. As Mutton et al. (2007) discuss, authors have defined fluency differently, ranging from closer to grammaticality (Pan and Shaw, 2004) to an intuitive reaction (NIST MT Evaluation Plan Guidelines, 2005), as well as including attributes such as rhythm and flow, among others (Coch, 1996). The LDC (2003) defines fluency as the "degree to which the translation is well-formed according to the grammar of the target language", thereby bringing it close to the definition of grammaticality. Since the research was being conducted in an industrial setting, our aim was to learn whether the translation generated by the RBMT system was ready for publication. The standard acceptable for publication depends on the expected function of the translated text. For our context, the minimum quality required for publication was set as a grammatical text which transferred the same information as the original text.

The use of human evaluators limited how many examples could be judged. We used a stratified systematic sampling technique to extract an evaluation set of 1,800 examples. Evaluators were asked to judge the translation of the -ing words only. They were presented with a source segment in which the -ing form to be judged was highlighted (so that it could be easily identified), together with the machine translation of the segment and a post-edited version, which they were told to use for reference purposes as an example of what could be accepted for publication. Due to the novelty of the constituent-based approach, evaluators were provided with some guidelines. This allowed for better understanding of our aim and, we hoped, a higher level of consistency.

The analysis of the results was performed by a native-speaker linguist for each target language. They were asked to examine the examples that the evaluators had judged as incorrect. They were provided with guidelines to ensure that the results from all four target languages could be compared.

2.4. Testing for Correlations between Human and Automated Metrics

Human evaluation is time-consuming and expensive, and its reliability has been a hot topic in recent years (Vilar et al., 2007). As an alternative, automated metrics have been proposed to measure the quality of MT output. Most of these metrics compare the machine translation output against one (or more) reference translations and report a score based on their similarity. The most widespread within MT evaluation experiments are string-based metrics, such as BLEU and NIST. These metrics, however, report the results for the text or sentence level, and their usefulness for calculating scores for a sub-sentential linguistic feature remains largely unexplored. Therefore, we decided to test correlations between the constituent-based human evaluation and a constituent-based automatic evaluation.[5]

We chose 5 different metrics that could be run using short constituents, namely, n-gram-based NIST (NIST Report, 2002), word-based GTM (Turian et al., 2003), TER (Snover & Dorr, 2006; Przybocki et al., 2006) and METEOR (Banerjee & Lavie, 2005), and character-based edit-distance (NLTK). The most widespread BLEU metric did not allow us to work on short constituents, as it uses a geometric mean to average the n-gram overlap (therefore, if one of the values of n produces a zero score, the total score is nullified). NIST, however, combines the scores for 1 to 5 n-grams using the arithmetic average and can be used with short segements. The GTM metric, based on precision and recall and the composite f measure instead of n-grams, pays less attention to word order. Thus there is no penalty for short segments and it can be used with constituents. We chose TER because it also calculates the distance between the MT-generated output and the reference translation, but does so by counting the number of insertions, deletions and substitutions required, based on edit-distance techniques. The last word-based metric used was METEOR. This metric diverges from the previous ones in that it uses a stemmer to calculate the scores. Finally, we included a character-based edit-distance metric, to examine whether better correlations could be found by using a character-based metric instead of a word-based metric in short constituents.

In order to obtain the -ing constituents, we asked the native-speaker linguists to read the 1,800-sentence evaluation set provided to the human evaluators and to highlight the translation of the -ing words in the MT output and the post-edited versions. They were required to do so according to the same criteria given to the human evaluators in the guidelines. The highlighted segments were extracted and treated as sentence units for input to the metrics. The segments obtained from the post-edited version were used as reference segments.

3. Results

The results of the human evaluation showed that for German, Japanese and Spanish, 72%-73% of the -ing forms were grammatically and accurately translated (see Figure 1). The average for French was lower, with 52% of the examples classified as correct. This lower score was mainly due to two frequently occurring -ing constituents, which were consistently translated incorrectly by the RBMT system for French. The human evaluation outcome, although impossible to compare with other problematic structures due to lack of similar exhaustive research, demonstrates that this RBMT system handles -ing words quite well. Yet there is clearly room for improvement.

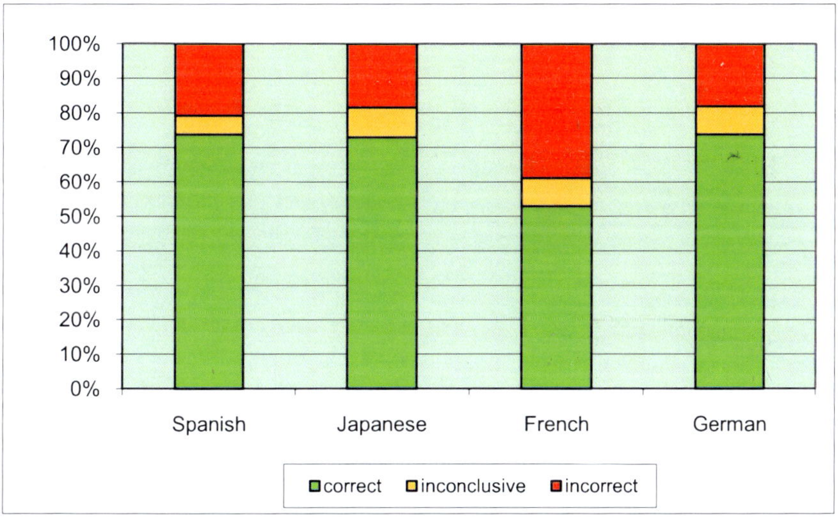

Figure 1: Percentage of correct and incorrect examples across the 4 target languages

We tested the validity of the evaluation by using the (Fleiss) kappa inter-rater measurement to calculate the reliability of the answers provided by the evaluators. The agreement was good for French (K=0.702), German (K=0.630) and Spanish (K=0.641) and moderate for Japanese (K=0.503). The results were satisfactory for two reasons. First, they confirm that the constituent-based approach to evaluation can obtain good inter-rater correlations (Callison-Burch et al., 2007). Second, the constituent-based approach is suitable for evaluating an attribute such as grammaticality and accuracy and does not need to be restricted to a ranking evaluation.

The first group in our classification were titles. The evaluation showed that for French (61%), Japanese (32%) and Spanish (36%) titles were problematic. For German, correct translations were more frequent, but 20% remained incorrect. Two types of problem arose with titles. First, a number of gerund-participles were analysed as participial adjectives and translated as modifiers into all target languages. Second, generation problems were observed, in which apparently correctly analysed gerund-participles were incorrectly translated as gerunds into Spanish, as infinitives and present participles into French and as nouns and gerunds functioning as subjects of the misanalysed plural nouns following the -ing form into Japanese. See Figure 2 for the percentage of correct examples, per category and target language.

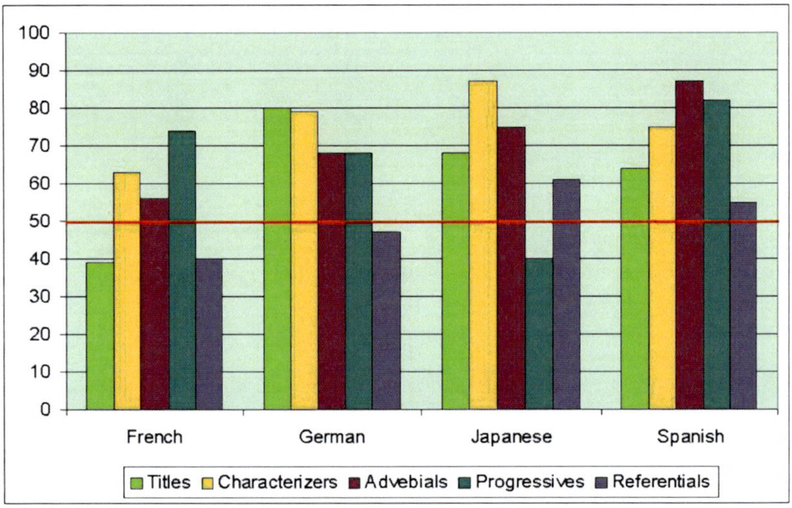

Figure 2: Percentage of correct examples for each -ing constituent category per target language

Characterizers were our second group. Whereas pre-modifiers were generally correctly analysed and translated when the terms were included in the MT system's dictionaries, we observed that post-modifiers presented more problems. The MT system generated post-modifying structures for the target languages; these structures, however, were not completely grammatical. For instance, for French, passive voice reduced relative clauses were translated into a combined structure of passives and participles. For Japanese, post-modifiers tended to show dependency errors. Equally, the MT system often failed (across all four languages) to generate correct prepositions and word classes following adjuncts.

The third group covered adverbial clauses with an -ing head. Spanish and Japanese performed better, with respective averages of 87% and 75% correct examples. German obtained a lower number of correct examples, at 68%. The target language most affected by these constituents was French, for which only 56% of the examples were translated correctly. All target languages showed problems with the choice between preposition or subordinate conjunction. Japanese and German, in particular, displayed ambiguity issues with gerund-participles translated as modifiers. Japanese encountered dependency errors, and the German output used incorrect pronouns to refer to the implicit subjects. French performed poorly in the translation of the constituent "*when + -ing*" as, when trying to generate an impersonal subordinate clause, the MT system created gerunds, which is incorrect for this context.

The -ing forms which combine with verbal tenses to introduce progressive aspect were our fourth group. For French and Spanish, this group performed well with respectively 74% and 82% of examples evaluated as correct. The issues found for these target languages were mainly due to the combination of continuous tenses and the passive voice and, in particular for French, the loss of progressive aspect. For German, the number of examples translated correctly was 68%, mainly due to these -ing forms being translated as nouns. For Japanese, the translation of the -ing forms in this group was predominantly incorrect, with only 40% of output correct. Despite the poor performance for Japanese, on average this group performed well across languages.

Finally, let us review the group of referential -ing forms. This was by far the worst-performing group, with 61% correct examples for Japanese, 55% for Spanish, 47% for German and 40% for French. We noticed that most issues were due to lack of translation resources. For instance, gerundial nouns were incorrectly translated in the cases where the MT system did not have the appropriate terminology available. Another example is catenative constituents, in which -ing forms were translated into incorrect word classes, leading to a literal translation that was often incorrect in the target languages. Similar issues were noted for phrasal verbs as for gerundial nouns, whereas prepositional verbs behaved more like catenatives. We observed that the particular constituents within each subgroup performed differently for each target language.

3.1. Correlation between human evaluation and automatic metrics

Our aim was to examine whether the -ing constituent evaluation could be performed using some of the existing automatic metrics. We isolated the constituents and their translations and we calculated the NIST, TER, GTM, METEOR and character edit-distance scores. Because we had four evaluators, the examples were therefore divided into 5 categories in which, in the worst case, none of the evaluators considered the example correct (0), and in the best case, all four evaluators considered the example correct (4). When one evaluator considered a translation to be correct, this corresponds to 1 on our x axis (See Figures 3 and 4); where two said it was correct, this is equal to 2; and so on. We then calculated the average automatic metrics score for each category.[6]

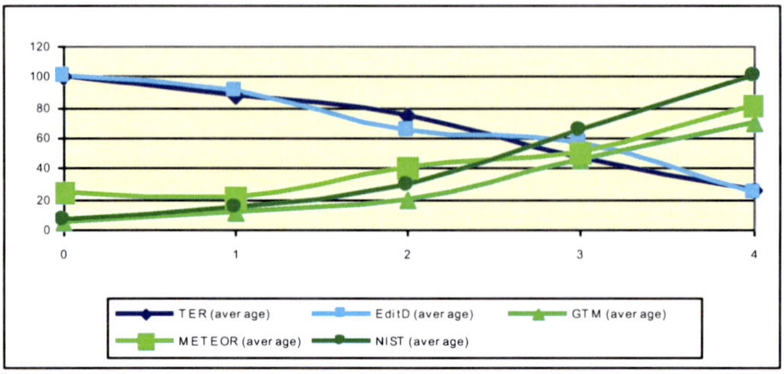

Figure 3: Automatic scores for the -ing constituents classified according to the number of evaluators who considered them correct for French

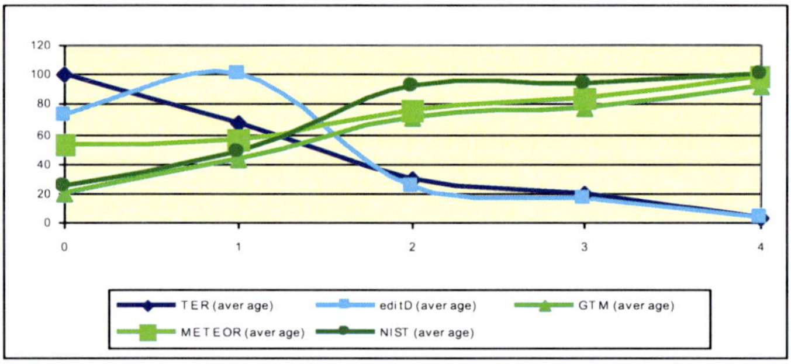

Figure 4: Automatic scores for the -ing constituents classified according to the number of evaluators who considered them correct for Spanish

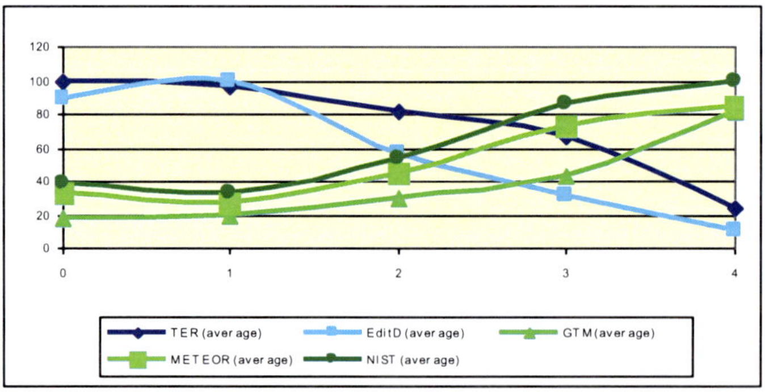

Figure 5: Automatic scores for the -ing constituents classified according to the number of evaluators who considered them correct for German

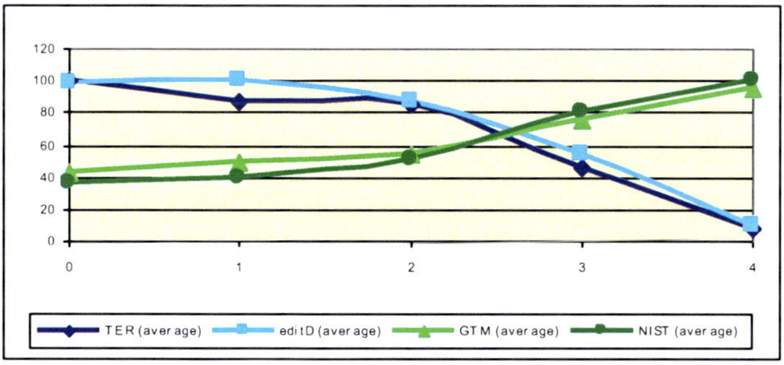

Figure 6: Automatic scores for the -ing constituents classfied according to the number of evaluators who considered them correct for Japanese

From the results we can clearly see that the tendency for each category correlates with the response of the human evaluators. According to the automatic metrics, while the examples classified as incorrect by all the evaluators (0) need higher numbers of changes to convert to the reference translation, the examples classified as correct by all four evaluators (4) need hardly any changes. We calculated the Pearson r-correlation between the mean human scores and the mean automatic metric scores to see if we could verify the trend shown above (see Table 2).

Table 2: Pearson r-correlation for the human evaluation score means (H) and automatic metrics score means (NIST, TER, GTM, METEOR, EditD) where all results are significant at the 0.01 level.

Pearson r-correlation	French	Spanish	German	Japanese
H / NIST	0.97	0.93	0.97	0.96
H / TER	-0.99	-0.97	-0.93	-0.94
H / GTM	0.96	0.97	0.92	0.96
H / METEOR	0.93	0.98	0.92	N/A
H / EditD	-0.98	-0.86	-0.94	-0.92

It is agreed that correlation is weak if the coefficient is less than 0.5 and strong if the coefficient is greater than 0.8. Our results are in the region of 0.86 to 0.99. Therefore, we observe that, even if the difference between them is statistically significant at 0.01, the agreement between human scores and automatic metrics is strong regardless of the automatic metric and the target language used.[7]

4. Conclusions

-ing forms are functionally very flexible, yet we conclude that they do not deserve their reputation for being classified as highly problematic for RBMT. The MT system has proven to be able to translate -ing forms grammatically and accurately 72-73% of the time for German, Japanese and Spanish. French performed worse, achieving correct translation for half the samples. However, closer examination allowed us to pinpoint the reason for the 20-point difference. Two highly frequent constituents were found to be systematically incorrect for French but not for the other target languages. Had these two constructs obtained similar results to those of the other target languages, the overall results would have been similar for all four.

A comparison between the human evaluations and NIST, GTM, TER and Edit-distance, showed good correlations. This may be an interesting avenue for further investigation.

A fined-grained analysis of the translation of the -ing constituents helped us detect the most problematic categories. The issues we found varied in type and we have considered solutions that could be implemented at different stages in the machine translation process. Firstly, we considered the use of controlled language at the content authoring stage. CL is most beneficial for the issues shared across all languages. Such was the case for titles, reduced relative clauses and prepositional phrases, and we have fine-tuned existing rules in the CL rule set for some of these categories.

Not all our -ing categories were problematic across all languages and, therefore, CL rules are not an appropriate solution. Hence, alternative ways should be explored and additional pre-processing stages are suggested. For example, the RBMT system we tested detects participial adjectives correctly but occasionally translates gerund-participles as modifiers. Our current research examines whether it would be possible to tag gerund-participles in such a way that the MT system could understand the tags and disambiguate appropriately.

Another obvious avenue of exploration for language-specific issues is to simply post-edit the MT output. We are investigating how to semi-automate the post-editing process so that recurring problems can be quickly fixed using find-and-replace rules crafted for each target language, based on our knowledge from this research. Another possibility we are considering is to "post-edit the source text" (Somers, 1997). This would involve editing the source text to eliminate known problems for specific target languages. This is different from implementing CL rules, which are normally implemented by technical writers at the time of writing, and the resulting documentation is published in English and is machine translated. A major advantage of post-editing the source text is that the modified source, because it would not be published, could contain any sort of "ungrammatical" changes in the source text, which would, hopefully, produce grammatical MT output.

Our future work will involve implementing and testing the effectiveness of these proposed solutions for the different categories of -ing forms across all four target languages.

Bibliography

Balkan, L., Netterz, K., Arnold, D. & Meijer, S. (1994). Test suites for natural language processing. In Proceedings of Language Engineering Convention (pp. 17-22);, Paris, July 6-7, 1994.

Banerjee, S. & Lavie, A. (2005). METEOR: An automatic metric for MT evaluation with improved correlation with human judgments. In Proceedings of Workshop on Intrinsic and Extrinsic Evaluation Measures for MT and/or Summarization at the 43rd Annual Meeting of the Association of Computational Linguistics (ACL-2005 (pp. 65-72); Ann Arbor, Michigan, June 29, 2005.

Bernth, A. & Gdaniec, C. (2001). Mtranslatability. *Machine Translation, 16*, 175-218.

Biber, D. (1988). *Variation across speech and writing*. Cambridge: Cambridge University Press.

Bowker, L. & Pearson, J. (2002). *Working with specialized language. A practical guide to using corpora*. London/New York, NY: Routledge.

Callison-Burch, C., Osborne, M. & Koehn, P. (2006). *Re-evaluating the role of BLEU in machine translation research*. In Proceedings of the 11th Conference of the European Chapter of the Association for Computational Linguistics (pp. 249-256); Trento, Italy, April 3-7, 2006.

Callison-Burch, C., Fordyce, C., Koehn, P., Monz, C. & Schroeder, J. (2007). *(Meta-)Evaluation of machine translation*. In Proceedings of the Second Workshop on Statistical Machine Translation (pp. 136-158); Prague, Czech Republic, June 23, 2007.

Cieri, C., Strassel, S., Glenn, M. L., & Friedman, L. (2007, September). *Linguistic resources in support of various evaluation metrics*. Presentation at MT Summit XI Workshop: Automatic Procedures in MT Evaluation, Copenhagen, Denmark.

Coch, J. (1996). Evaluating and comparing three text-production strategies. In Proceedings of the 16th International Conference on Computational Linguistics (COLING 96) (pp. 249-254); Copenhagen, Denmark, August 5-9, 1996.

Dervišević, D. & Steensland, H. (2005). *Controlled languages in software user documentation*. M.A. thesis, Department of Computer and Information Science, Linköpings University. Linköping, Sweden.

Elliott, D., Hartley, A. & Atwell, E. (2004). A fluency error categorization scheme to guide automated machine translation evaluation. In R.E. Frederking & K.B. Taylor (Eds.), *AMTA 2004* (pp. 64-73). Berlin/Heidelberg: Springer-Verlag.

Estrella, P., Popescu-Belis, A. & King, M. (2007). A new method for the study of correlations between MT evaluation metrics. In Proceedings of the 11th Conference on Theoretical and Methodological Issues in Machine Translation (pp. 55-64); Skövde, Sweden, September 7-9, 2007.

Huddleston, R. & Pullum, G. (2002). *The Cambridge grammar of the English language*. Cambridge: Cambridge University Press.

Huijsen, W.O. (1998). Controlled language – An introduction. In Proceedings of the Second Controlled Language Applications Workshop (CLAW 1998) (pp. 1-15); Pittsburgh, Pennsylvania, May 21-22, 1998.

Izquierdo, M. (2006). *Análisis contrastive y traducción al español de la forma -ing verbal inglesa*. M.A. thesis, Department of Modern Philology, University of León, León, Spain.

Kennedy, G. (1998). *An introduction to corpus linguistics*. London/New York, NY: Longman.

LDC (2003). *Linguistic data annotation specification: Assessment of fluency and adequacy in translation*. Project LDC2003T17.

McEnnery, T., Xiao, R. & Tono, Y. (2006). *Corpus-based language studies*. London/New York, NY: Routledge.

Microsoft Corporation (1998). *Microsoft manual of style for technical publications* (2nd ed.). Redmond, WA: Microsoft Press.

Mutton, A., Dras, M., Wan, S. & Dale, R. (2007). GLEU: Automatic evaluation of sentence-level fluency. In Proceedings of the 45th Annual Meeting of the Association of Computational Linguistics (pp. 344-351); Prague, Czech Republic, June 23-30, 2007.

National Institute of Standards and Technology (2002). *Automatic evaluation of machine translation quality using N-gram co-occurrence statistics*. Retreived January 26, 2009 from http://www.nist.gov/speech/tests/ mt/2008/doc/ngram-study.pdf

NLTK (Natural Language Toolkit). Retrieved January 26, 2009 from http://www.nltk.org/

O'Brien, S. (2003). Controlling controlled English: An analysis of several controlled language rule sets. In Proceedings of the 4th Controlled Language Applications Workshop (CLAW 2003) (pp. 105-114); Dublin, Irelend, May 15-17 ,2003.

Olohan, M. (2004). *Introducing corpora in translation studies*. Abingdon/New York, NY: Routledge.

Pan, S. & Shaw, J. (2004). Segue: A hybrid case-based surface natural language generator. In Proceedings of the International Conference on Natural Language Generation (INLG04) (pp. 130-140); Brighton, UK, July 14-16, 2004.

Papineni, K., Roukos, S., Ward, T. & Zhu, W.J. (2002). *BLEU: A method for automatic evaluation of machine translation*. In Proceedings of the 40th Annual meeting of the Association for Computational Linguistics (ACL-2002) (pp 311-318), Philadelphia, PA, July 7-12, 2002.

Pierce, J.R., et al. (1966). *Language and machines: Computers in translation and linguistics. A report by the Automatic Language Processing Advisory Committee*. .Washington, D.C.: National Academy of Sciences – National Research Council.

Przybocki, M., Sanders, G. & Le, A. (2006). *Edit distance: A metric for machine translation*. In Proceedings of LREC 2006: Fifth International Conference on Language Resources and Evaluation (pp. 2038-2043); Genoa, Italy, May 24-26, 2006.

Quirk, R., Greenbaum, S., Leech, G. & Svartvik, J. (1985). *A comprehensive grammar of the English language*. London: Longman.

Snover, M. & Dorr, B. (2006). A study of translation edit rate with targeted human annotation. In *Visions for the Future of Machine Translation* (pp. 8-12): Proceedings of the 7th Conference of the Association for Machine Translation in the Americas (AMTA 2006) (pp. 223-231);,Cambridge, UK, August 8-12 ,2006.

Somers, H. (1997). A practical approach to using MT software – "Post-editing" the source text. *The Translator, 3(2),* 193-212.

Turian, J., Shen, L. & Melamed, I.D. (2003). Evaluation of machine translation and its evaluation. In Proceedings of the Machine Translation Summit IX (pp. 386-393); New Orleans, LA September 23-27, 2003.

Vilar, D., Leusch, G., Ney, H. & Banchs, R.E. (2007). Human Evaluation of Machine Translation Through Binary System Comparisons. In Proceedings of the Second Workshop on Statistical Machine Translation (pp. 96-103); Prague, Czech Republic, June 23, 2007.

Appendix: Numbers of Extracted –ing Forms and Their Classifications

titles 2,603	**beginning with -ing**	**no quotations**	**1,255**			
		within quotations	**BOS**	**530**		
			embedded in sentence	**620**		
	beginning with about + -ing	**no quotations**	**100**			
		within quotations	**BOS**	**60**		
			embedded in sentence	**38**		
referentials 594	**nouns**	**252**				
	comparatives	**46**				
	objects of prepositional verbs	**116**				
	objects of phrasal verbs	**13**				
	catenatives	**167**				
characterizers 2,488	**pre-modifiers**	**participial adjectives**	**1,873**			
	post-modifiers	**reduced relatives**	**377**			
		nominal adjuncts	**226**			
		adjectival adjuncts	**12**			
progressives 661	**present**	**active**	**501**			
		passive	**117**			
		questions	**2**			
	past	**active**	**9**			
		passive	**3**			
	future	**2**				
	modal	**22**				
	infinitive	**5**				
adverbials 1,970	**manner 763**	**by - 516**	**without - 88**	**ϕ - 159**		
	contrast 11	**instead of - 11**				
	time 728	**before- 179**	**after – 139**	**when – 313**	**while – 65**	**between – 4**	**upon - 1**

		on – 8	**in – 2**	**during – 2**	**prior – 1**	**along with – 2**	**in the middle of - 2**
		from – 2	**through – 5**	**ϕ - 3**			
	concession 1	**besides - 1**					
	place 1	**where - 1**					
	purpose 444	**for – 443**	**in - 1**				
	condition 20	**if - 20**					
	cause 2	**because 2**					

[1] For an overview of the different functional categories of –ing words, see Izquierdo 2006.

[2] We draw on our experience here with the editors and technical writers in Symantec.

[3] CL checkers are software programs that allow checking for specific syntactic or lexical occurences which are disallowed, according to the specific CL rule set.

[4] The unclassified 20.17% can be accounted for by -ing forms which do not fall into any of the syntactic patterns proposed by Izquierdo due to long-distance occurrence, that is, the -ing form is not directly followed/preceded by the syntactic anchors used to retrieve them using the CL checker. We also expect that there is a large number of gerundial nouns acting as subjects or objects in the remaining group. No specific search was carried out for this group for two reasons. Firstly, because unless they are preceded by a determiner they are difficult to find automatically. Secondly, because they behave as genuine nouns and should be included in the RBMT system's dictionary, thus not creating problems for translation.

[5] Note that we use "-ing form" to refer to words that end in -ing whereas we use "-ing constituents" when we refer to the -ing form in context.

[6] Given that the automatic scores express the results on different scales, we normalized them in order to compare the trends. Note that there is no upper bound for the TER and Edit-distance scores. For those metrics the highest score, i.e. the worst-performing score, was taken as the upper bound. Note also that these two metrics score best when the result is zero, as opposed to NIST, GTM and METEOR, for which a zero score is the worst possible result. This is the reason why the metrics appear to go in opposite directions on the graphs.

[7] Note that the negative sign refers to the direction of the correlation.

Can Machine Translation meet the needs of official language minority communities in Canada? A recipient evaluation

Lynne Bowker
University of Ottawa

Canada is an officially bilingual country, but the only legal requirement is for federal services to be offered in both official languages. Therefore, services provided by provincial and municipal governments are typically offered only in the language of the majority, with cost being cited as the main obstacle to providing translation. This paper presents a recipient evaluation designed to determine whether machine translation could be used as a cost-effective means of increasing translation services in Canadian official language minority communities. The results show that not all communities have the same needs, and that raw or rapidly post-edited MT output is more suitable for information assimilation, while maximally post-edited MT output is a minimum requirement when translation is intended as a means of cultural preservation and promotion. The survey also suggests that average recipients are more receptive to MT than are language professionals.

1. Introduction

Evaluation of machine translation (MT) can and must take many forms depending both on the goal of the evaluation and on which stakeholders are involved (White, 2003). Common types of evaluations include developer evaluations, researcher evaluations and end-user evaluations (Dorr et al., 1999, pp. 48-54). However, Chesterman and Wagner (2002, pp. 80-84) describe another way of approaching MT evaluation, noting that it is possible to view translation as a service, intangible but wholly dependent on customer satisfaction; therefore, to measure translation quality, one needs to measure customer satisfaction. Such an approach to evaluating MT is referred to as a *recipient evaluation*, which is described by Trujillo (1999, p. 255) as an evaluation performed by the recipients of the translation in order to evaluate quality, cost and speed. According to Loffler-Laurian (1996, p. 69), the recipients of MT output are in the best position to judge whether this output satisfies their requirements.

Although the literature on MT evaluation is extensive, comparatively little attention is paid to recipient evaluations. While it is likely that many organizations that employ MT conduct some type of recipient evaluation, the details of these evaluations are not widely published. A literature survey presents several indirect references to recipient evaluations (e.g. Nuutila, 1996; Senez, 1998; Brace, 2000), but for many of these, little specific information about the evaluation procedure is provided, and the sparse information that is available is largely anecdotal in nature. Notable exceptions are Henisz-Dostert et al. (1979) and Vasconcellos and Bostad (1992) who furnish more detailed reports on recipient evaluations. Although these reports are valuable, they have become somewhat dated given the pace at which MT technology is both improving and taking hold.

Despite the shortage of references to recipient evaluations, there is no doubt that there are many recipients of MT output. In this era of globalization, increased demand for translation has been coupled not only with shorter deadlines but also with a shortage of human translators available to meet this demand (ABI, 2002; Shadbolt, 2002, pp. 30-31). One way to ease the burden has been to make greater use of MT systems for certain types of translation tasks. MT systems can produce translations far more quickly, and often more cheaply, than human translators; however, in the vast majority of cases, the quality of raw MT output is inferior to that produced by human translators.

Nevertheless, there are documented cases when MT fills a genuine need, such as automatic translation of product knowledge bases carried out in order to reduce the number of technical support calls to companies such as Intel and Microsoft (Dillinger & Gerber, 2009). Moreover, a growing body of evidence demonstrates that use of MT is rising. For example, the Allied Business Intelligence (ABI) report of 2002 identified MT as an area with "exponential growth potential" (ABI 2002: 5.21) and predicted that by 2007 the global translation market would be worth US$11.5 billion and the MT market worth US$133.8 million (ABI, 2002, 5.23). According to Brace (2000, p. 220), use of MT at the European Commission has soared since the early 1990s: In 1996, 220,000 pages were run through the MT system; and by 2000 this number had more than doubled to 546,000 pages (ABI, 2002:, p. 5.14). A more recent account (DePalma, 2007, p. 46) notes that the city of San Francisco has experimented with MT to provide translations in various languages to residents who have limited English proficiency. The following caveat appears on the city's Web site: "We prefer to provide automated translation rather than no translation at all in order at least to provide speakers of other languages an overall sense of the information available on a web page."

The experiment in San Francisco raises an important point, one underscored by Somers (2003, p. 88) in a paper on translation technologies and minority languages: Speakers of non-indigenous minority languages are typically not well served in their local communities. In the case outlined by DePalma (2007), MT is offered as a sort of 'bonus' for residents with limited English. In other words, the city of San Francisco is not obliged to translate texts, but offers the service as a sort of goodwill gesture. Many other municipalities are considerably less generous in attempting to meet the needs of linguistic minorities.

This difficulty of accessing information in one's own language can be witnessed even in countries such as Canada that officially mandate bilingualism,. In Canada, MT does not seem to be heavily used as a means of providing access to text in both official languages.[1] This could be because MT is generally associated with lower quality results as compared to human translation; so offering MT as a solution for translating an official language may be perceived as an indication that one of the languages is somehow "less official" or of lower status than the other and therefore does not deserve high quality translation. To the best of our knowledge, no serious investigation has been conducted into the reception of MT in a context where bilingualism is officially legislated. Would the use of MT be rejected outright for reasons of perceived loss of status or equality? Or would the case of "having an automated translation is better than having no translation at all" apply as it did in the San Francisco experiment described by DePalma (2007, p. 46)? Would speakers of the two official language groups react to MT in the same way? The goal of this paper is to move towards filling this knowledge gap by reporting on a large-scale recipient evaluation that specifically targets members of Canada's official language minority communities (OLMCs).

The paper begins with an overview of what it means to be an OLMC in Canada, introducing two different communities as examples: a French-speaking OLMC in Saskatchewan, and an English-speaking OLMC in West Quebec. Next, the costs of providing translation services to OLMCs are considered, followed by description of an experiment that investigates whether MT could be used as a means of partially meeting the translation needs of these OLMCs. The experiment takes the form of parallel recipient evaluations conducted in the Saskatchewan and West Quebec OLMCs, and the results of these evaluations are discussed and compared.

2. Official bilingualism and official language minority communities (OLMCs) in Canada

Canada is a country with two official languages: English and French. The French language is used predominantly in the province of Quebec, while English is more prevalent elsewhere in the country. In Canada, OLMC designation therefore refers to an English-speaking community within Quebec or a French-speaking community outside Quebec.

There is sometimes confusion about precisely what it means to be an officially bilingual country. In the case of Canada, English and French became recognized as the official languages of all federal institutions in the country following passage of the *Official Languages Act* in 1969. In 1988, a new *Official Languages Act* came into force, which sets the following three basic objectives of the Government of Canada:

- To ensure respect for English and French as the official languages of Canada and ensure equality of status and equal rights and privileges as to their use in all federal institutions;
- To set out the powers, duties and functions of federal institutions with respect to the official languages of Canada;
- To support the development of English and French linguistic minority communities and generally advance the equality of status and use of the English and French languages within Canadian society.

In November 2005 the Parliament of Canada passed additional amendments to the *Official Languages Act*, which now requires all federal government agencies to adopt measures to foster growth and development of OLMCs.

For the most part, the federal government has done a reasonable job of meeting the first two objectives. Canadians generally have access to information about federal services in both languages, and they can usually interact with federal institutions in the official language of their choice. However, Canada is divided into ten provinces and three territories, with the result that the Canadian federal structure of government is extremely decentralized. Although this decentralization affords flexibility, in the case of official languages it also brings complexity. Provincial governments have broad responsibilities and they vigorously defend their almost exclusive jurisdiction over important areas that, in other countries, would be strongly influenced or controlled by central national authorities. For example, in Canada, healthcare, education, social welfare, and civil rights all fall under provincial rather than federal jurisdiction.

Although the federal government can encourage development and equal treatment of OLMCs in the 13 provinces and territories, 12 of these are not legally required to provide provincial or territorial services in both official languages.[2] The same is true of the vast majority of municipal governments. As a result, provincial and municipal services are generally offered only in the language of the majority. Understandably, this approach does not sit well with members of the OLMCs. In a cross-Canada consultation exercise conducted by the Office of the Commissioner of Official Languages (OCOL), members of such communities were severe in their judgments of the behaviour of provincial governments with respect to the official languages of Canada (Adam, 2000, p. 5). The OCOL went on to criticize the situation, noting that "all too often, the federal government transfers its responsibilities to other levels of government, or to the private sector, without ensuring continued respect for the language rights of the persons receiving these services" (Adam, 2001, p. 39). These observations have since been echoed by the Standing Joint Committee on Official Languages in a report to the Parliament of Canada (SJCOL, 2002, p. 2) and by Lord (2008, pp. 16-17) in the *Report on the Government of Canada's Consultations on Linguistic Duality and Official Languages*.

Given this situation, we set out to conduct a preliminary investigation into whether MT could offer at least a partial solution for addressing the unmet translation needs of Canadians living in OLMCs. A recipient evaluation is highly appropriate in this case because in order for use of MT to be considered viable, the intended recipients of the target texts must accept the output produced by MT systems. We selected two different communities for this parallel study of the reception of MT output in French and English OLMCs: the Fransaskois and West Quebecers. The following sections introduce these two OLMCs and describe the respective contexts in which they have evolved. By gaining deeper understanding of some of the challenges facing these OLMCs, we can better interpret their reactions to MT output.

2.1. The Fransaskois

The first of the two OLMCs studied is the Fransaskois[3], a community of Francophones living in the predominantly English-speaking province of Saskatchewan, located in the midwest of Canada. Data from Statistics Canada's 2006 census show that the province of Saskatchewan has a total population of 968,157, with approximately 19,500 inhabitants (roughly 2% of the total population) having French as a native language. This figure has declined from 1951, when approximately 4.4% of the residents of Saskatchewan were Francophones (OCOL, 2007, p. 22).

Historically, Francophones settled in small rural pockets across Saskatchewan, and according to the OCOL (2007, p. 15), statistics indicate that the majority of Fransaskois still reside in predominantly rural areas. As Churchill (1998, p. 68) notes, rurally located OLMCs such as the Fransaskois face particular challenges. They are threatened by assimilation, especially if existing levels of federal and/or provincial support for community organizations are reduced. Moreover, provincial governments have proved themselves largely reticent when it comes to adopting measures to assist development of OLMCs. Churchill (1998, p. 40) also notes that in provinces like Saskatchewan, which have an English-speaking majority and are primarily rural, the expansion of public services in French has been driven primarily by legal and constitutional pressures rather than by provincial politicians seeking to improve the status of the French language. Francophone residents of Saskatchewan who participated in the OCOL's cross-Canada consultations in 2000 were very clear that this lack of political support is keenly felt in their province (Adam, 2000, p. 114).

Furthermore, it would seem that members of the Fransaskois community are also facing an uphill struggle to gain recognition and support outside the political arena. Several investigations and surveys have revealed that Anglophones living in Saskatchewan do not find the French community to be prominent and have less interest in participating in bilingual education than do Anglophones from other provinces (OCOL, 2007, p. 4-13). The Fransaskois community thus faces a considerable challenge in raising its visibility and promoting the value of its language and culture to the Anglophone majority living in Saskatchewan.

Another issue that may be perceived as a factor diminishing the importance of French in Saskatchewan is the significant presence of Aboriginal or First Nations language use in the province. Similarly, as increasing numbers of immigrants from various countries come to live in Canada, members of many OLMCs, including the Fransaskois, have concerns about the long-term effects of the country's rapidly changing demographic composition. The situation in the province of Saskatchewan is particularly striking: While approximately 2% of the population is Francophone, over 12% report that their mother tongue is something other than one of Canada's two official languages. As noted by Lesage et al. (2008, p. 37), many members of OLMCs are concerned that their status as founding peoples will diminish if their numbers decline in relation to those of other cultures, and that protection granted under the *Official Languages Act* could be diluted by special measures to promote cultural diversity. Although multiculturalism policies and the *Act* are not incompatible, members of OLMCs "increasingly feel like a link in the cultural diversity chain and, as a result, fear losing whatever gains they have achieved under the *Act*" (Lesage et al., 2008, p. 37).

2.2. West Quebecers

The second OLMC studied is the community of West Quebec[4]. This community consists of English-speakers who live in the Outaouais region, the southwestern region of the predominantly French-speaking province of Quebec. Data from Statistics Canada's 2006 census show that the Outaouais region has a total population of 281,650, with approximately 35,815 inhabitants (roughly 12.7%) having English as a native language. However, according to both Jedwab and Maynard (2008, p. 167) and the Quebec Community Groups Network (QCGN, 2004, p. 8), the English-speaking community of Quebec requires a broader definition than simply "native speaker". According to the QCGN (2004, p. 8), "The English-speaking community of Quebec is made up of multiple communities that are diverse, multicultural and multiracial. These communities include citizens throughout Quebec who choose to use the English language and who identify with the English-speaking community".

The QCGN goes on to note that, according to this broader definition, the total number of English speakers in West Quebec in 2001 was approximately 53,948. This means that in addition to the 12.7% of the Outaouais region's inhabitants who claim to be native English-speakers, another 6.4% of the region's total population use English as their preferred official language. Therefore, the region's total percentage of English speakers is 19.1%, of whom approximately one-third are non-native speakers. It is notable that this inclusiveness within the English-language community seems to differ somewhat from the attitude in French-speaking OLMCs, where, as discussed earlier, speakers of other languages are sometimes viewed as competing with the OLMCs in the context of multiculturalism policies.

If multiculturalism is seen as less of a threat in the English-speaking OLMCs, one issue of great concern is that the population of English-speakers is both declining and aging. This situation has arisen largely as a result of language laws introduced in the province of Quebec. Bill 101 (the *Charter of the French Language*), for example, had the objective of ensuring that French-speaking Quebecers had the right to receive services in French, not only in the narrow domain of provincial and municipal services but also in all sectors of industry, commerce and the professions. For the French-speaking majority, the objective was to protect the French language; for the English-speaking minority, it appeared that the primary *de facto* objective was to reduce the visibility, utilization and attractiveness of the English language. One of the most serious effects of the introduction of Bill 101 has been the demographic impact on Quebec's non-Francophone population. In this province, Bill 101 has become a source of irritation and frustration for much of the English-speaking minority, which has suffered. This has contributed to drastic decline in the English-speaking population, especially the youth population, due to out-migration (NHRDCELM, 2000, p. 11; QCGN, 2004, p. 5). Moreover, as Churchill (1998, p. 37) reports, the traditional in-migration flow of English-speakers to Quebec from other provinces has simultaneously been seriously reduced, largely in reaction to Bill 101.

Interestingly, Churchill (1998, p. 47) observes that Quebec's language laws have also produced a more positive consequence: Among the young English-speakers who remain in the province, there appears to be consensus that French has a pre-eminent place in all aspects of life in Quebec, and that being a Quebec English-speaker in the future implies the practical necessity of being bilingual in French. This observation is echoed by Jedwab and Maynard (2008, p; 168), who credit dramatic rise in bilingualism in OLMCs in Quebec (from 37% in 1971 to 69% in 2006) to the determination of those in the English-speaking community who have chosen to remain in the province.

The National Human Resources Development Committee for the English Linguistic Minority (NHRDCELM, 2000, p. 17) reports that another challenge facing West Quebecers is the serious need in the OLMCs of Quebec for development and maintenance of services, such as business development, health and social services, in the English language. As Jedwab and Maynard (2008, p. 175) report, the majority (64.2%) of English-speakers living in Quebec are very satisfied with access to English services offered by the federal government, but only 24% are very satisfied with the English-language services provided by the Quebec provincial government, which include healthcare and social services. Likwise, only 17% of Quebec's English-speakers felt that English-language services provided by the Quebec government had improved in the previous five years.

In a related vein, because the English language is extremely strong at the global level, there often arises a false impression that English-speaking communities in Quebec have a healthy vitality. However, as several examples demonstrate, this perception obscures the actual situation at the level of community vitality. For example, there are no English-language hospitals in the province of Quebec, although research has shown that being unable to communicate in one's own language with health professionals is a considerable barrier to accessing adequate healthcare (Pottie et al., 2008). Moreover, as both the NHRDCELM (2000, p. 49) and Jedwab and Maynard (2008, p. 168) note, in West Quebec, English-speakers do not have access to any regional English-language daily newspapers or radio coverage, and thus which means that they receive little English-language media coverage of information about what affects them most in their daily lives: decisions and events in their hometown and home province.

3. Examining the cost of providing translation to OLMCs

A principal reason that provincial and municipal governments within Canada are reluctant to provide bilingual documents (such as Web sites) is that translation can be both costly and time consuming (OCOL, 2005, p. 58; OCOL, 2007, p. 57). One of the recurring criticisms levelled at bilingualism in Canada since the 1960s has been its cost to taxpayers (Adam, 2005, p. 107). Churchill (1998, p. 63) emphasizes that for official languages policies to succeed, their costs must be kept to a reasonable level. Moreover, it is not simply a matter of finding a lump sum of money to pay for a one-off translation of existing Web sites. Rather, ongoing commitment is required because it is exceedingly difficult (and unpopular!) for a government to curtail a service once it has been offered, and the Web is a dynamic resource that updates constantly.

Another oft-cited reason for not translating such Web sites is that there is a recognized shortage of professional translators in Canada (Clavet, 2002, p. 13; Lord, 2008, p. 15). This is exacerbated by the fact that many of the country's current translators belong to the Baby Boom generation, who will soon be retiring (CTISC, 1999, p. 79).

Given these circumstances, the challenge of providing bilingual Web sites is becoming increasingly intractable because, as the Internet's popularity grows, the volume of documents awaiting translation also grows. As noted by the OCOL (2005, p. 27), the advent of the Web has given rise to a 15% increase since 1996 in the volume of content to be translated. Clavet (2002, p. 13) notes that this number may be closer to 25%.

As early as 1999, when the Internet was still a relatively new phenomenon, the OCOL found the lack of resources (both financial and human) a systemic obstacle blocking translation of documents to be posted to the Web. The OCOL initially suggested that larger budgets were required if the volume of documents to be translated for inclusion on the Web was to be increased (OCOL, 1999). However, the OCOL (2005, p. 58) also recognizes that institutions do not have endless supplies of financial and human resources for translation, and that, as a result, these institutions often face difficult choices that usually entail some form of selective translation.

Therefore, in addition to recommending budget increases where they are possible, the OCOL has repeatedly suggested that technology be explored as a partial solution to helping bridge the gap between supply and demand for translation[5] (Adam, 2001, p. 27; Adam, 2005, p. 55; Clavet, p. 2002: 52; OCOL 2005: 58-59). For example, the OCOL proposes that

> the government should also explore new avenues to increase its effectiveness and efficiency in creating, managing, and translating documents. Specifically, it should substantially step up its use of technolinguistic tools and adapt its organizational policies and practices to maximize the impact of its software. (OCOL, 2005, p. 58)

This type of strategy has since been echoed by others, including Lord (2008, pp. 15-16).

In fact, the OCOL cites the Pan American Health Organization as an example of the success that can be achieved by using the output of MT software in combination with revision by professional translators:

> Since 1985, the Pan American Health Organization (PAHO) has been using automatic translation software called ENGSPAN to translate most of its documents from English into Spanish. While fully aware that this technology cannot produce perfect results on its own, PAHO management has put in place a process whereby ENGSPAN supports the work of translators rather than eliminates it: the document to be translated is first subject to an automatic correction and/or human revision; it is then translated automatically by the automatic translation software before finally being revised by a professional translator. The results of this approach are conclusive: PAHO has been able to reduce its translation costs per word by 31%; most translations are delivered within specified deadlines; and most readers find the quality acceptable. (OCOL, 2005, p. 59)

However, the Government of Canada's Translation Bureau reacted negatively to this suggestion, stating that it would be unreasonable to use MT systems to translate the content of government Web sites automatically because any reduction in translation costs would inevitably come at the cost of a dramatic drop in quality (OCOL, 2005, pp. 60-61). This is in line with observations made by Guyon (2003), for example, as part of an investigation into whether MT could be a viable option for translating the Web site content of a Canadian museum. Guyon concluded that

> Permanently displaying a machine translation would tarnish the prestigious image the museums enjoy because of the customary quality of their content. We recommend that the museums post appropriate

> warnings if they wish to add links to one or more machine translation engines and that they resist the temptation to use machine translation for permanent content. (Guyon, 2003, p. 173)

The need for quality is not in question. The OCOL maintains that linguistic duality reflects a major commitment that involves not only promoting the equal status of the two official languages throughout Canada, but also the quality of services offered to the public in both English and French (Adam, 2001, p. 17; OCOL, 2005, p. 32). To this end, the OCOL recommends that if an institution is to focus on providing quality service in both official languages, it should adhere to a series of guiding principles, which include, among others:

- Establishing contacts with OLMCs to determine their need for the services offered; and
- Measuring client satisfaction. (Adam, 2001, p. 76)

4. Recipient evaluations in two OLMCs

In summarizing the ideas outlined in the preceding sections, we can identify a number of key points. Firstly, it is clear that members of OLMCs have substantial unmet translation needs at the level of provincial (and municipal) services. It is also clear that tight budgets coupled with a shortage of professional translators present a substantial roadblock to having this material translated professionally. For this reason, the OCOL has suggested that translation technology should be investigated more fully to determine if it can be used to increase the effectiveness and efficiency of translation services for OLMCs. At the same time, however, the OCOL warns that a more cost-effective translation solution should not come at the expense of translation quality. Finally, the OCOL recommends that members of the OLMCs should be consulted to determine their needs and their level of satisfaction with proposed solutions.

With these points in mind, we set out to conduct an investigation into whether MT can provide a faster and more cost-effective means of translation that would in turn enable provincial and municipal governments and agencies to offer a wider range of translation services to OLMCs.

As noted above, MT is unquestionably faster and cheaper than human translation but, in the vast majority of cases, unedited MT output is of lesser quality than human translation. A key question to be answered is whether members of the OLMCs will accept some form (either raw or edited) of MT output. In order for MT use to be considered viable, the intended recipients of the target texts must be willing to accept the output produced by MT systems. As noted by the OCOL (Adam, 2001, p. 76), as well as by MT researchers Loffler-Laurian (1996, p. 69) and Trujillo (1999;

p. 255), the intended recipients of the translated texts are in the best position to decide whether their needs can be suitably met by those texts. Thus, to ascertain whether members of the Fransaskois and West Quebec OLMCs would be accepting of MT, we conducted parallel recipient evaluations in order to determine the extent to which MT can help to meet some of their translation needs.

Experience has clearly shown that MT is not a viable option for all types of texts or situations (Church & Hovy, 1993; L'Homme, 2008, p. 273). It is generally accepted that MT is better viewed as a translation aid, rather than as outright replacement of human translators. With this in mind, our investigation has two main goals; to identify the translation needs of the two OLMCs that are currently not being met; and to evaluate the potential of some form of MT for meeting those particular needs. Note that the investigations in the two OLMCs were conducted a year apart: The Fransaskois community was investigated first, followed by the West Quebec community the next year. Nevertheless, the two studies are largely parallel in nature, so the general methodology described in the following sections applies to both.

4.1. Preparatory work

As a first step, an initial survey was sent to members of the two OLMCs asking them to specify the types of texts currently made available to them only in the official language of the majority but which they would like to have made available in their own official language. This initial survey was sent by email to two active community associations — the *Assemblée communautaire fransaskoise (ACF)* and the Regional Association of West Quebecers (RAWQ) — with the request that it be distributed among their members.[6] Responses to this initial survey totalled 25 from the Fransaskois community and 27 from the West Quebec community.

For the Fransaskois community, suggestions received included tourism-related texts, news items of local interest, and various types of general information posted on the Web sites of the provincial and municipal governments and agencies. The third suggestion was most frequently given.

In regard to the West Quebec community, suggestions received included municipal by-laws, news items of local interest, health-related information, and information posted on the Web sites of provincial and municipal governments and agencies. The last was again the most frequently cited.

We gathered samples of these various types of texts and ran preliminary tests using three commercially available desktop MT systems[7] (Power Translator Pro, Reverso Pro and Systran) to see which of these types of texts were most amenable to MT, and which system would produce the highest quality output for these texts.

Based on these initial system tests, the best candidates were the Web sites of the provincial and municipal governments and agencies because the texts that they contained were informative and written in a relatively clear, neutral style with reasonably short sentences. This style of text proved quite amenable to being processed by an MT system. Many words in the texts were already in the system dictionaries, and additional terms could easily be added. Specific issues cited by OLMC members who responded to the initial survey included disaster planning, justice and business (for the Fransaskois community), and health, social services and business (for the West Quebec community). Accordingly, six texts[8] (three in English and three in French, and each approximately 325 words in length[9]) were selected as the basis for the surveys. All the texts were taken from relevant municipal or provincial government Web sites.

Of the three MT systems, Reverso Pro produced the highest quality results[10] during the preliminary testing phase in each language, and so this system was retained for use during the next phase, where for each of the six texts, four translations were produced:

- A raw or unrevised machine translation (MT);
- A rapidly post-edited (RPE) machine translation (i.e., a translation where content errors were corrected, but stylistic changes were not made)[11];
- A maximally post-edited (MPE) machine translation (i.e., a translation where both content and style were corrected to produce a text that resembles as closely as possible a human translation);
- A human translation (HT).

The time and cost for producing each of the four versions was also calculated, because whenever a text needs to be translated, the competing parameters of quality, time, and cost must always be considered. The methods used for determining the time and cost are described in the following paragraphs, and the actual time and cost required to produce each version are summarized in Tables 1 and 2 for the Fransaskois and the West Quebec OLMCs, respectively.

The raw machine-translations were produced by running the texts through the Reverso Pro MT system. Tests revealed that the time required to produce the raw output for each text was approximately two minutes, which included opening the software, importing the source text, and running it through the translation engine. Since each text was relatively short (approximately 325 words), in practical terms there was no difference in the processing time required to produce each of the raw machine-translations. Of course, an initial investment of time would be required in order to install the MT system and to learn how to use it, but this was not factored into the equation since it would be a once-off investment of time, and since even use of conventional translation resources, such as dictionaries or term banks, require investment of time for learning their proper use.

Four professional translators were hired to help produce the remaining target texts. Two of these translators worked from English to French to produce texts for the Fransaskois OLMC, and the others worked from French to English to produce texts for the West Quebec OLMC. Clearly it is not possible for different translators to have precisely the same ability, but every effort was made to find translators with comparable backgrounds and levels of experience. For each language direction, one translator produced the human translations, and the other did the post-editing (both RPE and MPE) of the raw MT output[12]. All translators were instructed to keep careful track of the time needed to complete their tasks.

In the case of post-editing, the post-editors began by taking the raw MT output and conducting the RPE. Once the RPE was complete, the post-editors saved a copy of the RPE text and recorded the amount of time that had been required for this task. Next, with the clock still running, the post-editors revisited the RPE text and gave it a more thorough revision to produce an MPE text, and recorded the total amount of editing time required. The editing time varied from text to text depending on the number and types of problems the MT system encountered in each text. Then, for both the RPE and MPE texts, the time required to produce the raw MT output (i.e. two minutes) was added to the time required for editing. This yielded the total time required to produce the two types of post-edited target text.

The cost of producing each version was also calculated. For the raw MT output, the price was set at $1.68[13], on the basis that it took less than two minutes to launch the program, import the text and generate a raw translation. Obviously, this cost does not include the software's purchase price or time spent building dictionaries. However, we felt justified in excluding these costs for the following reasons. As noted previously, the texts used in this experiment required relatively few entries to be added. In any case, although dictionary-building is not strictly a once-off investment of time, it is an activity that will lessen considerably over time as the dictionaries grow larger and fewer entries need be added. Therefore, the amount of time spent on dictionary building in an early stage of an experiment such as ours would not be representative of the typical amount of time required to use the system on a long-term basis.

For the other versions, the cost was calculated using the average hourly rates charged by translators ($53.73) and editors ($50.16) as reported in the "Sondage de 2004 sur la tarification et les salaires" published by the professional translators' association the Ordre des Traducteurs, Terminologues et Interprètes Agréés du Québec (OTTIAQ). Although we calculated the post-editing costs using the full rate normally charged by editors, we could potentially have used a lower rate, since evidence in the literature suggests that post-editors are not always paid the full rate. For example, Chesterman and Wagner (2002, p. 125) note that freelance translators contracted by the European Union institutions to post-edit output produced by the Systran MT system are paid "at a rate equivalent to about half the normal rate for freelance translation." Similarly, Vasconcellos and Bostad (1992, p. 67) report that freelance translators hired to post-edit the output of the ENGSPAN MT system used by the PAHO "were being paid 55 percent of the HT rate." Had we used lower rates to calculate the costs of post-editing, then these texts, which had already proved less expensive to produce than HT, would have been even less expensive as compared to HT. However, for these experiments we decided to be conservative in calculating the costs and so opted to use the full rate charged by editors as reported in the OTTIAQ survey of rates (OTTIAQ, 2004). The production times and costs for each of the texts are summarized in Tables 1 and 2.

Table 1. Time and cost required to produce French versions of English source texts for members of the Fransaskois OLMC

	Text 1	Text 2	Text 3
Time raw MT	2 min	2 min	2 min
Cost raw MT	$1.68	$1.68	$1.68
Time RPE	28 min	18 min	22 min
Cost RPE	$23.52	$15.12	$18.48
Time MPE	69 min	53 min	82 min
Cost MPE	$57.96	$44.52	$68.88
Time HT	107 min	110 min	111 min
Cost HT	$96.30	$99.00	$99.90

Table 2. Time and cost required to produce English versions of French source texts for members of the West Quebec OLMC.

	Text 1	Text 2	Text 3
Time raw MT	2 min	2 min	2 min
Cost raw MT	$1.68	$1.68	$1.68
Time RPE	23 min	31 min	27 min
Cost RPE	$19.32	$26.04	$22.68
Time MPE	62 min	79 min	74 min
Cost MPE	$52.08	$66.36	$62.16
Time HT	98 min	112 min	108 min
Cost HT	$88.20	$100.80	$97.20

The data show that, not surprisingly, raw MT was always the fastest and cheapest method of producing a text, followed by RPE, then MPE, and finally HT. For the texts used in these two experiments, it is notable that those produced using MP (which aims to produce texts comparable in quality to HT) were between 30% and 55% cheaper than HT and were also produced in a much shorter timeframe.

4.2. Survey and findings

Once the various translations had been generated, the next step was to consult members of each OLMC to try to identify the reasons why they wanted the texts to be made available in the other official language, and to determine which of the four translated versions presented to them (MT, RPE, MPE or HT) best met their needs. To this end, two parallel online surveys were developed and made available[14] – one aimed at members of the Fransaskois OLMC; the other at members of the West Quebec OLMC.

Members of the Fransaskois OLMC were contacted and invited to participate in this survey via mass electronic mailing through groups such as the Assemblée communautaire fransaskoise (ACF), the Conseil culturel fransaskois, the Association canadienne-française de Regina, the Fédération des francophones de Saskatoon, the Association communautaire Fransaskoise de Moose Jaw, the Association des Parents Fransaskois, and the Institut français at the University of Regina. The recipients of this invitation were invited to redistribute it to other potentially interested parties. As a result of these efforts, a total of 104 respondents participated in the survey aimed at the Fransaskois OLMC.

Similarly, members of the West Quebec OLMC were contacted and invited to participate in this survey via mass electronic mailing through groups such as the Regional Association for West Quebecers (RAWQ), the Community Table, the Outaouais Health and Social Services Community Network for the English-speaking Population, the English Network Resources in Community Health (ENRICH), the English Language Arts Network (ELAN), and the Quebec Community Groups Network. This effort netted a total of 119 responses to the survey aimed at the West Quebec OLMC.

4.2.1. General profile questions

The survey was posted on the Web and participants were able to respond anonymously. Because the surveys specifically targeted adult members of the Fransaskois and West Quebec OLMCs, participants were first asked to confirm that they were indeed members of the respecitive OLMCs and that they were over the age of 18.

They were also asked to provide their gender (M or F), age bracket (18-25 years; 26-40 years; 41-60 years; 61 years and over) and whether they considered themselves "language professionals" (e.g. translators, interpreters, terminologists, revisers, writers, language teachers, etc.). Unfortunately, no data were collected regarding the respondents' educational profiles, although in hindsight this data would have been informative.

4.2.2. Reasons for wanting texts to be translated

Survey participants were then invited to read the source texts and to indicate why they would like such texts made available in their own language. As stressed by Edwards (1992, p. 48), probing the underlying reason, rather than simply asking Yes/No-type questions, can provide valuable insight into an OLMC. The findings for each of the two OLMCs are presented in the following sections.

4.2.2.1. Fransaskois

Members of the Fransaskois OLMC were asked to specify one or more reasons why they would like the English texts used in this study to be translated into French. A list of possible reasons was provided in the survey, but participants were also able to suggest their own reasons. The responses received are summarized in Table 3 in order of frequency.

Table 3. Reasons given by members of the Fransaskois OLMC for wanting translations (note that respondents were allowed to select more than one reason). Based on a population size of 19,500 and a sample size of 104 respondents, the margin of error is ± 8% with a confidence level of 90%.

Reason for wanting translation	**# of responses**
Cultural preservation	80 (76.9%)
Faster processing of information	38 (36.5%)
Greater confidence in comprehension	24 (23.1%)
Teaching material (e.g. for children, students)	24 (23.1%)
Improvement of 2nd language skills (verifying information in translation)	12 (11.5%)
Do not fully understand original	6 (5.8%)
Other: Equity – it should be my right	8 (7.7%)

Reviewing the data for the Fransaskois community, we see that the most common reason for wanting to have the texts translated into French was as a means of cultural preservation. In other words, a considerable number of the Fransaskois participants tended to view translation not as a necessary tool for the functional transfer of linguistic content but rather as a public acknowledgement of the presence of their language and culture, and as a measure of it strength. As Lesage et al. (2008, p. 15) observe,

> The ability of official language minorities to identify with their culture is enhanced when that culture comes out of the shadows of private life and assumes a public face. Only then are citizens able to feel a sense of belonging to something greater than themselves—a collective history, a common endeavour, an ambitious future.

Bernard Lord (2008, p. 21), in reporting the results of his cross-Canada consultations with members of OLMCs, also underscores the value of culture for these communities, noting "the importance of culture is undeniable, not only for community vitality but also as a source of economic development and a way of fostering openness toward others." Accordingly, Lord (2008, p. 12) recommends that culture be given special attention in the new strategy for the next phase of the federal government's *Action Plan for Official Languages*[15] Similarly, François Paré (1997, p. 14) notes that "Whatever its colonial, minority or insular context, the development and prestige of a culture are connected to the survival and the strategic importance of its language in the global linguistic economy." Paré's observation focuses in particular on literary works, but the general principle can be extended to the situation encountered in this experiment. In this case, members of the Fransaskois community viewed the translation of material on provincial and municipal government Web sites as a means of preserving and promoting their culture not so much because of the content of these sites *per se*, but rather because having greater amounts of material available in French will help to increase the visibility and vitality of their community, which in turn will help to revitalize linguistic duality. Indeed, this is supported by Churchill's observation (1998, p. 13) that the motivating force in seeking policies for official languages has been the "search for status and recognition of identity by different communities and constituencies of citizens."

Other reasons were provided that dealt more specifically with translation as a tool for linguistic transfer; however, these reasons were selected less frequently than the view that translation has an important role to play in the linguistic and cultural preservation of the Fransaskois community. These other reasons included the fact that some people felt that although they could understand English they processed information more quickly and easily in their native language, and had greater confidence that they had understood all the details of the text. Some respondents said that they would like to have more French-language texts available to use as teaching material, either to teach their own children or to use in more formal classroom settings. This may be explained in part by the fact that a relatively high proportion (48%) of the respondents identified themselves as members of the language profession, which includes language teachers. A few others said they were trying to improve their own English-language skills and would appreciate having a French translation available so that they could verify if they had fully understood the English text. Only a very small number of people claimed not to have been able to understand the English texts sufficiently, and the remaining participants stated that they simply felt that, as Canadians, it should be their right to have this information available in French regardless of how well they could understand the English text.

4.2.2.2. West Quebecers

In regard to the survey of the West Quebec OLMC, participants were asked to provide one or more reasons why they would like to have the English-language texts used in this study translated into French. A list of possible reasons was again provided in the survey, but participants could also suggest their own reasons. The responses received are summarized in Table 4 in order of frequency.

Table 4. Reasons given by members of the West Quebec OLMC for wanting translations (note that respondents were allowed to select more than one reason). Based on a population size of 35,580 and a sample size of 119 respondents, the margin of error is ± 8% with a confidence level of 90%.

Reason for wanting translation	**# of responses**
Greater confidence in comprehension	72 (60.5%)
Faster processing of information	60 (50.4%)
Do not fully understand original	34 (28.6%)
Improvement of 2nd language skills (verifying information in translation)	22 (18.5%)
Cultural preservation	13 (10.9%)
Teaching material (e.g. for children, students)	0 (0%)
Other:	N/A

In contrast to the Fransaskois respondents, far more respondents from West Quebec (28.6%) claimed not to be able to understand the source language text and therefore to need the translation in order to access the content. In addition, 60.5% felt they would be more confident that they had understood the text if they could read it in English, while 50.4% believed that they would be able to process the information more quickly. Moreover, another 18.5% would have appreciated the opportunity to verify their understanding of the French-language text by being able to refer to the English translation. These findings seem to be supported by research carried out by Bishop (1999), who undertook a human resources development needs assessment for the English-speaking minority in the region of West Quebec.

As Bishop (1999, p. 23) reports, there appears to be a lack of confidence among English speakers in West Quebec regarding their ability to function in French. In discussing the results of a survey about employment opportunities for English-speakers in the Outaouais region, Bishop (1999, p. 28) explains in more detail that

> Another contributing factor to unemployment in the English-speaking community in the Outaouais may be an existing perception among Anglophones that the level of French they possess is not sufficient enough to warrant even the search for employment. Respondents indicated that the prevailing political situation in the province

> has caused them to lose confidence in their abilities to function bilingually. Even if a person has a high level of French, he may not perceive himself to be sufficiently proficient in his second language to apply for positions requiring French language skills. (Bishop, 1999, p. 28)

Bishop's findings are supported by Lord (2008, p. 16), who notes that Anglophones in Quebec have difficulty finding employment because their level of bilingualism is considered imperfect; however, many of those who leave the province subsequently find bilingual jobs elsewhere, where their knowledge of French is considered above average. Although Bishop (1999) and Lord (2008) are discussing employment opportunities in particular, it is quite likely that the lack of confidence that West Quebecers have developed about their abilities to function in French spills into other aspects of their lives, such as their self-perceived ability to read and understand French-language provincial and muncipal Web sites.

In addition, it is notable that among those West Quebec OLMC members who responded to the survey, 59% were in the age bracket for 41-60 years, and 16% were in the 61-and-over age bracket. As noted by the National Human Resources Development Committee for the English Language Minority (HRDCELM, 2000, p. 11) and by the Quebec Community Groups Network (QCGN, 2004, p. 5), shifting demographics, such as those in reaction to Bill 101 (discussed above), have resulted in disproportionately fewer youth and more seniors in English-speaking Quebec. Churchill (1998, p. 57) observes that an increasing number of English-speaking parents are beginning to enrol their children in French-immersion programs[16], but notes that this is a relatively recent trend. The majority of English-speaking Quebecers over the age of 40 are thus less likely to have learned French intensively from an early age or to consider themselves bilingual.

In regard to other reasons, no respondent felt it was necessary to translate the texts to use them as teaching material. This is doubtlessly because vast amounts of original English-language material can be obtained relatively easily from other sources (e.g. the Internet, the nearby and predominantly anglophone province of Ontario). Relatively few of the respondents (9.2%) identified themselves as members of the language profession, which includes language teachers.

Furthermore, a comparatively small percentage of West Quebecers (10.9%) identified cultural preservation as a reason that motivated their desire to have the texts translated. This may be because West Quebecers, although not wishing to relinquish their right to use English as the official language of their choice, seem to acknowledge that their situation is somewhat different than that of their counterpart francophone OLMCs. As the Quebec Community Groups Network (QCGN, 2004, p. 5) notes, English-speakers in Quebec are beginning to more readily acknowledge that the global (rather than local) influence of English is a threat to Quebec. Moreover, as discussed previously, there appears to be growing consensus among English-speakers that French has a pre-eminent place in all aspects of life in Quebec and that bilingualism is becoming increasingly important for English-speakers.

4.2.3. Preferred type of translation

In the next step, participants were asked to read the four translated versions of a text. Then they were asked to choose, taking into account the quality of the translations and the time and cost required to produce them, which version they felt would best meet their needs. The results of the responses from members of the two OLMCs are presented in the following sections.

4.2.3.1. Fransaskois

Members of the Fransaskois OLMC were asked to indicate, keeping in mind the associated production time and cost, which translated version of a text (a raw machine-translated text, a rapidly post-edited machine-translated text, a maximally post-edited machine-translated text or a human translation) would best meet their needs,. The responses are summarized in Table 5.

Table 5. Preferences for type of translation among the Fransaskois OLMC. Based on a population size of 19,500 and a sample size of 104 respondents, the margin of error is ± 8% with a confidence level of 90%.

Type of translation	**# of respondents selecting this option**
Human translation (HT)	74 (71.1%)
Maximal post-editing (MPE)	22 (21.2%)
Rapid post-editing (RPE)	8 (7.7%)
Raw machine translation (MT)	0
Total	*104 (100%)*

On the basis of this survey, it is clear that unrevised MT output is unacceptable to members of the Fransaskois OLMC. None of the respondents selected the option, many of them took time to voice their dissatisfaction with the quality of the raw MT output in the comments section of the survey. Such comments included the following:

- "Je ne vois sincèrement pas l'utilité de traduire un texte de façon automatique sans révision. À ce moment, aussi bien le lire en anglais."
- "On peut remarquer que la traduction automatique a une couleur de mot à mot."

- "Les traductions automatiques sans révision sont absolument à éviter si l'on veut que les francophones en milieu minoritaire améliorent leurs connaissances du français écrit."

At first glance, it seems that a significant majority of Fransaskois community members (71.1%) do not appear willing to accept any form of MT output, even if it has been post-edited, feeling that only HT can fully meet their needs. However, a closer look at the data reveals interesting information.

As noted earlier, respondents were asked to indicate if they were language professionals. In the case of the Fransaskois OLMC, of the 104 respondents, 50 (48%) consider themselves language professionals, and the remaining 54 (52%) are Francophones who do not work in the language industry. If, as illustrated in Table 6, the data are broken down according to these categories, then a somewhat different picture is revealed.

Table 6. Translation preferences of language professionals vs non-language professionals in the Fransaskois OLMC.[17]

Type of translation	**# of language professionals selecting this option**	**# of non-language professionals selecting this option**
HT	44 (88%)	30 (55.6%)
MPE	6 (12%)	16 (29.6%)
RPE	0	8 (14.8%)
Raw MT	0	0
Total	*50 (100%)*	*54 (100%)*

In the survey, language professionals, who clearly have extremely high standards and expectations for language production, insist 88% of the time that HT is the only acceptable means of producing a target text. In contrast, members of the Fransaskois OLMC who do not work in the language industry are willing to accept some form of post-edited MT close to half the time. That nearly half the respondents to the survey are language professionals could be skewing the results since it is unlikely that half the members of the overall Fransaskois community work in the language industry. However, no reliable information about the actual number of Fransaskois working as language professionals could be found.

Detailed analysis of correlations has not been carried out, and so definitive conclusions cannot be drawn based on the data reported in this recipient evaluation. Nevertheless, it is possible to speculate that language professionals may harbour prejudices against MT for a number of reasons. As Hutchins (2001) and Yuste Rodrigo (2001) report, some translators seem to feel threatened by MT, fearing that it may cost them their livelihoods. Church and Hovy (1993, p. 249) report that others fear MT will contribute to reduced job satisfaction, noting that many translators do not wish to become post-editors, a task they perceive as tedious and dreary. Moreover, translators may fear that use of MT will result in production of lower-quality texts, thus hurting the general reputation of their profession. As Gerber (2008) explains;

> Translators also tend to judge MT very harshly. This is often seen as self-preservation, and there is certainly an element of that. But professional translators are trained to adhere to a very high standard of accuracy. And professional ethics prevent them from accepting any translation job that they cannot deliver at the highest levels of quality. Is it any wonder that they find MT offensive? (Gerber, 2008, p. 16)

The survey findings appear to provide some broad support for Hutchins's (2001) observation that the general population may be more willing than language professionals to accept MT. According to Hutchins (2001, p. 8), "While poor quality output is not acceptable to translators, it is acceptable to most of the rest of the population, if they want immediate information, and the on-line 'culture' demands rapid access to and processing of information." This observation that the intended recipient of a text may have different needs, and therefore different standards, than a language professional has been confirmed in various instances.

For example, in describing customers who work in the business field, where "time is money," Allied Business Intelligence (ABI, 2002) reports that

> Often, an MT program can generate the gist of an email or other message and allow a rapid reply with a reasonable degree of accuracy. This has become more acceptable in business, where the tolerance for low-quality texts has risen [...] and users are more willing to concede some quality to achieve expediency in communication. (ABI, 2002: 5.3)

In another example, experiments using MT in intelligence agencies and in the military produced similar observations. Holland et al. (2000, p. 246) note that agents who work as language professionals in intelligence agencies have relatively high degrees of translation training and considerable translation experience. In general these agents are much less tolerant of MT than are soldier-linguists in the military, who have considerably less formal training and experience in translation. In fact, when compared to intelligence agents, it has been observed that "soldiers seem disproportionately welcoming of automatic translation" (Hernandez et al., 2004, p. 95) and that "they [soldiers] are tolerant of lower quality translations" (Holland et al., 2000, p. 246).

Similarly, Gerber (2008, p. 16) reports a project at Intel Corporation that seeks to provide fully automated translation of technical knowledge base articles from English into Spanish in order to provide self-serve support. The results have been relatively impressive: Adoption of English-Spanish MT for certain technical support articles has succeeded in deflecting support calls, and the quality is high enough that some human translation efforts have discontinued. As Gerber explains,

> Sometimes the end user's standard isn't "the highest level of quality". In the case in point, Intel's standard was the ability to deflect support calls for a language that had very little technical support content before the project began. When the company was evaluating machine translation output to assess feasibility of an MT solution, human linguists rated the MT generally inadequate. But the company's representatives in central and South America evaluated the MT output as quite adequate for the purpose at hand – to provide better support to a Spanish-speaking audience and reduce the number of calls that resulted from the lack of Spanish-language self-help content. When the system was deployed, user responses to the question "did this information help answer your question" actually exceeded the satisfaction levels projected even by the regional representatives. (Gerber, 2008, p. 16)

Returning to our own experiment, the following comments were made by survey respondents who were language professionals. These comments display significant intolerance towards MT and clear preference for HT.

- "À mon avis la seule solution est de traduire tout texte par un traducteur humain, ou ne pas traduire du tout."
- "Aller vers un système de traduction automatique met notre langue à risque dans des contextes de vie où les 2 langues officielles se côtoient et crée pour celle-ci des interférences et nous en perdons parfois les mots justes."
- " Moi je préfère la traduction faite par un traducteur."
- " Les 'systèmes de traduction automatique' sont des monstres qui défigurent la langue française."

4.2.3.2. West Quebecers

Let us now turn our attention to the results gathered from the survey conducted in the West Quebec OLMC, summarized in Table 7. Participants were asked to indicate which translated version of a text (a raw machine-translated text, a rapidly post-edited machine-translated text, a maximally post-edited machine-translated text or a human translation) would best meet their needs, keeping in mind the associated production time and cost.

Table 7. Preferences for type of translation among the West Quebec OLMC members. Based on a population size of 35,580 and a sample size of 119 respondents, the margin of error is ± 8% with a confidence level of 90%.

Type of translation	# of respondents selecting this option
Human translation (HT)	10 (8.4%)
Maximal post-editing (MPE)	45 (37.8%)
Rapid post-editing (RPE)	59 (49.6%)
Raw machine translation (MT)	5 (4.2%)
Total	*119 (100%)*

Unlike the survey results of members of the Fransaskois OLMC, wherein no respondents felt that raw MT output could meet their needs, a small number (4.2%) of West Quebecers felt that machine-translated texts represented a viable option. One might have expected this number to be higher because, as discussed above, a considerable number of respondents from West Quebec indicated that lack of ability and/or confidence in understanding the source text was a motivator for wanting it to be translated. In such circumstances, one might assume that MT could do a sufficiently good job of helping readers to understand the gist of the text. However, in this experiment the respondents were asked to choose which text among the four versions best met their needs, taking into account the time and money required to produce it. Presumably, therefore, they found the edited texts easier to read and process than the raw MT output. It would have been highly interesting to conduct a similar experiment in which the choice was simply between raw MT output and no translation (as was the case in the San Francisco experiment described by De Palma (2007)). In such circumstances, it is possible that more respondents might have been willing to accept raw MT output rather than nothing.

At the other extreme, however, it is revealing that fewer than 10% of the West Quebec respondents felt that HT offered the best value for money. This contrasts starkly to the responses of Fransaskois respondents, of whom a clear majority felt that only HT could truly meet their needs. In the survey of the West Quebec OLMC, only 9.2% of the respondents identified themselves as being language professionals (as compared to 48% of the Fransaskois respondents), and among the language professionals, all opted for either HT or MPE. Again, no formal correlation analysis was carried out as part of this research, and it would have been complex to do so given the different sample sizes of self-reported language professionals in the two OLMCs. Nonetheless, we can speculate that the relatively low number of West Quebecers insisting on HT may be related to the fact that, as Hutchins (2001) and Gerber (2008) observe previously, the standards of the average intended recipient of these texts are likely to be less exacting than the standards of a language professional. In the case of the West Quebecers, more than 85% of the respondents were willing to entertain some form of post-edited MT output, and among these, nearly 50% were content with MT output that had been rapidly post-edited rather than maximally post-edited. Again, if we consider the observations of Bishop (1999) and Lord (2008) regarding the fact that many West Quebecers are in fact quite bilingual but simply lack confidence in their ability to function in French, then it seems reasonable that a rapidly post-edited text could suffice as a sort of crutch that would allow those respondents to feel more confident that they had indeed understood the text.

It is also worth considering that, as noted previously, almost one-third of the English-speakers in the West Quebec OLMC are not native speakers of English and, as such, it is possible that they may have higher tolerance for lower-quality English than do native speakers. Unfortunately, survey respondents were not asked to indicate whether they were *native* speakers of English, so it is not possible to confirm this hypothesis using data generated from this experiment.

Another interesting observation about the respondents from West Quebec is that those who identified themselves as belonging to the older age brackets (i.e. 41-60 years and 61 years and older) were more likely to opt for either MPE or HT, while the vast majority of respondents who selected RPE or raw MT were under the age of 40. This would seem in-line with Churchill's (1998) observations that among the English-speaking residents of Quebec, the younger generations are typically more comfortable with the French language. The younger respondents may have been better equipped to process an English-language text that retains traces of French syntax or style, such as text translated by an MT system and only rapidly post-edited.

5. Concluding remarks

The recipient evaluation of MT output in two different OLMCs in Canada revealed a number of interesting points and seems to support several earlier observations made by other researchers.

Among the first things to note is that MT cannot simply be adopted wholesale as a solution for meeting the needs of Canada's OLMCs. Although some recipients are simply seeking functional translation, there are many other factors to be considered in a context of official legislation of the use of two languages..These include factors that are quite sensitive (e.g. politics, citizens' rights, historical developments and the strength of a given language in a global context) and which therefore must be addressed carefully. Tt is critical to keep in mind a fact observed by other researchers, including Church and Hovy (1993), Lewis (1997), and Miller et al. (2001): The acceptability of MT output is not absolute but varies according to the purpose for which the text will be used. In our experiment, the two OLMCs had quite different overall reactions to the possibility of using some form of

MT output to meet their translation needs. In examining these reactions, we can observe possible connections between the reasons why the translation is desired and the level of acceptance of MT output.

As Vasconcellos and Bostad (1992, p. 69), O'Hagan and Ashworth (2002, p. 9) and Wagner et al. (2002, p. 90) point out, MT seems most useful when the recipients simply want a general understanding of a text (i.e. personal assimilation of information). Our data support these observations and reveal that there was greater willingness to accept raw or rapidly post-edited MT output when the respondents wanted translations primarily to be able to understand a text, process information more quickly and with greater confidence, or to improve their own knowledge of the source language, all of which can be considered forms of information assimilation. A general willingness to accept some form of MT output, and most often a relatively cheap and quick RPE text, was best exemplified by the West Quebec OLMC, in which the majority of participants were seeking functional translations that could help them to understand a text quickly and confidently.

In contrast, respondents who view translation as a means of preserving or promoting a culture, of providing equity for the two official languages, and of furnishing material that could be used to teach a language (all of which are forms of information dissemination rather than assimilation) are more likely to insist on the need for high-quality texts, even if it comes with a higher price tag and slower turnaround time. In this experiment, this type of need was expressed by most surveyed members of the Fransaskois OLMC, and the majority opted for HT or MPE.[18]

It is interesting, however, that the main group calling for HT rather than some form of post-edited MT output were language professionals. This would seem to provide additional confirmation that typical or "average" recipients are more open to the idea of MT than are language professionals. Even in the Fransaskois OLMC, where the main reasons for seeking translation were for dissemination rather than for information assimilation, almost half the respondents who were *not* members of the language industry felt that post-edited MT output could be a viable means of meeting their translation needs. Among the respondents receptive to considering some form of MT-based solution, two-thirds felt that the higher-quality MPE (rather than RPE) would be the most appropriate option.

Overall, the results of this recipient evaluation seem to indicate that, in the case of Canada's OLMCs, machine translation is a valid option that is worth exploring as a more cost-effective means of offering a greater range of translated materials to members of these communities. However, the needs in all OLMCs are not exactly the same across the country, so different forms of MT-based solutions would need to be developed for different OLMCs. Based on this research, it would seem that raw or rapidly post-edited MT output could be effectively used in English-speaking OLMCs[19], where translation needs are mainly for personal assimilation of information. In the French-speaking OLMCs, where recipients tend to view translation chiefly as a means of helping to preserve and promote their culture, there is a need for higher quality texts such as those produced through maximal post-editing of MT output. In both cases, however, an MT-based solution would offer considerable cost savings over an HT solution, which should make it possible to increase the overall amount of material made available in both official languages at the provincial and municipal level.

This is an important finding because, in Canada the members of OLMCs are considered to have equality of status as citizens. Recognition of the rights of Canadian citizens should be a provincial and a municipal responsibility, as well as a federal responsibility. If members of one community (the numeric majority in a given province) agree to provide services and support for citizens of a numeric minority (of the other official language group), the majority's agreement to such services should not be seen as granting a 'privilege'. The majority are recognizing the rights of citizenship that are not limited to a given place of residence – rights which they themselves should expect to enjoy if they move to a province where they would be in the numeric minority. However, it is clear that the budget for providing such services is not unlimited, so a cost-effective means of doing so must be sought. The results of this recipient evaluation seem to indicate that carefully considered use of MT could play an important role in the development of a cost-effective solution for offering a wider range of translation services to meet certain needs of Canada's OLMCs.

Acknowledgements

Funding for this research was provided by two separate grants awarded by the Social Sciences and Humanities Research Council (SSHRC) of Canada. In addition, seed funding for a pilot project with the Fransaskois community was provided by the Centre canadien de recherche sur les francophonies en milieu minoritaire (CRFM) de l'Institut français at the University of Regina in Saskatchewan. Thanks are also due to Nicolle Sauvage and Brian Gibb, who acted as community contacts in the two OLMCs, and to the two anonymous reviewers, who provided constructive and insightful feedback.

Bibliography

Adam, D. (2000). *A call for action: Cross-Canada consultations by the Commissioner of Official Languages*. Ottawa, ON: Office of the Commissioner of Official Languages.

Adam, D. (2001). *Annual report of the Office of the Commissioner of Official Languages (2000-2001)*. Ottawa, ON: Minister of Public Works and Government Services Canada. Retrieved from OCOL: http://www.ocol-clo.gc.ca/html/ar_ra_2000_01_e.php

Adam, D. (2005). *Annual report of the Office of the Commissioner of Official Languages (2004-2005)*, Vols 1 and 2. Ottawa, ON: Minister of Public Works and Government Services Canada. Retrieved from OCOL: http://www.ocol-clo.gc.ca/docs/e/2004_05_e.pdf

Allen, J. (2003). Post-editing. In H. Somers (Ed.), *Computers and translation: A translator's guide* (pp. 297-317). Amsterdam/Philadelphia, PA: John Benjamins.

Allied Business Intelligence (ABI) (2002). *Language translation, localization and globalization: World market forecasts, industry drivers and eSolutions*. Oyster Bay, NJ: Allied Business Intelligence, Inc.

Bishop, L. (1999). *Human resources development needs assessment for the English-speaking minority of the Outaouais*. Huntingdon, QC: Community Table of the National Human Resources Development Committee for the English Linguistic Minority.

Bowker, L. (2008). Official language minority communities, machine translation, and translator education: Reflections on the status quo and considerations for the future. *TTR: Traduction, Terminologie, Rédaction, 21*(2), 15-61.

Brace, C. (2000). Language automation at the European Commission. In R. Sprung (Ed.), *Translating into success. Cutting-edge strategies for going. multilingual in a global age* (pp. 219-224). American Translators Association Scholarly Monograph Series. Volume XI. Amsterdam/Philadelphia, PA: John Benjamins..

Canadian Translation Industry Sectoral Committee (CTISC) (1999). *Survey of the Canadian translation industry: Human resources and export development strategy*. Retrieved January 23, 2009 from http://www.uottawa.ca/associations/csict/princi-e.htm

Chesterman, A. & Wagner, E. (2002). *Can theory help translators? A dialogue between the ivory Tower and the wordface*, Manchester: St. Jerome Publishing.

Church, K.W. & Hovy, E.H. (1993). Good applications for crummy machine translation. *Machine Translation, 8,* 239-258.

Churchill, S. (1998). *Official languages in Canada: Changing the language landscape*. Ottawa, ON: Department of Canadian Heritage.

City of County of San Francisco. Translation services Accessed May 27, 2008 from http://www.sfgov.org/ site/translated.asp?lp=en_zt

Clavet, A. (2002). *French on the Internet: Key to the Canadian identity and the knowledge economy. Follow-up study by the Commissioner of Official Languages*. Ottawa, ON: Minister of Public Works and Government Services Canada. Retrieved from OCOL: http://www.ocol-clo.gc.ca/docs/e/fr_Internet_id_can-2002_e.pdf

DePalma, D.A. (2007). Limited English proficiency not a bar to citizen access. *MultiLingual, 18*(4), 46-50.

Dillinger, M. & Gerber, L (2009). Success with machine translation: Automating knowledge-base translation. *ClientSide News Magazine, 9*(1), 10-11.

Dorr, B.J., Jordan, P., & Benoit, J. (1999). A survey of current paradigms in machine translation. In M. Zelkowitz (Ed.), *Advances in computers* (Vol. 49, pp. 1-64). London: Academic Press.

Edwards, J. (1992). Sociopolitical aspects of language maintenance and loss: Towards a typology of minority language situations. In W. Fase, K. Jaspaert & S. Kroon (Eds.), *Maintenance and loss of minority languages* (pp. 37-54). Amsterdam/Philadelphia, PA: John Benjamins.

Gerber, L. (2008). Recipes for success with machine translation: Ingredients for productive and stable MT deployments. *ClientSide News Magazine, 8*(11), 15-17.

Guyon, A. (2003). Machine translation and the virtual museum of Canada (VMC). Retrieved August 30, 2009 from http://www.chin.gc.ca/English/Pdf/Digital_Content/Machine_ Translation/Machine_Translation.pdf

Henisz-Dostert, B., Ross Macdonald, R., & Zarechnak, M. (1979). *Machine translation*. The Hague: Mouton Publishers.

Hernandez, L., Turner, J. & Holland, M. (2004). Feedback from the field: The challenge of users in motion. In R Frederking & K. Taylor (Eds.), *Machine translation: From real users to Research* (pp. 94-101). Berlin: Springer.

Holland, M., Schlesiger, C. & Tate, C. (2000). Evaluating embedded machine translation in military field exercises. In J. White (Ed.), *Envisioning machine translation in the information future* (pp.239-247). Berlin: Springer.

Hutchins, J. (2001). Machine translation and human translation: In competition or in complementation? *International Journal of Translation, 13*(1-2), 5-20.

Jedwab, J. & Maynard, H. (2008). Politics of community: The evolving challenge of representing English-speaking Quebecers. In R. Bourhis (Ed.), *The vitality of the English-speaking communities of Quebec: From community decline to revival*. Montreal, QC: CEETUM, Université de Montréal. Retrieved January 1, 2009 from http://www.ceetum.umontreal.ca/pdf/Jedwab&Maynard.pdf

Langlais, P., Leplus, T., Gandrabur, S. & Lapalme, G. (2005). From the real world to real words: the METEO case. In Proceedings of the 10th European Association for Machine Translation Conference: Practical applications of machine translation; Budapest, Hungary,

May 30-31, 2005. (pp. 166-175). Retrieved August 31, 2009 from http://www.mt-archive.info/EAMT-2005-Langlais.pdf

Lewis, T. (1997). Do you have a translation tool strategy? *Language International, 9*(5), 16-18.

L'Homme, M. (2008). *Initiation à la traductique, 2e édition*. Brossard, QC: Linguatech.

Loffler-Laurian, A.(1996). *La traduction automatique*. Villeneuve d'Ascq: Presses Universitaires du Septentrion.

Lord, B. (2008). *Report on the government of Canada's consultations on linguistic duality and official languages*. Retrieved from Canadian Heritage web site: http://www.canadianheritage.gc.ca/pc-ch/consultations/lo-ol_2008/lord_e.pdf

Meta4 Creative Communications & Micheline Lesage & Associates (2008). *Federal government support for the arts and culture in official language minority communities. Report prepared for the Office of the Commissioner of Official Languages*. Retrieved from OCOL Web site: http://www.ocol-clo.gc.ca/docs/e/ arts_culture_e.pdf

Miller, K., Gates, D., Underwood, N., & Magdalen J. (2001). Evaluation of machine translation output for an unknown source language: Report of an ISLE-based investigation. In Proceedings of the Machine Translation Summit VIII; Santiago de Compostela, Spain (September 18-22, 2001). Retrieved December 19, 2008 from: http://www.eamt.org/ summit-VIII/papers/miller-2.pdf

National Human Resources Development Committee for the English Linguistic Minority (NHRDCLEM), (2000). *Community economic development perspectives: Needs assessment report of the diverse English Linguistic minority communities across Quebec*. Huntingdon, QC: Community Table of the National Human Resources Development Committee for the English Linguistic Minority.

Nuutila, P. (1996). Roughlate service for in-house customers. In Proceedings from the Aslib Conference: Translating and the Computer 18; London, UK, November 14-15, 1996).

Office of the Commissioner of Official Languages (OCOL), (1999). *The Government of Canada and French on the Internet*. Ottawa, ON: Minister of Public Works and Government Services Canada. Retrieved January 23, 2009 from OCOL Web site: http://www.ocol-clo.gc.ca/ html/gov_fr_internet_gouv_fran_e.php

Office of the Commissioner of Official Languages (OCOL), (2005). *Bridging the digital divide: Official languages on the Internet*. Ottawa, ON: Minister of Public Works and Government Services Canada. Retrieved January 27, 2009 from OCOL Web site: http://www.ocol-clo.gc.ca/html/stu_etu_092005_e.php

Office of the Commissioner of Official Languages (OCOL), (2007). *French culture and learning French as a second language: Perceptions of the Saskatchewan public*. Ottawa, ON: Minister of Public Works and Government Services Canada. Retrieved January 16, 2009 from OCOL Web site: http://www.ocol-clo.gc.ca/docs/e/perceptions_e.pdf

O'Hagan, M. & Ashworth, D. (2002). *Translation-mediated communication in a digital world*. Clevedon: Multilingual Matters.

Ordre des Traducteurs, Terminologues et Interprètes Agréés du Québec (OTTIAQ), (2004). *Sondage de 2004 sur la tarification et les salaires*. Document distributed to OTTIAQ members.

Paré, F. (1997). *Exiguity: Reflections on the margins of literature*. L. Burman (Translated in English. French original *Les littratures de l'exigut: Essai*, 1993). Waterloo, ON: Wilfred Laurier University Press.

Pottie, K., Ng, E., Spitzer, D., Mohammed, A., & Glazier, R. (2008). Language proficiency, gender and self-reported health: An analysis of the first two waves of the Longitudinal Survey of Immigrants to Canada. *Canadian Journal of Public Health, 99*(6), 505-510.

Quebec Community Groups Network (QCGN), (2004). *Community development plan for the English-speaking communities of Quebec*. Ottawa, ON: Department of Canadian Heritage. Retrieved January 19, 2008 from http://www.westquebecers.com/Community_Outreach/ QCGN/aCommunity_Development_Plan_published_version.pdf

Senez, D. (1998). Post-editing service for machine translation users at the European Commission. In Proceedings from the Aslib Conference: Translating and the Computer 20; London, November 12-13 1998.

Shadbolt, D. (2002). The translation industry in Canada. *Multilingual Computing and Technology, 13*(2), 30-34.

Somers, H. (2003). Translation technologies and minority languages. In H. Somers (Ed.), *Computers and translation: A translator's guide* (pp. 87-103) Amsterdam/Philadelphia, PA: John Benjamins.

Standing Joint Committee On Official Languages (SJCOL), (2002). *The Official Language Minority Communities Told Us...* Ottawa, ON: Minister of Public Works and Government Services Canada. Retrieved January 23, 2009 from: http://cmte.parl.gc.ca/cmte/ CommitteePublication.aspx?COM=223&Lang=1&SourceId=37139

Statistics Canada. 2006 Retrieved January 25, 2009 from: http://www12.statcan.ca/english/ Search/secondary_ search_index.cfm

Thouin, B. (1982). The METEO system. In V. Lawson (Ed.), *Practical experience of machine translation* (pp. 39-44). Amsterdam/New York, NY/Oxford: North-Holland Publishing Company. Retrieved August 31, 2009 from: http://www.mt-archive.info/Aslib-1981-Thouin.pdf

Trujillo, A. (1999). *Translation engines: Techniques for machine translation*. London: Springer.

Vasconcellos, M. & Bostad, D. (1992). Machine translation in a high-volume translation environment. In J. Newton (Ed.), *Computers in translation: A practical appraisal* (pp. 58-77). London/New York, NY: Routledge.

Wagner, E., Bech, S. & Martínez, J. (2002). *Translating for the European Union institutions*. Manchester: St. Jerome Publishing.

White, J. (2003). How to evaluate machine translation. In H. Somers (Ed.), *Computers and translation: A translator's guide* (pp. 211-244). Amsterdam/Philadelphia, PA: John Benjamins.

Yuste Rodrigo, E. (2001). Making MT commonplace in translation training curricula: Too many misconceptions, so much potential! In Proceedings of the Machine Translation Summit VIII; Santiago de Compostela, Spain, September 18-22, 2001. Retrieved January 6, 2009 from: http://www.dlsi.ua.es/tmt/docum/TMT7.pdf

Appendix

This appendix contains samples of the texts used as source texts for the experiments described in this paper.

ENGLISH-LANGUAGE SOURCE TEXT: Staying Safe During Disasters

Source: http://www.regina.ca/content/info_services/emergency_services/ during.shtml

During a Tornado

- If you are in a building go to the basement immediately. If there isn't one, crouch or lie flat under heavy furniture in an inner hallway or small inner room or stairwell away from windows. Stay away from large halls, arenas, shopping malls, and so on as their roofs could collapse.
- If you are outside and there is no shelter, lie down in a ditch or ravine, protecting your head.
- If you are driving, get out of and away from the car. It could blow through the air or roll over on you. Lie down as above.

During a Severe Lighting Storm

- If you are in a building, stay inside and away from windows, doors, fireplaces, radiators, stoves, metal pipes, sinks or other electrical charge conductors. Unplug TVs, radios, toasters and other electrical appliances. Do not use the phone or other electrical equipment.
- If you are outside, seek shelter in a building, cave or depressed area. If you are caught in the open, crouch down with your feet close together and your head down (in the "leap-frog" position). Don't lie flat – by minimizing your

contact with the ground you reduce the risk of being electrocuted by a ground charge. Keep away from telephone and power lines, fences, trees and hilltops. Get off bicycles, motorcycles and tractors.
- If you are in a car, stop the car and stay in it. Do not stop near trees or power lines that could fall.

During a Flood
- Turn off basement furnaces and the outside gas valve. Shut off the electricity. If the area around the fuse box or circuit breaker is wet, stand on a dry board and shut off the power with a dry wooden stick.
- Never try to cross a flooded area on foot. The fast water could sweep you away.
- If you are in a car, try not to drive through floodwaters. Fast water could sweep your car away. However, if you are caught in fast rising waters and your car stalls, leave it and save yourself and your passengers.

During a Winter Power Failure
- Turn the thermostat(s) down to a minimum and turn off all appliances, electronic equipment and tools to prevent injury, damage to equipment and fire. Power can also be restored more easily when the system is not overloaded.
- Use proper candleholders. Never leave lit candles unattended.

Remember: Do not use charcoal or gas barbecues, camping heating equipment, or home generators indoors.

FRENCH-LANGUAGE SOURCE TEXT: Notre santé et notre environnement en Outaouais

Source: http://www.santepublique-outaouais.qc.ca/app/DocRepository/ 1.doc

Dans l'ensemble, nous pouvons dire que l'Outaouais est privilégiée au point de vue environnemental. L'air extérieur, l'eau de nos plans et cours d'eau ainsi que nos sols sont relativement peu pollués, si nous les comparons à d'autres régions du Québec et du monde.

Quelques points saillants

Entre 2002 et 2006, on a enregistré 58 jours de mauvaise qualité de l'air à Gatineau. Les véhicules constituent la principale source de pollution atmosphérique et produisent près de 50 % des gaz à effet de serre. Aussi, la ville de Gatineau doit-elle davantage développer les transports en commun et inciter ses citoyens à réduire l'utilisation de leur véhicule.

L'air intérieur est un élément sur lequel les citoyens ont un contrôle encore plus grand. Comme nous passons 90% de notre temps à l'intérieur, il est important de s'assurer de la qualité de l'air intérieur que nous respirons. Chaque année, on dénombre une trentaine de cas d'intoxication au monoxyde de carbone (CO) en Outaouais. Environ 60% de ces intoxications se produisent dans les résidences, les autres surviennent au travail ou ailleurs. Outre le CO, les éléments les plus menaçants à l'intérieur sont : les moisissures et les particules émises par certains matériaux de construction.

Un autre risque vient des émanations de radon dans le sous-sol de certaines maisons. Le radon est un produit de la désintégration naturelle de l'uranium. Certains endroits de notre territoire comme Chelsea, Cantley, le Pontiac et la Haute-Gatineau sont caractérisés par une concentration importante d'uranium. Par conséquent, les possibilités d'avoir de fortes concentrations de radon dans les sous-sols des maisons sont plus grandes dans ces endroits.

Dans ces mêmes secteurs de l'Outaouais, l'uranium peut aussi constituer un problème de santé dans l'eau des puits. Comme 27% de la population de l'Outaouais est approvisionnée en eau potable par des puits, il est important de sensibiliser les propriétaires de puits aux risques tels que les bactéries et les fortes concentrations de nitrates et d'uranium dans leur eau. Une étude réalisée en 2002 a permis d'identifier des taux élevés d'uranium dans l'eau de 11 puits sur 160 dans la Haute-Gatineau.

---

[1] A notable exception is, of course, the well-known Météo machine translation system, which has long been used to translate weather forecasts issued by Environment Canada from English into French. For a historical overview of the development and application of the Météo system, see Thouin (1982), and for more recent discussion, see Langlais et al. (2005).

[2] The exception is province of New Brunswick, whose provincial constitution mandates that it be an officially bilingual province.

[3] The study of the Fransaskois OLMC was undertaken in 2006-2007 with the help of a one-year grant from the Social Sciences and Humanities Research Council (SSHRC) of Canada (858-2005-0002). Preliminary results were reported in Bowker (2008).

[4] The study of the West Quebec OLMC was undertaken in 2007-2008, one year after the study of the Fransaskois OLMC, with the the help of another one-year grant from the Social Sciences and Humanities Research Council (SSHRC) of Canada (858-2006-0008). The results of this study are being reported here for the first time.

[5] MT systems have already been used to help translate a number of different documents for the federal government, including weather forecasts produced by Environment Canada (translated by the Météo MT system) and job advertisements for the JobBank operated by Service Canada (translated using the Reverso Pro MT system); however, these represent quite restricted sublanguages. MT systems have not yet been widely used by the Canadian government to translate texts containing less restricted language.

[6] We were not given direct access to the membership lists of these two associations, and so it is not possible to know exactly how many people received the invitiation to participate in this initial survey. Both associations claim, however, to have over 200 members each. In addition, as part of the information letter accompanying the survey, potential participants were invited to forward the invitation to other potentially interested parties.

[7] Commercial systems were selected because they typically offer better quality translation than the systems freely available on the Internet. However, given the emphasis placed on the need to ensure that official languages policies be kept to a reasonable cost, it is important to note that all the systems tested are available for a very moderate price (less than Cdn$500) and all permit customization of the dictionaries in order to allow for improved output quality.

[8] Samples of some of the texts used in this research are found in the Appendix.

[9] Ideally, it would have been preferable to use a greater number of texts and/or longer texts; however, we had to take into account that we were asking volunteers to read four versions of each text, and we did not want the overall task to become too onerous.

[10] System quality was determined using subjective measures by taking the raw translations produced by each of the three MT systems and, for each text, asking three certified translators to rank the translated versions according to basic guidelines of accuracy and style. For four of the six texts, all the translators gave the highest ranking to the Reverso Pro output. For the remaining texts, two of the three translators ranked the Reverso Pro output as the highest quality, while the third translator ranked it as second. Note that the texts were labelled with a reference number only, and not the system name. In addition, the translators had access to the source text as a point of departure for determining the accuracy of the translated versions.

[11] As Allen (2003, p. 302) explains, RPE is "strictly minimal editing on texts in order to remove blatant and significant errors and therefore stylistic issues should not be considered. The objective is to provide the minimum amount of necessary correction work that can be made on a text in order for the text to be fully understandable as a comprehensible element of information.

[12] Note that in the case of post-editing, both translators had prior experience in this area.

[13] Prices are given in Canadian dollars since these experiments took place in Canada.

[14] Surveys were conducted in accordance with the ethics policies of the Research Grants and Ethics Services (RGES) of the University of Ottawa (Ethics certificate number 09-05-06).

[15] The original *Action Plan for Official Languages* (2003) was introduced to give new momentum to the federal policy on official bilingualism. Presented as a 5-year plan (2003-2008), its goal is to enhance and promote linguistic duality and to foster the development and vitality of OLMCs. It addresses issues relating to health services, immigration, education and literacy; however, it has been criticized for making no specific mention of culture. According to Lesage et al. (2008, p. 8), this omission was deeply disappointing to OLMC members and left them feeling vulnerable.

[16] French immersion programs are those where English-speaking students study most subjects of the school day through French as a medium of instruction.

[17] Note that it was not possible to calculate a margin of error or confidence level for this data because no reliable information could be found about the population of language professionals in the Fransaskois OLMC as a whole.

[18] Note that in this experiment, recipients were conducting a comparative evaluation in which they were assessing the acceptability of different versions of a translated text. It would be interesting to conduct a slightly different survey, in which the respondents were limited to choosing between MT and no translation at all (i.e. to set up a situation similar to that described by DePalma (2007) for the city of San Francisco Web site mentioned in the introductory section of this paper). It would be of interest to see how this might affect the outcome. Based on the results of the present research, we might hypothesize that most members of the West Quebec OLMC would tend to favour MT given that their needs are mainly for information assimilation, whereas members of the Fransaskois OLMC would more likely opt for no translation since their needs are more oriented to information dissemination.

[19] Even here, we must be very careful about over-generalizing in regards to the needs of English-speaking OLMCs since it is quite likely that different English-speaking OLMCs have different needs. For example, the needs of a largely urban, English-speaking OLMC, such as that found in the Montreal region, are likely to be quite different than the needs of a more rural or isolated, English-speaking OLMC, such as the one located on the Magdalen Islands in the Gulf of St. Lawrence. This means that any MT-based solution must be tailored to the specific needs of the intended recipients.

II EVALUATION OF TRANSLATION TOOLS

Social and economic actors in the evaluation of translation technologies. Creating meaning and value when designing, developing and using translation technologies

Iulia Mihalache
Université du Québec en Outaouais, Canada

Evaluation of translation technologies is a social activity, which involves the establishment of knowledge communities as well as the creation of competition to produce better tools. Companies developing translation technologies need to encourage the evaluation of their tools (through online forums, discussion lists, blogs, product communities, community translation, etc.), since evaluating the technology implies spreading and sharing knowledge about it; and sharing the same knowledge or the same modes of thinking and operation, rather than sharing the same material resources, represents the basis of future economic competition. When exchanging knowledge about technologies, translators engage in social activity: they express their opinions and feelings about the technologies they are using, they make judgments about the worth or value of a specific technology, they influence others' decisions or they believe their thoughts will have an impact on decisions companies will make. This article investigates the use of translation technology evaluation criteria as they are represented in several translators' communities and it calls for a multidisciplinary approach when analysing translation technologies adoption, use and evaluation.

1. Introduction

To be highly competitive on the market, translation technology developers need to build strategies for spreading knowledge about their technologies, within and outside the organization. They also need to support the creation of collaborative environments where translators learn and exchange information and opinions about translation technologies. Yet, translation technology developers need to go beyond communicating contents so as to build social skills and change attitudes towards translation processes (which should be now crowdsourced) and towards translation technologies (move from individually oriented software to multi-user technologies, develop collaborative translation tools). The criteria and methods used for evaluating translation technologies[1] are not always the same when considering, for instance, freelance translators or translation agencies, on one side, and translation technology purveyors or translation technology developers, on the other side, since they have different sets of concerns and therefore need different sorts of information. However, it is essential for translation technology developers to understand translators' needs and try to respond to their concerns or explain innovation processes. This is what happened in June 2009, when many professional translators became outraged with a survey launched by LinkedIn aimed at determining translators' interest in collaborative translation *for free,* more precisely their interest in translating LinkedIn's website (a for-profit business) into other languages for free.

> The third question of the survey asked what "incentive" translators would prefer. However, the possible answers did not include payment. Choices included "because it's fun", "upgraded LinkedIn account", and "other" all of them indicating that LinkedIn was looking for volunteers to localize their website. (Selina 2009)

Following translators' reaction, Common Sense Advisory (an independent research and consulting firm), in a *Global Watchtower* posting entitled "Freelance Translators Clash with LinkedIn over Crowdsourced Translation" (Kelly, 2009), compared translators' perceptions with organizations' viewpoints and argued that crowdsourced translation (CT3) is not a threat to the translation profession. CT3 does not mean less quality, but faster, better end-user involvement boosts quality, global reach and community-building. While trying to convince translators of the advantages of collaborative translation (which implies the development of collaborative tools) and explain why translation practices are being overhauled, Common Sense Advisory stated: "A huge information gap separates the companies interested in carrying out CT3 projects and the enormous pool of professional translators who have yet to ever hear of such a thing." (idem). The analysis shows that while translators and translation technology developers may evaluate differently translation tools and processes, it is essential for organizations not only to develop user-oriented systems, but also achieve and implement innovation processes at specific times. Translators as users should therefore be able to participate in each of the steps of the technology lifecycle (product initialization, software development, product implementation and use, market penetration, product redesign). At the same time, translation technology developers and translators should have a concerted interest in the evaluation of translation technologies, throughout the entire software lifecycle.

While there are different evaluation methods for software in general, the methods are hardly standardized (Stowasser, 2006). The formal level of reflection includes theoretical evaluation methods (methods based on cognitive interaction models) and heuristic evaluation methods (expert appraisals based on a series of rules or criteria, such as checklists or guidelines). The empirical level of reflection includes subjective evaluation methods (where the user is called upon to give written or oral answers to questions regarding the software usability or user-friendliness) and objective evaluation methods (user behaviour observation, analysis of tests performed by the user). In this paper, we focus on subjective evaluation methods (group discussions and reflections) of translation technologies, as they are represented in several translators' online communities. We start by presenting a series of translators' opinions about translation technologies so as to show that the choices translators make in terms of tools are often shaped by the beliefs and values of the stakeholders involved in the software design, development and use. The way technologies are perceived – for example as simple tools or as actors[2] – can influence the design, application, outcome, interpretation and use of technology evaluation. After illustrating how perceptions vary among translators, we present a series of criteria that are recurrent when evaluating translation technologies as tools *per se*, as 'technical' instruments. We go on by presenting translators' comments that illustrate not only the different stages in the technology adoption process, but also the role technologies play as social actors, as agents organizations use in order to spread knowledge, build value and competitive advantage and achieve innovation in terms of translation processes, translation competences or translation social skills. We also exemplify how innovation related determinants, adopter related determinants as well as the marketing strategy have an impact on how translation technologies are perceived and evaluated by the users and on the decisions and choices translators make. Finally, we call for a multidisciplinary approach when analysing translation technologies adoption, use and evaluation.

2. Constructive interaction of translators within translation on-line communities

Consider the following comments about translation technologies from translators communicating on ProZ.com, "a comprehensive network of essential services, resources and experiences" (www.proz.com) for translators:

(1) "Generally, the more you pay for a product, the more support and development there is behind it (e.g. Trados, Déjà Vu)."
www.proz.com/forum/translator_resources/93005-should_i_buy_a_tool_like_trados.html

(2) "If you do a lot of work for agencies with big and/or ongoing projects allocated over several translators, then it is probably worth it. If you have a combination of direct customers and agencies that do not require it, then you don't. I bought it this year, but so far have not made a return on the investment. At the same time, 2007 was a record year for me, so, at this pace, I will not renew or upgrade Trados since for me it has had negative value." (idem)

(3) "I am content (and have sufficient reputation and work!) to simply refuse jobs that insist on the use of CAT tools, and

stick with the more interesting and lucrative jobs that I know I am best at." (ibid.)

(4) "I keep telling people to resist the pressure to use CAT tools [...] unless they are really interested in using them. In other words, don't you buy a CAT tool and painstakingly learn to use it only because your client said so. If you do it, do it for your own purposes - if you think a CAT tool can help you do your work better or faster, buy one. But it seems that the CAT tool end of the balance really is heavier because most of us bought the thing, afraid to miss out on opportunities. (ibid.)

(5) "I was forced to buy Trados by a translation agency, but they do not know how to handle it well." www.proz.com/forum/translator_resources/4371-is_trados_a_vital_tool_for_translating.html

(6) "When investing in any type of software, a translator needs to ask (at least) two questions: 1. Will it increase my productivity? 2. Will it provide me with access to work previously unavailable?" www.proz.com/forum/business_issues/120791-is_it_normal_to_be_asked_to_buy_software-page2.html

(7) "Translating is a business and you have to invest in your tools. [...] It seems to me that some of us are still stuck in the past. Translating does not mean being an 'artist' anymore [...]. The client has every right to ask for a specific tool; if you don't like it or don't want to pay for it, just decline the job. Translating has evolved immensely in the last few years and if you are happy with your luddite approach, then don't complain when clients go somewhere else." www.proz.com/forum/business_issues/110584-what_is_the_next_best_thing_to_trados-page3.html

(8) "Don't tell me that accepting to use the client's favorite CAT tool is added value. It doesn't in any case prove that your translation will be of high quality, as mentioned by several colleagues. Also, if you can give me one real world example of an agency paying you more because you did use their CAT tool, I'd really like to hear it." (idem)

These comments illustrate translators' attitudes, beliefs and behaviours related to translation technologies. They show variations in terms of technology adoption or use. They also show that a richer understanding of translation technologies use and evaluation is obtained when their implications for translators are jointly studied from social, economic, organizational and psychological perspectives. Comment 1 expresses the translator's conviction that paying/asking for more for the tool guarantees constant interaction with the company as well as continuous improvement of the tool. More money normally means more insights in user preferences and the guarantee that technology will not fail because of too much attention given to technical features and less attention given to user needs. The translator's adoption decision involves a rational analysis of costs and benefits. Comment 1 also gives visibility to two specific technologies: Trados and Déjà Vu. Comment 2 shows a translator's ambiguity about the real value the technology has; the work environment (partners, social motivations) seem to influence the translator's decision to buy that tool, while the market's decisions appear to produce negative outcomes. Comments 3 and 4 articulate the pressure social groups may have on translators' decisions to adopt a specific technology (even when its results are not proven) as well as the potential impact of a deeper experience in translation and a large client database on the decision to acquire a tool. Comment 5 shows how technology adoption involves power games and conflict between agents. Comment 6 highlights the link between the decision to buy the tool and the misconception that the tool will quickly help translators be more productive and therefore, earn more. Comment 7 reflects the market's impact on the translation practices and the need for translators not only to fit into a new social milieu and an innovative working environment but also to manage their work and relationships and accept innovation generated by technology. Finally, comment 8 expresses the resistance and lack of trust of some translators with respect to buying and using translation technologies.

3. Factors in technology adoption and use: translators' perceptions and attitudes

Technologies are not only tools, but also social agents. They allow companies to communicate with existing and possible users, and thus to gain a competitive advantage. To be first on the market, companies need to perform thorough analyses of user preferences, needs, expectations and motivations. Companies need to understand or be aware of translators' attitudes towards technological innovations. At the same time, companies need to use specific communicative strategies to persuade translators that technologies have actually been developed for them.

Technologies are first of all hardware. What are the features of 'proper software' and user's attitudes towards such a tool, according to different translators communicating in the Getting established forum of ProZ.com?

Table 1: Features of proper software

1. I have used and bought SDLX and find it extremely good:	

a. it's fast, b. easy to learn, c. has efficient technical support, d. and can export files in TRADOS format if your client asks for a TRADOS translation.	**+ processing speed** **- complexity** **+ satisfaction** **+ flexibility/adaptability**
2. You could try WordFast. a. It is free. b. and supposedly compatible with Trados, Transit, Déjà Vu and Cypresoft.	**- cost** **+ compatibility**
3. I've been working with it for 3 months and it has already more than saved me the initial investment.	**+ optimism** **+ return on investment**
4. If you do get Trados, then you should seriously consider going to a seminar to have someone explain the workings of the system to you.	**+ complexity; whether training is available**
5. Yes, it has some glitches, but I have yet to find a software package that has none.	**+ product knowledge** **+ familiarity with similar products** **+ willingness to accept some imperfections**
6. Yes, it can be expensive (although I find that the Freelance version is not that bad).	**+ variants at different costs** **+ adaptation to user's needs**
7. Yes, you need training to fully use the functionality - try grouping with others to reduce the cost (or ask Trados about their in-house training sessions, provided that you happen to be physically near one of their offices.	**+ complexity for specific functionalities (need to be part of the group to understand)** **+ collaborative use (sharing licenses)** **+ in-house training** **+ remote training**
8. The open discussion group is at http://groups.yahoo.com/group/wfisher.	**+technology community available**

Some other technical features are highlighted by translators connecting on ProZ.com: file conversion, translatable text extraction, aligning method and format, word count, ignoring HTML tags when counting words, compatibility with all types of computers, ease of installation, no data loss or corruption, file formats handled, multiple languages, need/possibility of TM exchange and so on.

4. Perceived attributes of innovation and the process of technology adoption

Most importantly, technologies are the information that goes with them, that is knowledge about how they can represent an advantage or a disadvantage in a specific work environment. This knowledge may remain coded, tacit and may therefore not be transferred[3].

When seeking information for improving a translation process, translators will adopt a technology faster if they are already **familiar** with other products in the same cluster (for instance, traditional translation memory systems versus context-based translation memory systems), if the technology shows **flexibility** and **compatibility** with other existing systems and if it offers the capacity of **adaptation** to customer specific workflows and company sizes. What is also needed in the technology adoption process is the presence of a **critical mass of adopters** who will convince the majority of the utility of the technology (Rogers, 1995). Here, this critical mass of translation technologies adopters could be represented by the *Top 25 Translation Companies* as identified in a Common Sense Advisory report[4], or by the key players in the translation technologies development industry, or by those companies that introduced new business models and technologies[5], or by some other "smaller firms like across, Alchemy, Lingotek, and MultiCorpora [that] will challenge the incumbent leader SDL-Trados on translation memory with rapid product turns and innovative distribution and market acceptance models" (DePalma & Beninatto, 2006). The critical mass of adopters could be also formed within virtual environments, such as social networks (DePalma & Kelly, 2008), (collaboration) translation portals/websites, translation communities, forums, discussion lists, or by independent market research firms.

The critical mass of adopters will be also able to influence organizational technological choices, asking for or imposing specific functionalities which can help translators perform better. They can be 'user-strategists' (Flichy, 2007, p. 90), that is "firms which negotiate with the designers within a formal framework" (idem), but also individuals who create pressure groups (for instance, translators communities) and modify technology frames of use.

In the light of the diffusion theory introduced by Everett Rogers in 1962, five characteristics of innovation form people's attitude toward a new technology and determine the timing of technology adoption decision: **relative advantage** (measured, for example, in economic terms, social prestige, convenience, or satisfaction), **compatibility** with the values of the community or past/existing experiences, **complexity** (the degree to which the innovation is perceived as difficult to understand and use), **trialability** (possibility to test it on a limited basis) and **observability** (the extent to which results of an innovation are visible to others). The tacit knowledge that may not be diffused with the innovation is related to both the complexity and the observability of the innovation; the **tacitness** of innovation represents the extent to which an innovation may be conveyed or communicated to the final users (Rothman, 1974). In the following statements, translators question SDL's real intentions when it comes to SDL/Trados certification, which raises questions about the **transferability** of the know-how coming with the innovation:

> In my opinion, they are not making this test only to earn more money; it seems that they want to employ some experienced people who may help them solve the bugs in the program.
> If they care so much about us and our knowledge of the product, AND the object is not money-making, why not make it free? www.proz.com/forum/business_issues/51328-sdl_trados_certification_what_do_you_think.html

Innovation transferability could explain why people adapt differently to technological change. According to Rogers (1962), people may be:

Translators' comments	
innovators and early adopters select the technology first: they have a higher perception of relative advantage than the (later) adopters as well as a lower perception of complexity (contrary to the late majority)	If you already lost projects due to not having this software, there is no reason for any further delay. Look for the best offer you can get (quite often here on ProZ.com as TGB) and invest some money in your future. And please, don't come with "it is so expensive"... This is an investment and not a piece of clothing or so. You will use it on long term basis - and so it is cheaper than smoking. www.proz.com/forum/business_issues/110584-what_is_the_next_best_thing_to_trados.html
early majority careful but accepting change more quickly than the average	As many agencies require to have a CAT, I did some research and ended up with SDLX (about US$120)… www.proz.com/forum/translator_resources/812-any_opinions_about_trados.html

late majority sceptic people who will use new products only when the majority is using them	1) My output is already very high - do CAT tools increase significantly the amount you can translate in a day? 2) My quality is already extremely high (according to my customers at least!) - presumably CAT tools make suggestions, which helps jog one's memory, but also encourage you to hand over some of the 'thinking responsibility' to the machine, if that makes sense. [...] 3) I have had agencies ask me if I use Trados, and say if so they would like to negotiate my rates... as a businessman, I see no reason to invest £500 (for example) in order to reduce my rates! Repetitions there may be in a text, but one still has to think 'is this the right translation'? In case it's not clear, I'm a little skeptical. www.translatorscafe.com/cafe/MegaBBS/thread-view.asp?threadid=12184&start=1
laggards traditional people who will only accept technology or innovation if it has become ordinary or tradition	In the meantime, I will not change my mind about this: forcing translators to use CAT tools is viewed as an obligation by most agencies, and not as an added value. The day I manage to be paid better when using Trados than when not using it, I will be one happy freelancer. Meanwhile, I have a list of added values that I use that work much better than the argument that I use Trados. www.proz.com/forum/business_issues/110584-what_is_the_next_best_thing_to_trados-page3.html.

The process of technology adoption passes over time: 1. from first knowledge of an innovation (the Knowledge stage – what is the information available to people), 2. to forming an attitude toward the innovation (the Persuasion stage – this attitude is created through a variety of communication channels, the interpersonal channels influence network having a much stronger impact on the forming and changing of attitudes that the mass media channels), 3. to a decision to adopt or reject (the Decision stage), 4. to the implementation of the new idea (the Implementation stage), and 5. to the confirmation of this decision (the Confirmation stage).

The technology adoption process as defined by Rogers shows us that companies developing translation technologies need to go beyond communicating intentions, contents and methods (the *Knowledge stage*) and stimulate cooperative technology evaluation and innovation in, for instance, web-based environments. By adopting a strategic thinking about the role technologies play, companies need to consider learning and evaluating capabilities as a way of creating value, and as a key competitive advantage. Companies therefore need to find ways of building social skills and technology perceptions (the *Persuasion stage*), enhancing translation competence (the *Implementation stage*), changing attitudes and values about translation processes (the *Decision stage*), which should be "collaborative", "simultaneous", "crowdsourced" or performed in "communities" as well as present confirmatory evidence (for instance, case studies) that the decision to adopt or reject the technology was the right course of action.

5. Attitudinal factors and the impact of the marketing strategy on technology adoption

Other theories approached the process of technology acceptance and use and included several other attitudinal factors that influence user's decision about how and when the technology will be used.

The *Theory of Reasoned Action* (TRA) (Fishbein, 1967; Fishbein & Ajzen, 1975) suggested that a person's behaviour is determined by their intention to achieve this behaviour. The intention is influenced by the **individual's attitude** (a series of beliefs about the consequences of performing the behaviour multiplied by a person's valuation of these consequences) as well as by the **subjective norm** (a combination of perceived expectations from relevant individuals or groups along with motivation to comply with these expectations). In other words, if people evaluate the suggested behaviour as positive (attitude), and if they think their reference groups wanted them to perform the behaviour (subjective norm), this results in a higher intention (motivation) and they are more likely to follow that behaviour. In the context of translation technologies use, the *subjective norm* would be the amount of influence translators' social networks, translation technology companies, translation agencies would have in influencing a choice to adopt and use a technology. In the following conversation, the translator is less motivated since he evaluates the suggested behaviour as negative, while the reference group wants him to perform that behaviour:

> Some of my clients specify the use of Trados. I always accept such jobs, translate them using an alternate TM-based program, produce a bilingual Trados compatible dirty - sorry, uncleaned - file and return it to the agency. Never, not once, has the agency reprimanded me for not using Trados. In fact, there is really no way for them to know whether I have or not. They have their uncleaned version, with which they can, I presume, update their client TM, and I have used a user-friendly program which has caused me considerably less headache than I suffer when using Trados.

> www.translatorscafe.com/cafe/MegaBBS/thread-view.asp?threadid=12184&start=11

The *Technology Acceptance Model*, developed by Fred Davis and Richard Bagozzi (Bagozzi et al., 1992; Davis et al., 1989), introduced two new technology acceptance factors: the **perceived usefulness** of the technology that will be used to enhance job performance and well as the **perceived ease-of-use** (the use of technology will not require an effort). In the context of translation technologies use, the *perceived usefulness* can be interpreted as whether or not translating texts by using translation technologies would help the translator achieve job outcomes (better quality, more efficiency, and even better quality of life):

> One of the first benefits I noticed was that the pain in my neck - from constantly consulting hard copy next to my keyboard and then looking up to the screen - disappeared! Stupid reason for using a CAT tool - but I really found it helped having the source text on the screen in front of me. [...] The benefits of the translation memory vary according to the job you are handling. [...] Then there is the business of terminology. [...] And one final thing: a good CAT tool will allow you to replicate the layout of the original source document - and that can save a lot of time.
> www.translatorscafe.com/cafe/MegaBBS/thread-view.asp?threadid=12184&start=1

Ease of use, in the context of translation technologies, can be construed as whether or not the translation tools are easy to work with in order for the translator to invest in such a technology, use it and accept to change his or her *translation behaviour*. One should notice in the following example not only the expression of this acceptance factor, but also the tacit competition between tools and behaviours: "I love Metatexis, as it is easy to work with, very stable and rarely crashes. You can convert the end result into an unclean Trados file and most agencies don't even notice it." (www.translatorscafe.com/cafe/MegaBBS/thread-view.asp?threadid=13129&posts=3)

The *Theory of Planned Behavior*, developed by Ajzen (1985; 1991), introduced the idea of "**perceived behaviour control**" and stated that the individual does not always have full control on behaviour: external factors may facilitate or constrain the performance of a specific behaviour as well as the individual's perception or confidence in self-efficacy and in achieving expected outcomes. In the case of technologies, the perceived behaviour control could have an impact on the intention to adopt or reject a technology. A translator observes:

> Also, if the main point of using a CAT tool is to help the translator, I really wonder why the agencies are requiring it... It's like forcing

> me to take vitamins when I say I'm fine without them. There must be some other reason why so many agencies require the use of Trados... like CAT rate schemes, that is, rebates on our work. Can somebody contradict this? Does anybody work with an agency who requires the use of Trados AND pays the full rate for every single word?
> www.proz.com/forum/business_issues/110584-what_is_the_next_best_thing_to_trados-page2.html.

Verdegem and De Marez (2008) extended the list of technology adoption determinants and distinguished ten innovation-related characteristics (perceptions), eight adopter-related characteristics, and the impact of the marketing strategy. They showed that the “perceived cost” and "tangibles” are the most important dimensions of “relative advantage”. They also included in the list of determinants the perceived enjoyment of using the technology and the reliability understood as a performance risk, as well as several other factors, such as the person’s ‘optimism’ towards technology, ‘product knowledge’, ‘willingness (and ability) to pay’, the ‘perceived impact on one’s personal image’, the ‘perceived control’, ‘impact of social influences’ and the ‘impact of marketing, advertising and promotional strategies’. And they stated that it is important not only to know why a technology is adopted, but also why people do not use a specific technology or why they lag behind in the adoption and use of new technologies. One translator says:

> There is the insidious phenomenon started by Trados, that tries to dictate the working relationship and economics of translators and clients. They have invented a formula whereby we go by “matches” and they – the software salespeople – are deciding what my quotes should be like. Moreover, they are telling my potential client that they have the right to impose a quote formula on me. (…) To some degree it is insulting to the work we do. www.translatorscafe.com/cafe/MegaBBS/thread-view.asp?threadid=12390&start=21.

We will quote here a series of translators’ comments that express some of the adoption determinants identified by Verdegem and De Marez, for which we have not offered examples so far.

Table 2: Innovation related characteristics

Compatibility	
Complexity	
Cost	

Enjoyment	You will find several online tutorials that will help you to get familiar with the software pretty quickly. You will also have the possibility to attend online sessions for free. www.translatorscafe.com/cafe/MegaBBS/thread-view.asp?threadid=10108&start=11
Observability	Trados is the market leader. It's reasonable to suppose that many translators who work mainly or exclusively for agencies use Trados for that reason, which is fair enough. http://arm.proz.com/forum/translator_resources/93005-should_i_buy_a_tool_like_trados-755233.html
Relative advantage	
Tangibles	They [CAT tools] allow you to get regular work from agencies using them. www.translatorscafe.com/cafe/MegaBBS/thread-view.asp?threadid=12184&start=1
Trialability (try out the software on a temporary or test basis)	Wordfast is the tool you may invest in. It is not at all expensive, you get unlimited period trial (with glossary limited to 500 words) and once comfortable go in for paid version. www.proz.com/forum/translator_resources/83225-can_we_share_a_tm_ietrados_as_a_group_of_community_translators.html
Visibility	Wordfast [...] has an excellent online user support community, including direct e-mail support from Wordfast's developer, Yves Champollion. www.translationdirectory.com/article511.htm

Table 3: Adopter related characteristics

Control/Voluntariness	I'm new to the CAT tool concept - and am willing to try. www.proz.com/forum/translator_resources/118211-demo_cat_tools_for_mac_os.html
Image/Prestige	My main reason for investing in such a tool is to become a more attractive partner for translation agencies. www.translatorscafe.com/cafe/MegaBBS/thread-view.asp?threadid=12184&start=11
Innovativeness	SDLX is the first CAT tool to support bi-directional languages such as Arabic and Hebrew. The program is highly robust and reliable. It has built a reputation over the years for these very characteristics. www.proz.com/forum/translator_resources/6726-cat_tools_comparison.html#41855

(product) knowledge	Being a legal Trados user since 2003 I decided to take this Trados certification and found it quite useful. First, it made me to go through some tough sections of Trados software (like DTD-settings files, etc.). Second, I raised my rates from 0.08 Euro per word to 0.10 Euro per word (quite a lot for English to Russian translations) and more and more clients agree with this rate seeing I'm Trados certified. The reason is many translators say they know Trados, but only some of them know "ins and outs" of it. And I must admit, the exam is not an easy thing to pass although I've been using Trados for a long time. www.proz.com/forum/business_issues/51328-sdl_trados_certification_what_do_you_think.html
Opinion leadership	That is why you are SDL Trados Workbench Certified. Thanks a lot! www.proz.com/forum/sdl_trados_support/73452-is_it_possible_to_batch_translate_to_fuzzy_in_sdl_trados_2006.html#574600
Optimism	Heartsome works with Linux and Mac. And that's the good thing about it. www.proz.com/forum/across_support/57014-does_anyone_have_experience_with_across_translation_suite_and_heartsome_translation_suite.html#431794
Social influence	If I pay Trados a considerable sum of money, I get accredited and have the right to give them free advertising on my business card and website... www.proz.com/forum/business_issues/51328-sdl_trados_certification_what_do_you_think.html
Willingness to pay	

Table 4: Impact of marketing strategy

Marketing (impact)	Certainly I share your objections to the growing tendency of agencies to demand both an investment in costly software and, when you have made that investment, expect you to charge less than you did before! How did this situation arise? Simply because SDL has adopted an extremely intelligent marketing approach: convince end-clients that they can reduce their translation costs if they insist on the use of Trados; get these end-users to put pressure on agencies and demand deductions for repetitions and fuzzy matches; get the agencies to use only those translators with the software; create the impression among the translator community that unless you have Trados you won't get any work. www.translatorscafe.com/cafe/MegaBBS/thread-view.asp?threadid=12390&start=21 Keep your head cool when you are attacked by overly aggressive marketing experts. www.proz.com/translation-articles/articles/222/1/Trados---Is-It-a-Must%3F

6. For a multidisciplinary approach when evaluating translation technologies

Konanaa and Balasubramanian (2005) introduce the Social-Economic-Psychological (SEP) Model to account for the need for a multidisciplinary approach when studying technology adoption and usage. While this model is used to study behaviour of online investors, we can use several of these determinants to analyze translational behaviours before, during and after adopting a specific translation technology:

(1) The *perceived operational competence* explains the responsiveness of translation technology companies (speed and means to provide feedback, customer support, and accurate information).
(2) The *convenience* explains translators' ability to quickly grasp knowledge about the technological product and interact with the company at any time.
(3) The *overconfidence* may reflect translators' misconceptions about a quick return on investment after buying the technology.
(4) The *risk attitude* determines how translators value a specific technology in terms of possible gains:

> I have seen surprisingly little monetary benefit from using Trados – other than the ability to work with clients who request that I do so. And with the varying economic conditions of the various countries where my contacts are located added into the mix, I know I have lost work because of rates and Trados discounting. www.proz.com/forum/business_issues/110584-what_is_the_next_best_thing_to_trados-page4.html

(5) The *normative social pressure* refers to the influence relevant groups (employers, translation agencies, translation communities) may have on the translators who have to fit into a social milieu: "The use of TM software is a must for every freelance translator working on domestic or worldwide markets." www.proz.com/translation-articles/articles/222/1/Trados---Is-It-a-Must%3F

(6) The *embarrassment avoidance* can explain translators' need to have a perfect technology and avoid uncomfortable situations (no bugs, same payment as without using technologies): "CAT tools have two sides - on one hand they facilitate your work, but on the other hand customers and agencies are using this argument to push down prices." www.proz.com/forum/translator_resources/4371-is_trados_a_vital_tool_for_translating.html

(7) The *pursuit of social class membership* captures translators' desire to become part of a social network using the technology.

(8) The *illusions of knowledge and control* express translators' belief that they can influence decisions made by companies or that they control the technology in their respective environment. "I do hope that newer CAT tools be developed to help more the translators' job. We translators do not care if those companies are spending billions of dollars to be first in the market; we do not want to be their sponsors!" (idem)

(9) The *perceptions of fairness* refer to the belief of different translators' communities (freelancers, small and mid-size companies) that they are treated in the same manner as large companies by the translation technology companies, which means they will participate in different activities (learning, training, buying) in a relaxed way.

(10) *Trust* captures the different ways translation technologies companies persuade or assure translators of positive outcomes when using their technologies and manage to develop relationships with translators. This is done without a face-to face or physical interaction.

(11) The *social/institutional safeguards* may explain the credibility strategies translation technology companies build when addressing translators.

While the technology acceptance models focus on the adoption of a new technology and the usage behavior, the sociology of innovation approaches (Science and Technology Studies and Actor-Network Theory: Bruno Latour, 1987, Michel Callon, 1989; Madeleine Akrich, 1987) focus on the specific moment of the development of innovations which presupposes a process of making decisions as well as social, technical, cultural or economic choices. These approaches try to identify the interactions between different social actors participating in the process of innovation and see innovation as the result of a competition between several projects, as a series of transformations and confrontations (for instance, usability tests or user performance tests may be considered as 'confrontations') which create links between human and non-human (technical) actors and generate knowledge. The absence of competition is equivalent to the absence of choice: "Several respondents worried that this deal creates an effective monopoly in the tools area and that SDL could do as it pleases", writes DePalma (2005) in an article reporting on the results of a Globalization and Localization Association (GALA) survey of language service providers about the impact of SDL's acquisition of TRADOS on 20 June 2005. "Some [language service providers] are afraid that SDL could limit access to the tool, give preferential levels of support, or even increase the price of tools and drive competitors out of business" (idem).

Developing an innovation implies knowledge about competitors and their products: "[…] before competitive strategies can be formulated, decision makers must have an image of who their rivals are *and on what dimensions they will compete*" (Hodgkinson, 2005, p. 2; italics ours). It also implies integrating in the technical device a definition of what the users are, of their identity, of their possible profiles. Transferring knowledge about an innovation towards the final users (by means of user guides, web-based training, web presentations, advertising printed material) is a didactic and strategic activity constrained by psychological conditions (who are the users – translators, terminologists, reviewers, project managers, what are their individual motivations and intentions, what are their competence levels in translation technologies, what are the tools they already use or they use most frequently) as well as by socio-cultural conditions (the situation in which the users are embedded, ranging from freelancers to language service providers, company owners, company employees, translation communities and large companies). In his paper "Rethinking the Dissemination of Science and Technology" (Woolgar, 2000), Steve Woolgar argues that technology transfer is not a solely technological process, but also a cultural, social, managerial and economic one, affected by the competition between representations and beliefs about people beyond the organization (the users) and the mediation between what different entities participating in the process think about the users: the success of technology transfer depends on the communication between producers and consumers (here, the communication between companies developing translation technologies and the users or the translators). This means that transfer will only occur if what is known separately about the users eventually becomes a well-defined body of users or 'configured users' (a *model*, a *pattern of relationships*) who have more confidence in the technology that the designers themselves.

7. Conclusion

Focusing on communication about translation technologies within translation communities (ProZ.Com, TranslatorsCafe) as well as on the role companies have in conveying and transferring knowledge about computer-assisted translation tools, we stated that a more complete understanding of translation technologies evaluation criteria is obtained if translators' attitudes, perceptions and behaviours related to technologies are jointly studied from sociological, economic, organizational, cultural and psychological perspectives. In presenting possible evaluation criteria for synthesizing translators' perceptions and attitudes, we appealed to different models of technology adoption and use as well as to other approaches able to explain the conflicts arising when developing and transferring innovations. Future work in the framework of this research could focus on detailed online surveys with different technology users, ranging from freelancers to language service providers, company owners and company employees, as well as on the strategies translation technologies companies use when teaching or training translators.

Bibliography

Ajzen, I. (1985). From intentions to actions: A theory of planned behaviour. In Kuhl & Beckmann (Eds.), *Action Control: From Cognition to Behavior*. Berlin, Heidelberg, New York: Springer-Verlag, 11-39.

Ajzen, I. (1991). The theory of planned behaviour. *Organizational Behavior and the Human Decision Process*, 50, 179-211.

Akrich, M. (1987). Comment décrire des objets techniques. *Techniques et Culture*, *9*, 49-64.

Bagozzi, R. P. (2007). The legacy of the technology acceptance model and a proposal for a paradigm shift. *Journal of the Association for Information Systems 8*, 244-254.

Bagozzi, R. P., Davis F. D. & Warshaw P.R. (1992). Development and test of a theory of technological learning and usage. *Human Relations 45(7)*, 660-686.

Callon, M. (1989). *La science et ses réseaux*. Paris: La Découverte.

Dautenhahn, K. et al. (Ed.) (2002). *Socially Intelligent Agents: Creating Relationships with Computers and Robots*. Series: Multiagent Systems, Artificial Societies, and Simulated Organizations, vol. 3, Norwell, Mass. / Dordrecht, The Netherlands: Kluwer Academic Publishers.

Davis, F. D. (1989). Perceived usefulness, perceived ease of use, and user acceptance of information technology. *MIS Quarterly 13(3),* 319-340.

Davis, F. D., Bagozzi R. P., & Warshaw P. R. (1989). User acceptance of computer technology: A comparison of two theoretical models. *Management Science 35*, 982-1003.

DePalma, D. & Kelly, N. (2008). *Translation of, by, and for the People*. Common Sense Advisory, Lowell, Massachusetts.

DePalma, D. (2005). "SDL-TRADOS Language Service Provider Reaction to SDL's Purchase of TRADOS", report for GALA. On line at: www.commonsenseadvisory.com/members/res_cgi.php/050730_R_gala_sdl_trados.php (retrieved November 2, 2008).

DePalma, D. & Beninatto, R.S. (2006). Predictions for 2007: Business and Website Globalization, Technology, and Business Models. *Global Watchtower™*. On line at: www.commonsenseadvisory.com/news/global_watchtower.php (retrieved November 11, 2007).

Eid, S. (2009). LinkedIn Translation Controversy. On line at: http://site.interpretereducationonline.com/2009/08/18/linkedin-translation-controversy/ (retrieved July 2, 2009).

Fishbein, M. & Ajzen, I. (1975). *Belief, Attitude, Intention, and Behavior. An Introduction to Theory and Research*, Reading: Addison-Wesley.

Fishbein, M. (1967). *Readings in Attitude Theory and Measurement*, New York: Wiley.

Flichy, P. (2007). *Understanding Technological Innovation. A Socio-Technical Approach*, Cheltenham/ Northampton: Edward Elgar.

Hodgkinson, G.P. (2005). *Images of Competitive Space. A Study of Managerial and Organizational Cognition*. Basingstoke/New York: Palgrave Macmillan.

Kelly, N. (2009). Freelance Translators Clash with LinkedIn over Crowdsourced Translation. *Global Watchtower™*. On line at: www.globalwatchtower.com/2009/06/19/linkedin-ct3/ (retrieved June 19, 2009).

Konanaa, P. & Balasubramanian S. (2005). The Social-Economic-Psychological model of technology adoption and usage: an application to online investing. In *Decision Support Systems 39*, 505– 524.

Latour, B. (1987). *Science in Action : how to follow scientists and engineers through society*. Cambridge, Mass.: Harvard University Press.

O'Neill, H.M., Pouder P.W. & Buchholtz, A.K. (2002). Patterns in the diffusion of strategies across organisations: insights from the innovation diffusion literature. *Academy of Management Review 23*, 98–114.

Rogers, E.M. (1962, 1995). *Diffusion of Innovations*. New York: Free Press of Glencoe.

Rothman, R. (1974). *Planning and Organizing for Social Change: Action principles from social science research*. New York: Columbia University Press.

Stowasser, S. (2006). Methods of Software Evaluation. Karwowski (Ed.), *International Encyclopedia of Ergonomics and Human Factors*, 2nd edition, 3rd volume, 3249-3253.

Verdegem, P. & De Marez, L. (2008). Conditions for technology acceptance: broadening the scope of determinants of ICT appropriation. *Proceedings of ICE-B, International Joint Conference on E-business and Telecommunications*, Porto, 26-29 July.

Woolgar, S. (2000). Rethinking the dissemination of science and technology. On line at: www.cirst.uqam.ca/PCST3/PDF/Communications/WOOLGAR.PDF (retrieved November 15, 2008).

---

[1] We are referring here to computer-assisted translation tools (conventional translation memories, advanced leveraging tools, terminology management systems, translator's workstations).

[2] "Tools react only when interacted with, while agents act autonomously and proactively, sometimes outside user awareness." (Dautenhahn (2002, 21)

[3] "Where knowledge is tacit, strategies will not travel well … visible elements of the strategy may travel across organisational borders, but the embedded context of the innovation stays with the originator." (O'Neill *et al.* 2002, 108)

[4] www.commonsenseadvisory.com/research/report_view.php?id=64.

[5] "This Quick Take describes four creative companies that are poised to shake things up in the language services space -- Adaquest, CSOFT, DotSUB, and ProZ", announces the report *Language Industry Movers and Shakers* by Common Sense Advisory. (www.commonsenseadvisory.com/research/reports_category.php?year=2008&id=0).

The role of Computer-Assisted Translation in the field of software localization

Alberto Fernández Costales
University of Oviedo

This article analyses the effectiveness of computer-assisted translation (CAT) in the field of software localization. In order to measure and assess the advantages of using translation tools, a program is localized using Passolo, a specialized software localization application. The study is intended to calibrate how CAT can improve translators' performance in a localization project and also to appraise the main features of the selected application, focusing on functionality, usability and reliability. The article outlines some of the challenges and difficulties of software localization, aiming to test how the process of adapting a product to a particular locale can be optimized by the use of computer assisted translation. The case study focuses on the main challenges of the process from the point of view of translation. To conclude, the study formulates a number of conclusions and evaluates the performance of the selected application.

1. Introduction

The development of new technologies in the latter half of the 20th century and the explosion of the Internet as a promotional, informative and communicative tool have modified how companies traditionally engaged in international trade. On the other hand, the political and economic changes occurring in recent decades have shaped a new global panorama involving new players and social agents.

Globalization has allowed small and medium-sized companies to increase their market shares by competing at an international level with the support of the Internet and new software applications.

In this scenario, translation is not only the basic tool for intercultural communication and a vehicle for understanding among nations but has turned into an essential element for the economy of any company seeking an international presence beyond the borders of its home country (Corte, 2002).

Companies adapting their products to a particular market will increase their sales figures as they improve their brand images. But a wrong Web site translation or a failure to localize software applications can lead to commercial failure even if the quality of the product is widely recognized.

As explained in this paper, localization involves not only textual adaptation but also modifying the non-verbal, semiotic and cultural elements of a product in order to make it suitable for the target audience. In order to achieve this goal, translators and localizers can rely on the support provided by computer-assisted translation (CAT)[1].

Traditionally, research in translation technology has been linked to machine translation. The lack of conclusive results in this area in the last decades of the 20th century opened new lines of research the target of which was not achieving machine translation but developing new tools to assist human translators. The application of CAT has been widely studied by translation scholars (Austermühl, 2001; Nogueira, 2002; Biau & Pym, 2006; Somers, 2003; Melby, 2006), and research in this field has contributed to improving and enhancing translation technology. One of the main advances in this field has been the setting of a standard format, known as Translation Memory eXchange, or TMX, which allows the exchange of translation memories among different applications (Abaitua, 2001). This implies that more than one single tool can be used to carry out a project, fostering competition among translation software providers and giving translators more flexibility and freedom of choice.

The main hypothesis of this paper is that the use of CAT is profitable for translators since it provides more efficiency and consistency in software localization. The more technical terminology is used and the more repetition occurs in a software application, the more suitable the use of CAT will be.

The basics of localization will be overviewed in section 2, focusing on the main methodological alternatives available in the case of software. The case study is detailed in section 3, where the key elements of the project will be explained and the way in which translation tools can effectively optimize localization from the translator's point of view will be analysed. In addition, the tool's performance will be evaluated, with comments on its strengths and weaknesses, and possible alternatives to Passolo will be suggested. Finally, conclusions are presented in section 4, where the initial hypothesis will be discussed.

2. Localization

Localization is the process of adapting a product to the local market where it is going to be sold, so that it seems that it has been originally designed for this particular audience. For a product to be effectively localized, users should not be aware that it has been designed in an other part of the world, with a different language and with an other cultural background. That is to say, the final consumer should not detect that a particular product has been created with other cultural parameters (Corte, 2002). Bert Esselink provides the following definition:

> Generally speaking, localization is the translation and adaptation of a software or Web product, which includes the software application itself and all related product documentation. The term "localization" is

derived from the word "locale" which traditionally means a small area or vicinity. (Esselink, 2000, p. 1)

The localization industry started to flourish in the 1980s, together with the development of new and more powerful translation tools, and it was consolidated in the 1990s with the creation of big multinational giants such as SDL (Esselink, 2003). Today, localization is a blooming sector, with a growing number of professionals and researchers working in the field. According to the Localization Industry Standard Association (LISA), the growth of the industry accounts for $30 billion per year (LISA, 2007, p. iii).

Localization has been approached from different viewpoints (Dohler, 1997; Esselink, 2000; Pym, 2006) and it is a meeting point for translators, linguists and professionals from the computer industry. The controversial question of the status of localization within Translation Studies has been widely discussed in the literature (Esselink, 2000, p. 2; Mangiron & O'Hagan, 2006; Pym 2006) but is beyond the scope of this paper.

Localizing a product goes beyond the textual adaptation of contents from the source to the target language. In addition, this process deals with the adaptation of multiple non-verbal elements to the target locale: Images and other visual components (icons) that the product may include, colours, cultural references, numbers, date formats, currency, flags, music and legal issues (Yunker, 2002, p.477).

2.1. Software localization

Localization deals with different fields, namely, Web sites, videogames and computer applications. Software is one of the most interesting targets since it allows millions of users to access computers in their own language.

Arguably, the US is the leading country in the computer industry (with the exception of videogames, where Japan rules the roost) and American English is the *lingua franca* for software. Original American programs are localized into the so-called FIGS languages (French, Italian, German and Spanish) (Esselink, 2000, p. 8).

In addition to the textual component (menus, help files, etc.), a computer application includes images and other non-verbal elements that should be localized. Colours, for example, must be adapted, taking into account the values they may express in the target culture: Green is a sacred colour in Arab countries, and white is used for funeral pyres in China (Yunker, 2002, p. 485). Even when these colours are harmless in the US or Europe, they must be adapted when localizing the product to different locales.

Cultural issues such as measurement units, currency, numbers, and date formats must be taken into account in the localization process. If we are working with a spreadsheet created in the United Kingdom, the pound will be the default currency. This element should be modified if the program is to be exported to Greece, Spain, France or any other member state of the euro zone.

Technical questions must also be addressed, as they can affect the correct functionality of an application. Dialogues and menus, for instance, must be edited due to possible enlargement of the text produced by translation. Such enlargements can create functionality problems in the user interface and affect the application's appearance (words exceeding allotted space, unreadable menus, etc.). When translating from English into other languages the text is expanded between 20% and 30% (Esselink, 2000, p. 33; Yunker, 2002, p. 176).

As explained in this paper, assisted translation tools provide a helping hand in many of the localization challenges here mentioned. One of the main advantages of CAT is commented on in the next section.

2.2. Source code or assisted translation?

There are two main alternatives to localize a computer application: Dealing directly with the source code file or localizing the binary files of the program once they have been compiled (that is, working with the translatable text).

The files used to create computer applications are known as "Resource Files", and are easily recognizable through the extension ".rc", which stands for "Resource Compiler" (Dohler, 1997). These files contain all information about the program's architecture, its functions, etc. Once the Resource Files have been compiled, the so-called "Executable Files" (usually with the ".exe" extension) are created[2].

2.2.1. First option: Source code file

If we work with the source code directly, we will have to cope with the previously mentioned Resource Files. This process requires expertise and technical skills since not all translators and localizers can read and master the source code file proficiently. This code is the language used by developers to design software and is based on instructions and commands in a specific programming language (such as C++). These instructions configure and adjust the parameters of the program and how it works.

```
IDD_SELECT DIALOG DISCARDABLE 0, 0, 167, 106
STYLE DS_MODALFRAME | WS_POPUP | WS_VISIBLE |
WS_CAPTION | WS_SYSMENU
CAPTION "Select an object"
FONT 8, "MS Sans Serif"
BEGIN
DEFPUSHBUTTON "OK",IDOK,108,8,50,14
PUSHBUTTON "Cancel",IDCANCEL,108,24,50,14
LISTBOX IDC_TOOLBAR_NAMES,8,8,92,88,LBS_SORT |
LBS_NOINTEGRALHEIGHT | WS_VSCROLL | WS_TABSTOP
PUSHBUTTON "&Help...",IDHELP,108,40,50,14
PUSHBUTTON "&Rename...",IDD_RENAME,108,64,50,14
PUSHBUTTON "&Delete",IDD_DELETE,108,80,50,1
        END
```

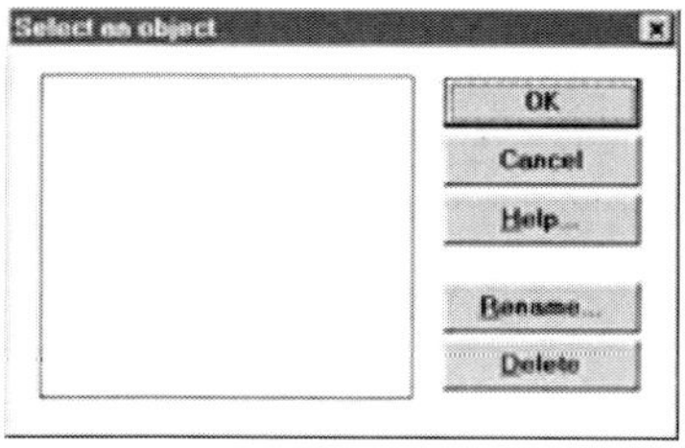

Figure 1: Example of a dialogue box and its source code file

A key problem in localizing the source code files is that working with the code requires surgical precision to accurately modify the translatable information without damaging peripheral text. Specific information (translatable strings) must be spotted very carefully since even a slight mistake can lead to functionality problems (the so-called "bugs") once the files have been compiled.

This is an extremely complicated process due to the difficulty of separating translatable text (usually between commas) and the code surrounding it. Given the hurdles and technical requirements involved in editing Resource Files, a more reliable alternative should be considered: Using computer-assisted translation to filter translatable strings.

2.2.2. Second option: translatable text

This alternative implies that we will not face the source code file, but will instead deal with the binary files once they have been created. Thanks to CAT, localizers are provided with a tool that supplies the same functions without requiring any editing of the source code. Translation tools use parsers and filters to detect translatable strings, thus allowing localizers to focus exclusively on software adaptation.

When extracting the translatable strings from the source files, translation tools perform a segmentation process in which the text is broken down into translation units. Segmentation rules can be adjusted according to the file format (for example, localizing a Web site in HTML may require different settings than a program in C++).

Furthermore, CAT supports localizers with translation memory systems, which allow previous translations to be re-used and recycled (leveraging). As translation units are stored by the application, localizers will be provided with suggestions for new translations according to the matching percentage (in Passolo, 100% coincidences provide exact matches and 75% fuzzy matches).

Moreover, translation quality can be improved by increasing coherence in the target text thanks to certain features such as "Translate Replicates", which are included in many applications. This is a useful tool for localizing software or Web sites, where there is a high level of textual repetition (and an important number of technical terms).

The next case study focuses on some of the most important features that use of CAT can add to the process of localization.

3. Case study

The aim of this case study is to test how CAT can support translators in localizing a software application and to provide evaluation of Passolo, a well-known localization tool. To do this, the user interface of a program from the field of logistics management was adapted from American English into Castilian Spanish. We will focus on the linguistic and technical aspects of the process. As this paper is written under the scope of Translation Studies, issues regarding marketing or project management are not addressed.

3.1. Localization tool

The localization software chosen for the case study is Passolo 6.0 Team Edition[3]. Selection of this particular tool was done according to several parameters. Firstly, we wanted to evaluate a Windows-based standalone application (Trados, Transit and Wordfast used Microsoft Word macros at the time this paper was written), with full-localization features (such as user interface resizing functionality, image and bitmap edition tools, automated localization tests, etc.). The best-known multi-faced localization tool meeting these requirements (together with Passolo) is Alchemy Catalyst, which offers a user-friendly interface and additional interesting features. However, using Catalyst was not possible since version 6 did not support 16-bit binaries (the format of the files to be localized). This circumstance made Passolo the most suitable candidate for this particular project.

The tool is evaluated mainly by its functionality, since the hypothesis in question asks how CAT can improve translators' performance in a localization process. Other aspects, such as usability and reliability, will also be commented upon.

Passolo can be used to localize 16-bit binary files (.exe, .dll) as well as software developed with 32-bit applications (Visual C++, Borland Delphi, and Borland C++ Builder). It also supports ASCII and Unicode (allowing localization to Asian languages). Additional features include Trados and Transit interface, terminology management, and a powerful tool for statistical analysis. The program has a rather short learning process (regarding the basic and most common localization functions) and the provided documentation is quite complete. Negative remarks regarding some of the mentioned features will be reported in the task description of the case study.

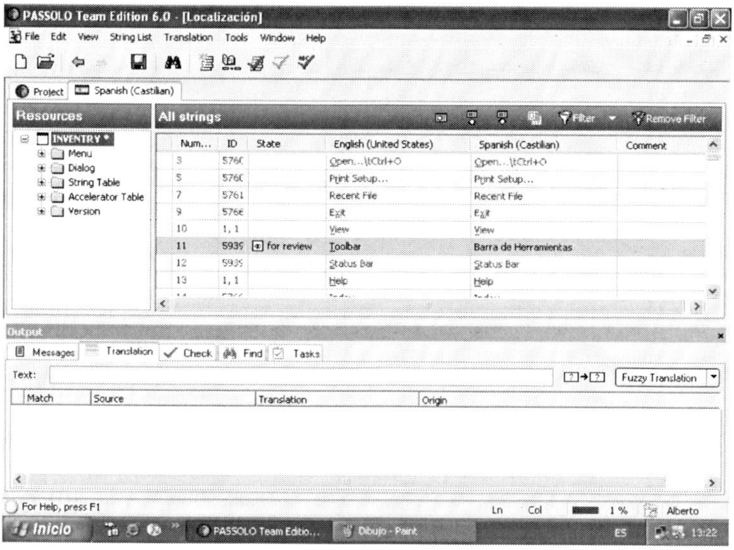

Figure 2: Passolo 6.0 user interface

3.2. Target application

The software to be localized is HOM (version 3.0), a widely known application in the field of transport and logistics management. This tool was developed at the Leonard N. Stern School of Business at New York University by Professors Michael Moses and Sridhar Seshadri, along with software consultant Michael Yakir[4]. The program was designed specifically for the Competitive Advantages course in the business school's Operation Management program and was released in November 1998.

HOM provides several tools designed to analyse a company's operations and services, and it helps to work out suitable solutions for specific problems regarding logistics and supply chain management. HOM comprises seven different modules: Quality Control, Inventory Management, Process Management, Forecasting Techniques, Project Management, Integral Planning and Queue Theory.

The program's seven modules share the same appearance, and the user interface is practically the same: The central part of the screen displays a table where data are introduced, and in the upper part is the classical toolbox with the typical menus (File, Edit, View, etc.) and 14 different icons. As seen in Figure 3, ten of these icons are common to any Windows-based application: New Document (a white sheet), Open File (a yellow folder), Save (a disc), Print (a printer), Preview (a magnifier and a sheet of paper), Cut (a pair of scissors), Copy (two pages overlapping), Paste (a clipboard), Help (a pointer with a question mark), and About (represented by a question mark). The other four icons of the toolbox have been specifically designed for HOM: Parameters (represented by a table), Run (a runner), Last Results (a graph) and Log (a writing hand).

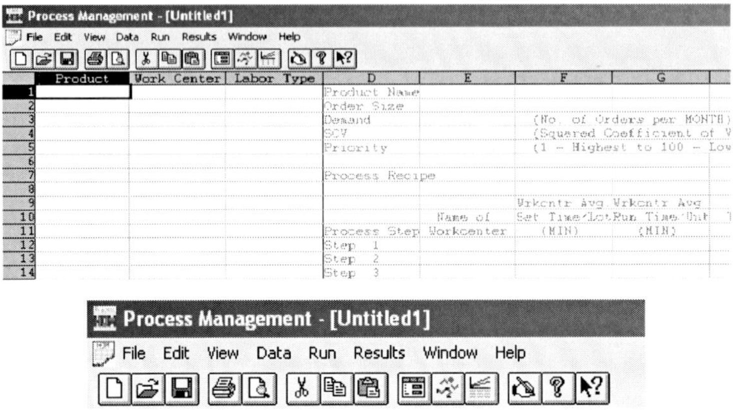

Figure 3: Screenshots of the Process Management Module and the toolbox of HOM 3.0.

3.3. Localizing the application

In order to achieve complete localization of the product, the seven modules of HOM were translated into Spanish and all non-verbal elements of the program were modified using Passolo: In addition to the translation of the text, the user interface was adjusted to the target language and some cultural elements (i.e. icons) were adapted.

Finally, when the localization stage was concluded, several quality and functionality tests were conducted using tools provided by Passolo (as we wanted to check whether the whole localization process could be completed with one single application). Quality tests included text proofreading, spell checking and terminology coherence. Passolo has simple tools (similar to those included in any text editor) to carry out the first two tests. As for coherence, the option Concordance Search allows the translator to check how a single term has been translated in all entries. Some possibilities of the program were not fully explored since we did not rely on the support of Trados or Transit.

On the other hand, functionality tests focused on user interface (size of windows, menus and boxes) and verification of shortcuts and other commands. In this sense, Passolo offers competitive advantage over its competitors: With a single option, all translations stored in the project can be checked. The command Check All performs a complete verification of the whole project (or a selection) and detects possible errors regarding size of menus and duplicate access keys (Figure 4). The application spots the exact line where a mistake was produced, making it is easy for translators to correct errors.

In this respect, CAT provides an important support, as functionality tests can be time-consuming for translators and localizers who do not rely on translation tools.

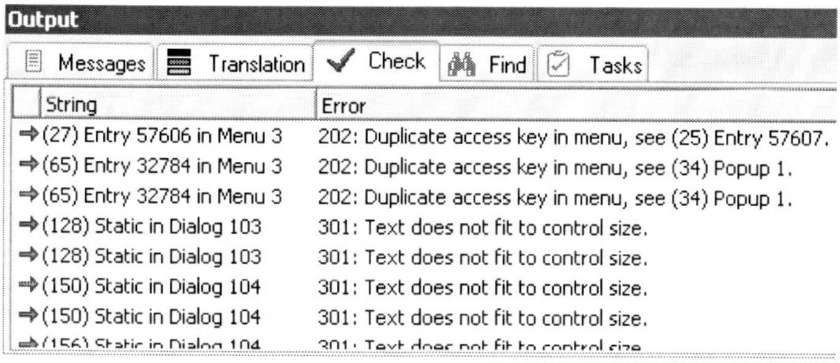

Figure 4: Functionality test in Passolo 6.0.

Arguably, textual coherence is an issue to be addressed in software localization: This is a key element not only for translation quality, but also for the program's functionality,as it is underlined in most localization guides (Lingo, 2000). Bert Esselink suggests the following:

> Create a glossary of terms relating to the product, company or industry, and apply this consistently across all documentation and online help sets. Use consistent phrases and terminology. The importance of simple, concise language is magnified when writing for translation. For example, decide at the outset if you want to use phrases like "click on", "click", "choose", or "select" when describing software commands. (Esselink, 2000, p. 28).

When starting a new project important decisions concerning terminology must be made. For example, if we are going to adapt an application from Spanish into English and we find the term *teléfono móvil* we will have to decide whether to use the British expression ("mobile") or the American one ("cellular", or even "cell"). Whatever the decision, it must be consistent and the same term must be used systematically throughout the translation of the application and all additional materials (manual, licenses, box, starting guides, etc.).

In order to maintain terminological coherence, Passolo provides the possibility of creating a technical glossary linked to the localization project. This can be extremely useful for two main reasons. First, by creating a glossary we contribute to maintaining coherence. Second, the glossary provides the translator with valuable information for new projects, making his or her job faster and more accurate.

In our project, the glossary was created after translating the first module of HOM, and it became a powerful tool for localizing the rest of

HOM since a huge amount of recurrent expressions was to be translated (even in the first module, Queue Theory, 40% of total strings were auto-translated by Passolo due to the high number of repetitions). Furthermore, glossaries can be stored for use in future translations with the same customer or similar projects.

Another interesting option is Translating Replicates. When translating a term for the first time, the program detects if there are more repetitions and asks the translator if he or she wants to export the translation and keep it for the rest of the entrances (see Figure 5).

This is a common option not only in Passolo but in CAT, and it can be extremely useful in large projects, especially if there is a high number of repetitions. Furthermore, it provides terminological coherence to the localized application.

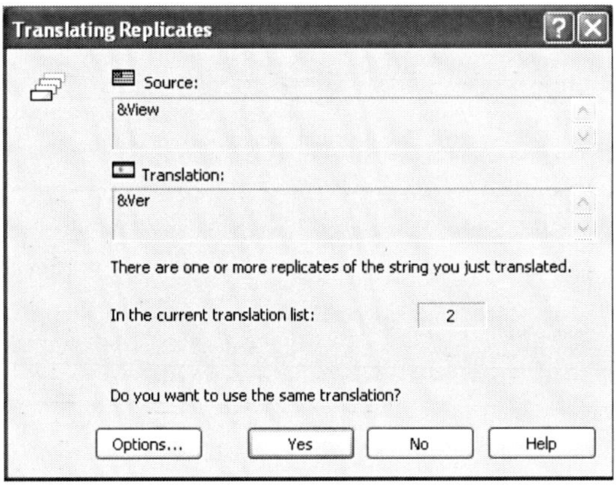

Figure 5: Translating replicates with Passolo

Other features included in Passolo (and in most localization tools such as Catalyst) are Auto Translation and Fuzzy Translation. The first option automatically translates the selected term if it has been previously translated in the project and there is 100% matching. The second option translates the term according to similar or partial expressions that have already been translated.

Some features described in this section support the idea that using CAT can improve the translator's performance in two different ways: By reducing the time needed to complete a project (thanks to leveraging, the re-use of previously translated strings) and contributing to maintaining textual coherence. It should be mentioned that in the case of software localization, functionality tests are a must: Passolo provided specific tools to perform these tests in a reliable and fast way.

In the next sections, some challenges faced in the program localization are commented upon, as are the solutions proposed for each case with the support of Passolo.

3.4. Linguistic aspects

Computer applications present a notable amount of technical terminology; this pool of terms should be translated so as to conform (as much as possible) to the standards of the sector (Windows operating system, in this case). If the string Out of Memory is translated as *Fuera de memoria*, Spanish native speakers would perceive it as an artificial expression. The sentence *No hay suficiente memoria* would be more accurate for users of computer applications. Similarly, the term Tile may not be translatable as *Teja* or *Azulejo* in the context of computers, where the word *Mosaico* refers to the layout and distribution of several windows in a computer screen.

Some of the most repeated terms in HOM can be found in any simple Windows-based application. Table 1 shows the most repeated terms in the Queue module of HOM:

Table 1: Recurrent terms in the Queue module of HOM 3.0.

Term	Repetitions
Help (*Ayuda*)	25
File (*Archivo*)	23
Open (*Abrir*)	21
New (*Nuevo*)	17
Print (*Imprimir*)	13

As mentioned earlier, Passolo provides several tools and options to deal with terms that are repeated in a text.

3.5. Technical issues

3.5.1. Shortcuts

Shortcuts allow users to execute an action or command without opening a menu with the mouse. By using a key combination (Alt and another key, in Windows-based applications), we can perform the same action with a few keystrokes. These elements are defined in the source code file and are meant to give users faster access to menus and dialogue boxes.

Shortcuts are usually represented in menus and toolboxes with an underlined letter (Open or *Abrir*) that indicates the combination required to perform that particular function with the keyboard. Computer-assisted translation tools (including Passolo) detect shortcuts in the source text, thereby allowing localizers to translate them into the target language in an effective way. By placing the character & before a specific letter we create a shortcut in the localized version (the command Open would appear in Passolo as &Open). As mentioned, Passolo is a rather functional tool regarding shortcuts, as it facilitates easy detection of duplicates.

3.5.2. Dialogue boxes

Another element to be tackled concerns the three dots (…) that appear after some translatable terms. The dots indicate that the term they accompany opens a dialogue box, and so the three dots should be kept in the target text for usability reasons. In this sense, Passolo does not allow Placeables translation. Placeables are elements (years, cities, proper nouns, etc.) that are not translated into the target text (they remain the same). When a term is marked as Placeable, it is copied into the target text without translation. This option can be useful when adapting dialogue boxes, as translators must copy (or type) the three dots into the target text. This function is common in translation memories (Trados, Wordfast) and even other localization tools (Catalyst).

3.5.3. Space restrictions

Space limitations are one of the most serious difficulties in localizing a software application. When translating from English into other languages, text can be expanded considerably: The Edit menu becomes *Bearbeiten* in German with a 100% expansion (Esselink, 2000, p. 33). This is a major concern for translators, as they must include long text-strings in limited spaces. However, translation tools enable redesign of the graphic user interface to adapt it to the target text.

This is an easy task with Passolo, since it includes a WYSIWYG (What You See Is What You Get) editor, where menus can be resized using drag-and-drop techniques, as shown in Figure 6.

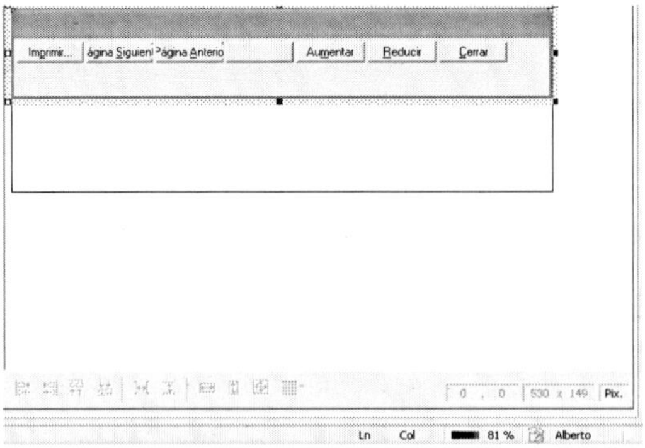

Figure 6: Redesign of a dialogue box using Passolo.

3.5.4. Icons

Despite the reduced number of images and icons in the user interface of logistics software, one specific bitmap was modified in the toolbox of HOM, where the following icon was found:

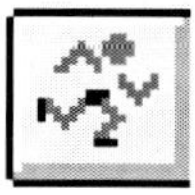

Figure 7: Icon of the Process Management module of HOM 3.0.

Although the expression *correr* (the Spanish equivalent for "run") is used in the field of computers as a synonym for *ejecutar* or *funcionar* ("execute" or "work")—as in the expression *la aplicación **corre** bajo Windows* ("the application runs in Windows")—a Spanish native speaker who is unfamiliar with this kind of (computer) language would not understand the meaning in this context.

The verb *correr* ("to run") does not refer to anything related to computer applications in Spanish, although the expression is widely used in the sector due to direct translation of the English "run", which is effectively meaningful in that context. However, the translation is not accurate and only minor numbers of people (computer industry professionals, advanced users, etc.) would understand *corer* in this sense.

In this particular case, there is a disruption between the meaning (execute, make something work) and the image representing it, since the icon of the runner will not make Spanish users understand its function. Noelia Corte (2000), in her research on Web site localization, notes that "Negative reactions may also come from the use of colour or icons. The metaphor of a person running to symbolise the running of a program does not work in all languages" (p. 19).

In the case of the HOM icon, the signifier (the image of the runner) is associated with the term "to run". When localizing the application into Spanish, the most suitable option is to adapt the icon to the target locale.

For this case study, the tool included in Passolo was used to redesign the icon. New versions were created so as to present better associations between the image and its function for the target audience: An icon with a finger pressing a button would match with the term *Ejecutar* ("execute" or "perform"), which is the way "run" is translated into Spanish.

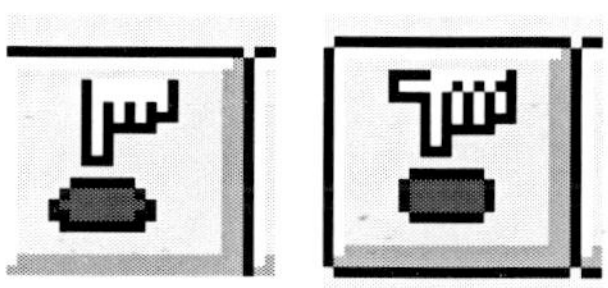

Figure 8: New versions of the Run icon

The adaptation of bitmaps or images is not an easy task, and Passolo's editor is not particularly functional as compared to similar tools in other localization software. Any other simple application (like Paintbrush, included in Windows) provides more functionality and contributes to more accurate results (apart from professional tools such as Photoshop).

3.6. Research output and assessment

The seven modules of HOM accounted for 2,789 segments, that is, 10,228 words (60,670 characters) that were translated from English into Spanish. 46% of the translatable strings were repeated in several modules and consequently auto-translated by Passolo. Due to the high rate of repetitions, we can conclude that the use of CAT clearly improved the translator's performance on this project. In addition, textual consistency was enhanced through some of the tools included in Passolo (concordance searches, glossaries, etc.). Besides, functionality tests were carried out using the same application.

In order to check the real user experience of the localized version of HOM, a copy of the program was delivered to students of the Master in Transport & Logistics Management of the University of Oviedo, as this application is used in several courses. The criticisms of the Spanish version were positive and users reported[5] having a better performance when using the application in their own language. Besides, adapted icons (Figure 8) seem to have improved usability in the target locale.

Passolo, the tool selected for the case study, can be positively evaluated according to several criteria. Regarding functionality, the application provides a number of features that clearly support localization and translation tasks: Translating replicates, fuzzy matches and auto-translation, shortcut edition, etc. are quite well implemented. Functionality tests are easily conducted with one single process. However, some interesting options (such as translation of placeables) are missing.

Reliability is one of the strengths of Passolo: Source text segmentation works properly and files can be successfully exported to other applications. No problems were detected regarding glossary management, and Trados interface works properly (although this was not used for the case study). The program supports a good number of file formats (although some problems have been detected with the HTML parser).

Regarding usability, Passolo is weaker than its main competitor, Catalyst, which has a much more user-friendly interface. Passolo's main layout is correct, but it is less intuitive and usable than those of other CAT tools. Furthermore, the image and bitmap editor is rather poor and some options (such as the possibility to modify background colours) are not available.

As a standalone Windows-based application, Catalyst seems to be the main alternative to Passolo in the field of software localization, offering a more usable interface but less file format compatibility. In the particular case of Web site localization, other alternatives may include small applications such as Catscradle or OmegaT (an open source option).

4. Conclusions

The use of CAT in software localization provides important benefits for translators and localizers. Besides improving text consistency and terminological coherence, assisted translation tools help to save time by recycling previously translated strings (leveraging). In addition, software can be completely localized using only one application, as it can be observed in our case study.

The target of translation tools is to improve translator's performance when completing a given project: Therefore, CAT is not a threat to professionals, since the quality of the final output will be strictly linked to the skills and competence of human translators. Learning curves for using CAT tend to be quite reasonable and multi-faceted applications (such as Passolo) can be handled in a short period of time (although extra time may be required to master it).

Obviously, relevant differences exist among translation tools in regards to not only functionality and usability but also other important issues (such as price, license conditions, etc.). The selection of a particular tool must be done in accordance with the specific requirements and necessities of translators. However, these applications clearly offer an advantage in order to achieve a truly localized product.

Bibliography

Abaitua, J. (2001). Memorias de draducción en TMX compartidas por Internet. *Tradumática, 0.* Retrieved August 25, 2009, from http://www.fti.uab.es/tradumatica/revista/articles/jabaitua/art.htm

Austermühl, F. (2001). *Electronic tools for translators*. Manchester: St. Jerome.

Biau, G., Ramón, J., & Pym, A. (2006). Technology and translation (a pedagogical overview). In Anthony Pym, Alexander , Perekrestenko, and Bram Starink (Eds.) Translation technology and its teaching (with much mention of localization). International Cultural Studies Group, Universitat Rovira y Virgili. Retrieved August 25, 2009, from http://www.tinet.cat/~apym/on-line/translation/BiauPym_TechnologyAndTranslation.pdf

Corte, N. (2000). *Web site localisation and internationalisation: A case study*. MsC thesis, City University London, London.. Retrieved August 25, 2009 from http://www.localisation.ie/resources/Awards/Theses/Theses.htm

Corte, N. (2002). Localización e internacionalización de sitios web. *Tradumática 1*. Retrieved August 25, 2009, from http://www.fti.uab.es/tradumatica/revista/articles/ncorte/art.htm

Dohler, P. N. (1997). Facets of software localization: A translator's view. *Translation Journal 1* (1). Retrieved August 25, 2009, from http://accurapid.com/journal/softloc.htm

Esselink, B. (2000). *A practical guide to localization*. Amsterdam/Philadelphia, PA: John Benjamins Publishing.

Esselink, B. (2003). The evolution of localization. Retrieved August 25, 2009, from Multilingual Computing, Inc. Web site: http://www.multilingual.com/articleDetail.php?id=646

Herrmann, A. & Florian, S. (2006). *Passolo 6.0*. [computer software]. Bonn: Pass Engineering.

Lingo Systems (2000). *The guide to translation and localization: Preparing products for the global marketplace*. Portland, OR: IEEE Computer Society.

LISA (2007). *The globalization industry primer: An introduction to preparing your business and products for success in international markets*. Retrieved August 25, 2009, from http://www.lisa.org

Mangiron, C. & O'Hagan, M. (2006). Game localisation: Unleashing imagination with 'restricted' translation. *The Journal of Specialised Translation 6*. Retrieved August 25, 2009, from http://www.jostrans.org/issue06/art_ohagan.php

Melby, A. (2006). MT+TM+QA: The future is ours. *Tradumática 4*. Retrieved August 25, 2009, from http://www.fti.uab.es/tradumatica/revista/num4/articles/04/04art.htm.

Moses, M., Sridhar, S. & Mikhail, Y. (1998). *HOM 3.0*. [computer software]. New York, NY: Stern School of Business, New York University. Retrieved August 25, 2009, from http://pages.stern.nyu.edu/ ~sseshadr/hom/

Nogueira, D. (2002). Translation tools today: A personal view. *Translation Journal 6*(1). Retrieved August 25, 2009, from http://accurapid.com/journal/19tm.htm

Pym, A. (2006). Localization, training and the threat of fragmentation. Retrieved August 25, 2009, from http://www.tinet.org/~apym/on-line/translation/translation.html

Somers, H. (Ed.). (2003). *Computers and translation: A translator's guide*. Philadelphia, PA: John Benjamins.

Yunker, J. (2002). *Beyond borders: Web globalization strategies*. Indianapolis; IN: New Riders Publishers.

[1] The term CAT can be associated with a wide variety of tools and applications, but in this article it is used mainly to refer to the general concept of memory tools. Although Passolo, the selected application for the case study, is included in the category of localization tools, providing a series of additional features (such as bitmap editor), translation memories are a core function of these applications (Austermühl, 2001, p. 146).

[2] In other operating systems, such as Linux or Mac OS, this process is performed in a different way. However, this paper focuses on the Windows platform because it is the standard in the field of software localization. New initiatives and research lines on localization of Mac, Linux and open source software are still needed and would contribute to enlarging the range of possibilities for translators.

[3] The case study was carried out before the release of SDL Passolo 2007, so no references are given to the new versions. However, it is notable that the latest release (Passolo 2009) shares the core features mentioned in the paper to support translators. Additional add-ons and characteristics (such as integration with Trados and Multiterm and streamlined and user-friendly interface) require further evaluation.

[4] In order to localize the software, permission was requested from the authors of HOM.

[5] 35 students were sent a questionnaire to appraise the localized version of HOM after one month using the program.

In search of the recurrent units of translation

Lieve Macken
University College Ghent/Ghent University

Translation memory systems aim to reuse previously translated texts. Because the operational unit of the first-generation translation memory systems is the sentence, such systems are only useful for text types in which full-sentence repetition frequently occurs. Second-generation sub-sentential translation memory systems try to remedy this problem by providing additional translation suggestions for sub-sentential chunks. In this paper, we compare the performance of a sentence-based translation memory system (SDL Trados Translator's Workbench) with a sub-sentential translation memory system (Similis) on different text types. We demonstrate that some text types (in this case, journalistic texts) are not suited to be translated by means of a translation memory system. We show that Similis offers useful additional translation suggestions for terminology and frequent multiword expressions.

1. Introduction

Translation memory systems aim to reuse previously translated texts. The basic idea is quite simple. Translation memory systems store source segments together with their translation in a database for reuse. During translation, the new text to be translated is segmented and each segment is compared with the source text segments of the database. When a useful match is found, the retrieved source-target segment pair is provided to the translator. If no useful match is found, the translator translates the segment manually and the newly translated segment is added to the database.

Two processes in the above description are important for fully understanding the potential value and limitations of translation memory systems: segmentation and matching. In translation memory systems of the first generation[1], a segment corresponds to a sentence or a sentence-like unit such as a title, header or list item. The text is segmented on the basis of punctuation and document-formatting information. However, there is a major problem with the idea of using sentences as basic units of translation. Because the matching process is sentence-based, the potential value of the use of a translation memory system depends on the degree of full-sentence repetition of the text to be translated in the database. Consequently, translation memories are mainly used for translating technical documents (e.g. user manuals) or texts with related content (related products) or text revisions.

Several researchers have explored the idea of creating sub-sentential translation memories (Gotti et al., 2005; Planas & Furuse, 2003; Simard & Langlais, 2001). In the domain of machine translation, the current best performing statistical machine translation systems are based on phrase-based models (Koehn, 2009), which in fact assemble translations of different sub-sentential units. The sub-sentential units are sometimes defined as "contiguous sequences of words"; in other cases more linguistically motivated definitions are used.

In this paper, we compare the performance of a sentence-based translation memory system of the first generation with a sub-sentential translation memory system of the second generation. We then compare the translation suggestions made by the two different systems.

The second important process mentioned above is matching. During translation, the translation memory system matches the new source sentence with the source sentences in its database and proposes previously translated sentences to the translator. The system can either return sentence pairs with identical source segments (exact matches) or sentences that are similar but not identical to the sentence to be translated (fuzzy matches).

In traditional translation memory systems, similarity is calculated by comparing surface strings, i.e. sequences of characters. In SDL Trados Translator's Workbench, the similarity threshold ranges from 30% to 99%. The user can change the similarity threshold in order to find the proper balance between precision and recall: If the similarity threshold is too high, potentially useful sentence pairs may be missed (high precision, low recall); if the similarity threshold is too low, the match can be based on high-frequency function words and the proposed translations may be of no use (low precision, high recall).

Because sentence-based translation memory systems calculate the similarity value on the whole surface string, sentence pairs that are very similar for humans may receive a low similarity value. Consider the following example:

(1) Oracle® is a registered trademark of Oracle Corporation.

For a human it is obvious that the following two sentences are very similar to the example above.

(2) Java® is a registered trademark of Sun Microsystems Inc.
(3) Unix®, X/Open®, OSF/1®, and Motif® are registered trademarks of the Open Group.

However, the translation memory system assigns a fuzzy match of 61% to the second sentence and a fuzzy match of less than 30% to the third. As these examples demonstrate, translation memories contain smaller segments than sentences that can be useful for translators. Bowker and Barlow (2004, p. 4) formulate this as follows: "There is still a level of linguistic repetition that falls between full sentences and specialized terms - repetition at the level of expression or phrase. This is in fact the level where linguistic repetition will occur most often."

In the following sections, we describe several experiments that were carried out to assess the usefulness of different types of translation memory systems. Because we were unaware of any comparative study on the degree of repetitiveness in different text types, an experiment was set up to quantify the recurrency level of complete sentences in different text types.

We also compare the performance of a sentence-based translation memory system with a sub-sentential translation memory system on different text types. As an example of a first generation system, we use SDL Trados Translator's Workbench[2], which is, according to the LISA Translation Memory Survey (Lommel, 2004), the most widely used TM tool. As an example of a second generation system, we use Similis[3]. According to Lagoudaki (2008), only two commercially sub-sentential translation memory systems are available: Similis and Masterin. Because Masterin only supports English, Swedish and Finish, we opted for Similis as sub-sentential translation memory system.

2. Corpus

Three subcorpora with parallel texts belonging to three domains and three different text types were selected from the Dutch Parallel Corpus (Macken et al., 2007). For each subcorpus, approximately 50,000 words of sentence-aligned parallel text was used to populate the translation memory, and approximately 2,000 words of source-text material was selected as text to be translated:

- The *medical* subcorpus contains European Public Assessments Reports (EPARs) originating from one pharmaceutical company. The texts are rather technical with a clear, repetitive structure. The texts were translated from English into Dutch.
- The *financial* subcorpus consists of a collection of newsletters from a bank that provide financial news for investors. The texts were originally written in Dutch and translated into English.
- The *journalistic* subcorpus contains articles originally published in *The Independent* and translated into Dutch for *De Morgen*.

We expect the highest degree of repetitiveness in the medical subcorpus; the lowest in the journalistic subcorpus.

The manually corrected sentence alignments available in the Dutch Parallel Corpus reveal that a different translation strategy was adopted for the medical and financial documents than for the journalistic texts (see Table 1.). In the medical and financial texts, most of the correspondences at sentential level are 1:1 alignments (98% and 97%, respectively). In the journalistic texts, the 1:1 alignments only account for 70%; 1:2 and 2:1 alignments for 11%; and null alignments (sentences that were added or deleted) for 16%.

Table 1: Number of different types of sentence alignments as extracted from the DPC

Domain	*0:n*	*n:0*	*1:1*	*1:2*	*2:1*	*n:m*	*Total*
Medical	1	0	1478	12	13	0	1504
Financial	3	7	1425	11	15	2	1463
Journalistic	122	83	881	135	12	19	1252

The selected source texts also differ in average sentence length: the average sentence length of the source texts is 16.3 words for the medical texts, 14.7 words for the financial texts and 21.5 words for the journalistic texts. As long sentences tend to be translated by more than one sentence, the difference in average sentence length explains the high degree of 1:2 alignments in the latter text type. As translation memory systems first segment the texts into sentence-like units and look for matching segments in their databases, the different sentence-alignment characteristics already indicate that some text types (i.e. journalistic texts) are less suited for translation with translation memories.

3. Sentence-based translation memory

In our first experiment, we used SDL Trados Translator's Workbench, a sentence-based translation memory system of the first generation. We created three translation memories (one for each subcorpus) and populated the translation memories with the sentence-aligned parallel texts. The obtained translation memories are a reduced version of the parallel corpora, as only unique sentence pairs without empty source or target segment (non-null alignments) are retained. Table 2 presents an overview of the size of the translation memories and the reduction rate.

Table 2: Size of the resulting translation memory actually used by SDL Trados Translator's Workbench

Domain	*Translation memory*
Medical	908 (60%)
Financial	1294 (88%)
Journalistic	1047 (83%)

A size reduction is seen in all three resulting translation memories, yet only for the medical and the financial translation memories is the reduction due to repetition at the sentence level. In the journalistic texts, the reduction is completely attributable to the removal of null alignments.

We used the analysis function of SDL Trados Translator's Workbench to count the number of exact and fuzzy matches in the respective original source texts. During analysis, SDL Trados Translator's Workbench segments the source documents, compares the segments with the selected translation memory and examines the source document for text-internal repetition. The results are presented in Tables 3, 4 and 5. Different match types are distinguished: text-internal repetitions (*repetitions*); exact matches (*100%*); and fuzzy matches within different threshold intervals (*95-99%*, *85-94%*, *75-85%* and *50-74%*). For each match type, the second column contains the number of segments covered; the third column the total number of words; and the fourth column the percentage of the number of words covered.

Table 3: Analysis statistics (SDL Trados Translator's Workbench) for medical texts

Match Type	*Number of segments*	*Number of words*	*Percentage*
Repetitions	0	0	0
100%	17	236	13
95-99%	4	47	3
85-94%	11	126	7
75-84%	16	87	5
50-74%	2	35	2
No match	70	1,334	70
Total	120	1,865	100

Table 4: Analysis statistics (SDL Trados Translator's Workbench) for financial texts

Match Type	*Number of segments*	*Number of words*	*Percentage*
Repetitions	4	14	1
100%	10	74	3
95-99%	3	37	2
85-94%	1	12	1
75-84%	3	15	1
50-74%	1	27	1
No match	122	1,980	91
Total	144	2,159	100

Table 5: Analysis statistics (SDL Trados Translator's Workbench) for journalistic texts

Match Type	*Number of segments*	*Number of words*	*Percentage*
Repetitions	1	1	0
100%	0	0	0
95-99%	0	0	0
85-94%	0	0	0
75-84%	0	0	0
50-74%	0	0	0
No match	126	1,981	100
Total	127	1,982	100

The analysis statistics show that for 30% of the segments of the medical source texts, a translation suggestion is available in the translation memory. The percentage of translation suggestions drops to 9% for the financial texts, and not a single suggestion is available for the journalistic texts.

To assess the usefulness of the suggested translations, we pre-translated the source texts with a fuzzy match threshold at 70% and manually inspected the translation suggestions. All suggested translations were considered to be either correct or useful, but the scope was considered limited:

- The EPARs (European Public Assessments Reports) of the medical subcorpus follow a clear, predefined structure. Apart from some introductory and closing paragraphs, the translation suggestions covered mainly the text headings, in which the name of a medicine was replaced (e.g. *What is the risk associated with <Xigris>?*).
- In the financial texts, the translation suggestions were only available for short headers and a few recurring paragraphs.
- In the journalistic texts, no translation suggestions were available.

From this small-scale experiment, we can conclude that some text types are more suited to be translated by means of a translation memory system than others. A second observation is that the analysis figures should be interpreteted carefully. In the medical texts, the statistics indicate that 30% of the segments recur. However, manual inspection of the sentence-based translation suggestions showed that the impact was considered rather low.

4. Chunk-based translation memory

In our second experiment, we compared the performance of Similis, a commercially available sub-sentential translation memory system of the second generation, on the same test set. Similis is a linguistically enhanced translation memory in that it contains monolingual lexicons and chunkers to group words into phrases (Planas, 2005). As a consequence, Similis is language-dependent. At present, Similis supports the following seven European languages: English, German, French, Italian, Spanish, Portuguese, and Dutch. Similis can be classified as a sub-sentential translation memory, as it can retrieve matches at the sub-sentential level. Translation memory systems working at the sub-sentential level face more challenges than sentence-based systems. In order to suggest matches at a sub-sentential level, the systems must be able to align source and target chunks (a non- trivial task); and must be able to identify (fuzzy) matches at sub-sentential level and have a mechanism to score multiple sub-sentential matches and select the best match.

In the following section we examine what type of structures Similis considers as chunks and we investigate the ability of Similis to align source and target chunks. In section 4.2, we evaluate the translation suggestions of Similis for our three text types; in section 4.3 we enlarge the size of the translation memories and examine how this affects our findings; in section 4.4 we compare the sub-sentential translation suggestions of Similis with the auto-concordance search of SDL Trados Translator's workbench.

4.1 Quality of sub-sentential alignments in Similis

Similis aligns not only sentences but also chunks below sentence level. In order to evaluate the quality of the aligned source and target chunks in Similis, a reference corpus was created, in which the translational correspondences were manually indicated. For each domain, we selected approximately 5,000 words from the parallel texts used to populate the translation memory.

During the manual annotation task the *minimal* language units in the source texts that correspond to an equivalent in the target texts, and vice versa, were aligned. Different units could be linked (words, word groups, paraphrased sections, punctuation). An example of a manually aligned sentence pair is found in Figure 1. Null links (Ø) are used for source text units that have not been translated or target text units that have been added. More details on the manual annotation process are found in Macken (2007).

It	Het
can	kan
not	niet
have been made	zijn
by	van
a	een
walking	wandelende
dinosaur	dinosaurus
because	aangezien
the	de
scratch marks	schrammen
are	zijn
quite	relatief
delicate	fijn
,	,
with	met
long	lange
grooves	groeven
made	Ø
in	in
the	het
sediment	sediment
indicating	die wijzen op
a	een
large	groot
,	,
swimming	zwemmend
animal	dier
, '' he said	Ø
.	.

Figure 1: Manually aligned source and target units for one sentence pair

Similis defines a chunk as a syntagma:

> SIMILIS met en correspondance non seulement les phrases mais aussi les chunks (ou syntagmes) avec leur traductions. Un syntagme est une unité structurelle du texte: un groupe nominal ou verbal. Il est défini grâce aux catégories grammaticales des mots qui le composent, et qui sont trouvées par l'analyseur linguistique. Un syntagme est parfois appelé "chunk". (Similis, Guide de l'utlilisateur, version 2, p. 4)

The Edit Alignment function of Similis allowed us to inspect the aligned chunks. As seen in Figure 2, Similis's chunks can consist of sequences of several words, but one-word chunks also occur. Table 6 presents an overview of the number of source chunks of different lengths that were aligned by Similis in the three test corpora. The majority of aligned source chunks are relatively short chunks: over 50% consist of maximally two words, and 75% contain maximally three words.

Table 6: Size of the source chunks expressed in number of words and percentage of each type in the test corpus

Size of the source chunk	*Percentage*
1	24
2	32
3	19
4	10
5	8
5-10	6
>10	0

Similis not only stores basic linguistic phrases, such as noun phrases (e.g. *the extinction of the dinosaurs* ~ *het uitsterven van de dinosaurussen*), prepositional phrases (e.g. *into a vein* ~ *in een ader*) and verb phrases (e.g. *were linked* ~ *gelieerd zijn*), but also stores larger units (e.g. *the full list is available in the Package Leaflet* ~ *zie de bijsluiter voor de volledige lijst van geneesmiddelen*) in the translation memory. In most cases, these larger units are extracted from parenthetical expressions in the text.

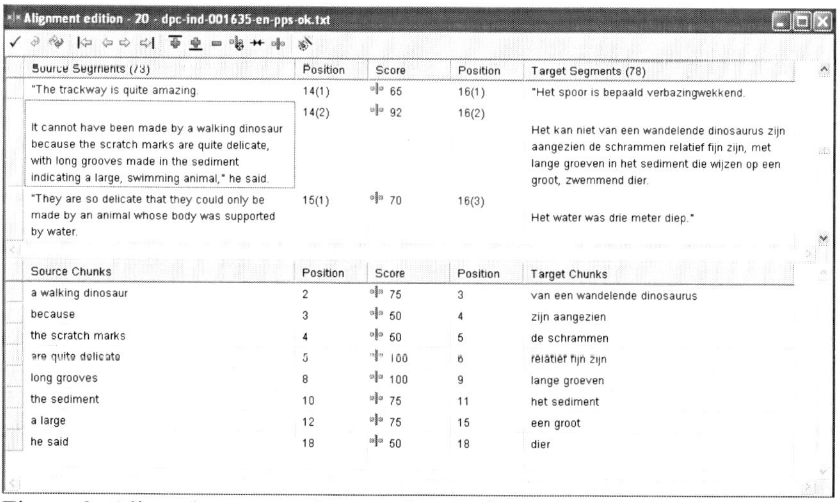

Figure 2: Aligned source and target chunks for one-sentence pairs in Similis

We used the Edit Alignment function of Similis to collect all aligned source and target chunks and compared the aligned chunks with the manual reference.

Each aligned chunk was given one of the following three labels:

- **Correct** if the aligned chunks were completely in line with the manually created reference alignment, e.g. *the scratch marks ~ de schrammen [the scratch marks]*)
- **Partially correct** if the source or target chunks contained extra words that were not aligned in the manually created reference alignment (e.g. *because ~ zijn aangezien [been because]*)
- **Wrong** if none of the words were aligned in the manually created reference alignment (e.g. *he said ~ dier [animal]*)

Table 7 summarizes the results of the analysis. The results demonstrate that word alignment (and hence chunk alignment) is a non-trivial task. For the medical texts, which are translated rather literally, 80% of the chunks align correctly, and 3% are wrong alignments. However, for the financial texts, which are characterized by a high percentage of idiomatic expressions, and the journalistic texts, which are translated more freely, the percentage of correctly aligned chunks drops to 70% and 67%, respectively; and the percentage of wrongly aligned chunks rises to 5% and 7%, respectively. Applying fuzzy match techniques on an already error-prone translation memory can lead to quite unexpected results.

Table 7: Percentages of correct, partially correct or wrongly aligned chunks

Domain	*Correct*	*Partially correct*	*Wrong*
Medical	80%	18%	3%
Financial	70%	25%	5%
Journalistic	67%	26%	7%

4.2. Coverage and quality of Similis's translation suggestions

We used the analysis function of Similis to count the number of exact and fuzzy matches at segment and chunk levels. The results are presented in Table 8. The upper rows present segment matches, which roughly correspond to the statistics given by SDL Trados Translator's Workbench. Minor differences due to application of slightly different segmentation rules and a different calculation of the fuzzy-match scores can be observed.

Table 8: Analysis statistics (Similis) for the three text types: percentage of segments and percentage of words per match type

	Medical texts		*Financial texts*		*Journalistic texts*	
Match Type	*Segments*	*Words*	*Segments*	*Words*	*Segments*	*Words*
Segment match						
100%	12.6	12.3	14.5	5.7	3.2	0.2
95-99%	1.7	1.7	1.4	1.3	0.0	0.0
85-94%	18.5	8.5	1.4	0.6	0.0	0.0
75-84%	3.4	2.5	2.1	1.9	0.0	0.0
65-74%	2.5	2.2	0.0	0.0	0.0	0.0
< 65%	0.0	0.0	0.0	0.0	0.0	0.0
Total	38.7	27.2	19.3	9.4	3.2	0.2
Chunk match						
100%		2.1		4.3		0.5
95-99%		0.0		0.0		0.0
85-94%		9.5		7.3		3.6
75-84%		2.8		4.3		0.8
65-74%		1.8		1.7		1.3
< 65%		0.0		0.0		0.0
Total		16.3		17.6		6.2

The lower rows present the additional matches at chunk level. As with the matches at segment level, matches at chunk level can be exact (100%) or fuzzy (ranging from 65-99%). Overall, the percentage of words for which sub-sentential translation suggestions are provided ranges from 16-17% (medical and financial texts) to 6% (journalistic texts).

Unfortunately, the statistics do not offer indication of the usefulness of the suggested translation. In many cases, the matched chunks are basic vocabulary words (e.g. *has ~ heeft, that ~ dat, came ~ kwam, had ~ had, more ~ meer, now ~ nu, worse ~ erger, wrong ~ erger, the world ~ de wereld*) and are thus of no use to an experienced translator.

To assess the usefulness of the sub-sentential translation suggestions, we pre-translated the source texts, manually inspected all translation suggestions at sub-sentential level and assigned to each chunk one of the following three labels:

- **Basic vocabulary** if the matched chunk contained only basic vocabulary words.
- **Useful** if the matched chunk and translation suggestion contained some usful suggestion. The match could be a fuzzy match, and the proposed suggestion is not always entirely correct.
- **Wrong** if the proposed translation did not make sense due to alignment errors (see section 4.1).

The results are presented in Table 9.

Table 9: Analysis of the sub-sentential translation suggestions

Domain	*Basic Vocabulary*	*Useful*	*Wrong*
Medical	15 %	79 %	6 %
Financial	20 %	78 %	2 %
Journalistic	54 %	37 %	9 %

We observe a high percentage of useful matches in the medical and financial texts and a low percentage of useful matches in the journalistic texts. This is because the medical and financial texts address similar topics and contain a high degree of recurring terms or recurring expressions. The journalistic articles have more diverse content, and thus less recurring expressions.

However, the percentage of useful sub-sentential suggestions must be interpreted as an upper bound. There are two reasons for this. First, *all* sub-sentential translation suggested were counted, not only the unique ones (e.g. in the financial texts, the word group *de aandelen* ~ *the shares* occurred several times). Second, whenever the translation suggestion made sense and did not belong to basic vocabulary, the proposed translation was labeled as *useful*. However, the usefulness of most fuzzy matches at sub-sentential level is questionable. For example, for the word group *de Europese nutsbedrijven* [*the European utility companies*], a fuzzy match leads to a translation suggestion of *de Europese beurzen* [*the European stockmarkets*], which is hardly useful, as the translation difficulty is in the noun *nutsbedrijven*, not the adjective *Europese*.

This limited experiment shows that the added value of the sub-sentential translation suggestions is mainly in providing translation suggestions for terminology and frequent multiword expressions. Given the importance of terminology for the translation of domain-specific texts, the added value of using a sub-sentential translation memory system is considered to be high in such cases. Examples of useful suggestions from the financial domain are *portefeuille* [*portfolio*], *Duitse obligatierente* [*German bond rates*], *rentewapen* [*interest-rate weapon*], *bedrijfsinvesteringen* [*corporate investments*]. As demonstrated above, the usefulness of fuzzy matches on sub-sentential translation suggestions is less clear. A mechanism to filter out basic vocabulary words by for example using a high-frequency word list or using measures like TF-IDF (Sparck Jones, 1979) would be beneficial.

4.3. Size of the translation memory

Because it is interesting to examine how the size of the translation memories affects our findings, we extracted additional parallel texts from the Dutch Parallel Corpus. We enlarged the translation memories from 50,000 words to 285,000 words of medical texts, 182,000 words of financial texts, and 289,000 words of journalistic texts. Table 10 presents the analysis results of Similis using the enlarged translation memories. The analysis statistics show that enlarging the translation memory has a positive effect at the level of segment matches for the financial texts: 18.6% exact matches versus 14.5% and 30.3% (all) matches versus 19.3%. Enlarging the translation memory has no effect at the level of segment matches for the jounalistic texts. For the medical texts, there is a slightly negative effect at the level of segment matches, but a positive effect at the level of chunk matches. It seems that if sentences contain fuzzy matches at both segment level and chunk level then the selection mechanism of Similis favours fuzzy matches with the highest threshold regardless of its type. For all text types, enlarging the translation memory has a positive effect on the chunk matches: 23.8% versus 16.3% for the medical texts; 22.2% versus 17.6% for the financial texts and 11.9% versus 6.2% for the journalistic texts.

Table 10: Analysis statistics (Similis) for the three text types using larger translation memories: percentage of segments and percentage of words per match type

	Medical texts		*Financial texts*		*Journalistic texts*	
Match Type	*Segments*	*Words*	*Segments*	*Words*	*Segments*	*Words*
Segment match						
100%	11.8	10.9	18.6	9.2	3.2	0.2
95-99%	1.7	1.7	2.8	3.1	0.0	0.0
85-94%	17.7	7.2	4.8	3.7	0.0	0.0
75-84%	3.4	2.5	2.1	1.9	0.0	0.0
65-74%	1.7	1.8	2.0	2.8	0.0	0.0
< 65%	0.0	0.0	0.0	0.0	0.0	0.0
Total	36.1	24.1	30.3	20.6	3.2	0.2
Chunk match						
100%		3.0		5.0		1.6
95-99%		0.0		0.0		0.1
85-94%		15.5		13.3		8.0
75-84%		3.5		2.7		1.9
65-74%		1.7		1.2		0.3
< 65%		0.0		0.0		0.0
Total		23.8		22.2		11.9

4.4 Autoconcordance (SDL Trados) versus sub-sentential translation suggestions (Similis)

SDL Trados Translator's Workbench also contains mechanisms to provide the translator with sub-sentential translation suggestions, viz. the autoconcordance search. If no match is found at segment level, the autoconcordance search retrieves from the translation memory all possible matches on the basis of the segment's lexical items and opens a concordance window showing all matching translation units. Figure 3 presents the autoconcordance result for the sentence "Excessive blood clotting is a problem during severe sepsis, when the blood clots can block the blood supply to important parts of the body such as the kidneys and lungs".

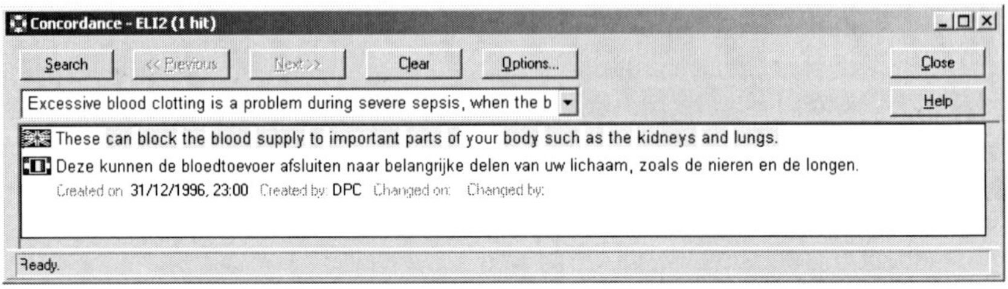

Figure 3: Autoconcordance result in SDL Trados Translator's workbench

A drawback of the auto-concordance search is that the system searches for all matches, even when the translator may not need help with a particular passage. A second shortcoming is that the system does not align source and target chunks. The translator must scan the provided target sentence(s) to locate the correct translation suggestions. Moreover, the autoconcordance results are presented in another window than the working window in which the translator is working.

Figure 4 shows how Similis presents sub-sentential matches to the user. In the sentence to be translated, the sub-sentential matches are indicated by colours. In the example, one exact match (*the kidneys and lungs ~ de nieren en de longen*), and two fuzzy matches (*important parts of the body such as ~ belangrijke delen van uw lichaam* and *severe sepsis ~ ernstige sepsis*) are presented. Contrary to the auto-concordance function of SDL Trados Translator's Workbench, Similis presents the sub-sentential translation suggestions together with the segment matches in the translation environment. Visually, this is less distracting. Moreover, as Similis aligns source and target chunks, translation suggestions below sentence level are presented to the translator and she or he does not need to read an entire series of potentially useful target sentences.

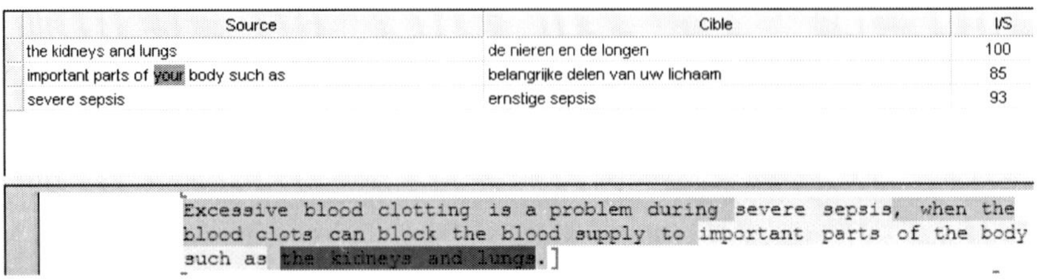

Figure 4: Sub-sentential translation suggestions provided by Similis

5. Bilingual concordance tools

A remaining shortcoming of the current sub-sentential translation memory systems is that they fail to provide translation assistance for idiomatic expressions and collocations. Such expressions are not always contiguous and can appear in various forms in the texts. Because it is very difficult to align such expressions (idiomatic expressions are often not translated literally in the target language), sub-sentential translation suggestions are in most cases not available.

Luckily, for such expressions, a bilingual concordance tool such as Paraconc[4], which offers more powerful searches than the concordance function available in SDL Trados Translator's Workbench, may provide assistance. A bilingual concordance tool performs searches on a sentence-aligned parallel corpus. The translator controls the search query and scans the target sentences to locate the translation.

If a bilingual concordance tool is used as a translation aid to solve *lexical* translation problems, relatively large parallel corpora are needed. A large, freely available parallel corpus is Europarl[5], which contains parallel texts in eleven European languages (Koehn, 2005). For the language pairs Dutch-English and Dutch-French, the Dutch Parallel Corpus (Macken et al., 2007) will be available soon.

Figure 5 presents an example of a concordance search for the expression "led the way" in a bilingual corpus. The parallel corpus search offers several Dutch translation suggestions: *de trend zetten*, *als eerste voor iets zorgen*, *het (goede) voorbeeld geven*, *het voortouw nemen*, etc.

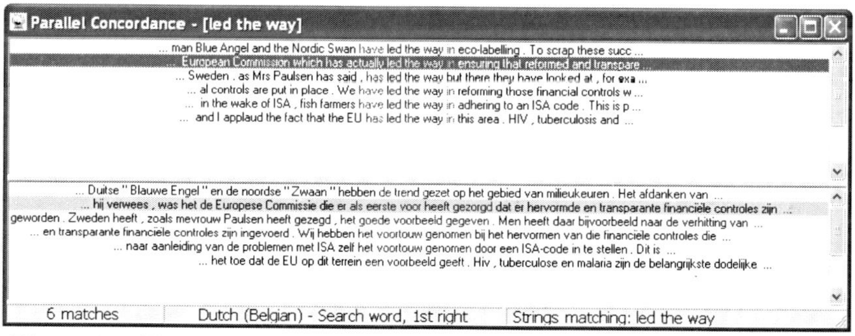

Figure 5: Bilingual concordance window in Paraconc with a contiguous search query

Figure 6 presents a concordance search that was performed for the discontiguous expression "dividend...uitkeren". Paraconc supports wildcards and discontinuity in its search queries, which makes it possible to look for variants of the verb *uitkeren* (*uitgekeerd*, *uitkeert*, etc.) by means of one search query.

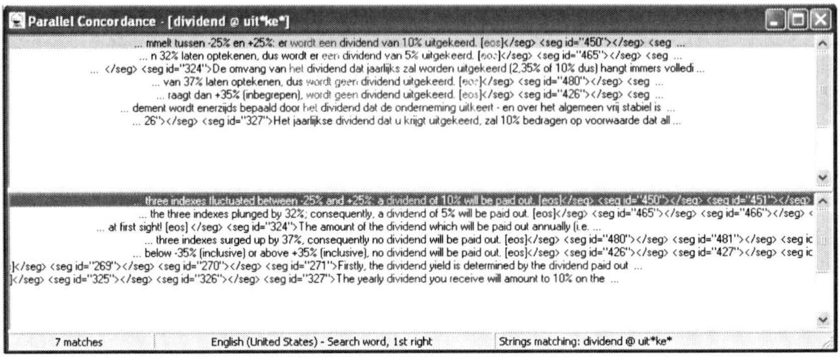

Figure 6: Bilingual concordance window of Paraconc with a discontiguous search query

Bilingual concordance systems cannot be seen as a replacement for translation memory tools. As Bowker and Barlow (2004) conclude, the two technologies may be considered complementary.

6. Conclusion

We carried out several experiments to assess the usefulness of two different types of translation memory systems (a sentence-based and a sub-sentential translation memory system) on different text types. We extracted three subcorpora of approximately the same size from different text types from the Dutch Parallel Corpus to populate the translation memories. We also extracted three source language texts to be translated.

We used the analysis functions of both translation memory systems to assess the usfulness of the translation memory for the given translation task. We pre-translated the source language documents to be translated and manually inspected the translation suggestions.

On the basis of the experiments we can conclude that sub-sentential translation memory systems are a move in the right direction. Because they look for matches at both the sentential and sub-sentential levels, they cover all functions of sentence-based translation memory systems. Furthermore, they provide useful translation suggestions for terminological units and other fixed expressions. For more flexible expressions (idiomatic expressions and collocations), less automated bilingual concordance programs may be more beneficial.

However, the performance of the sub-sentential TM system that we tested is not yet optimal, as less useful translation suggestions for basic vocabulary words and fuzzy chunk matches often offer translators more distraction than benefit.

In order for sub-sentential translation memories to exploit the full potential of translation memories, better word alignment algorithms are necessary so as to improve both precision (the quality of the chunk alignments) and recall (align more flexible units). Ideally, the matching mechanism would also take into account morphological variants, which is a major challenge and a problem unlikely to be solved in the near future.

Bibliography

Bowker, L., & Barlow, M. (2004). Bilingual concordancers and translation memories: A comparative evaluation. In: E. Yuste Rodrigo (Ed.), Proceedings of the Second International Workshop on Language Resources for Translation Work, Research and Training (pp. 70-83); Geneva, Switzerland, August 28, 2004.

Gotti, F., Langlais, P., Macklovitch, E., Bourigault, D., Robichaud, B., & Coulombe, C. (2005). *3GTM:* A third-generation translation memory. In: Proceedings of the 3rd Computational Linguistics in the North-East (CLiNE) Workshop (pp. 8-15); Gatineau, QC, August 26, 2005.

Koehn, P. (2005). Europarl: A parallel corpus for statistical machine translation. In: Proceedings of the Tenth Machine Translation Summit (pp. 79-86); Phuket, Thailand September 12-16, 2005.

Koehn, P. (2009). *Statistical Machine Translation*. Cambridge: Cambridge University Press.

Lagoudaki, E. (2008). The value of machine translation for the professional translator. In: Proceedings of the Eighth Conference of the Association for Machine Translation in the Americas (pp. 262-269); Waikiki, HI, October 21-25, 2008.

Lommel, A. (2004). LISA 2004 translation memory survey: Translation memory and translation memory standards. Romainmotier, Switzerland: LISA. Retrieved June 1, 2005, from http:// www.lisa.org/products/survey/2004/tmsurvey.html

Macken, L. (2007). Analysis of translational correspondence in view of sub-sentential alignment. In: F. Van Eynde, V. Vandeghinste, & I. Schuurman (Eds.), Proceedings of the METIS-II Workshop on New Approaches to Machine Translation (pp. 97-105); Leuven, Belgium, January 1, 2007.

Macken, L., Rura, L., & . Trushkina, J. (2007). Dutch Parallel Corpus: MT corpus and translator's aid. In: B. Maegaard (Ed.), Proceedings of the Machine Translation Summit XI (pp. 313-320); Copenhagen, Denmark, September 10-14 2007. Geneva, Switzerland: European Association for Machine Translation.

Planas, E. (2005). SIMILIS second-generation translation memory software. Proceedings of the 27th International Conference on Translating and the Computer (TC27), London, UK, November 24-25, 2005.

Planas, E., & Furuse, O. (2003). Formalizing translation memory. In M. Carl & A. Way (Eds.), *Recent advances in example-based machine translation* (pp. 157-188). Dordrecht: Kluwer Academic Publishers.

Simard, M. & Langlais, P. (2001). *Sub-sentential exploitation of translation memories*. In: Proceedings of the Machine Translation Summit VIII; Santiago De Compostela, Spain, September 18-22, 2001.

Sparck Jones, K. (1979). Experiments in relevance weighting of search terms. *Information Processing and Management*, *15*, 133-144.

---

[1] The terms *first generation TM* and *second generation TM* are widely used (Planas, 2005; Lagoudaki, 2008) to refer to sentence-based and sub-sentential translation memory systems, respectively. Only Gotti et al. (2005) make another distinction: first-generation systems are sentence-based translation memory systems without fuzzy matching techniques; second-generation systems are sentence-based systems supporting fuzzy matches; and third-generation systems are sub-sentential translation memory systems.

[2] www.trados.com

[3] www.lingua-et-machina.com

[4] www.athel.com/para.html

[5] http://www.statmt.org/europarl/

The effect of Translation Memory tools in translated Web texts: Evidence from a comparative product-based study

Miguel A. Jiménez-Crespo
Rutgers University, The State University of New Jersey

Translation Memory tools have been widely promoted in terms of increased productivity, quality and consistency, while translation scholars have argued that in some cases they might produce the opposite effect. This paper investigates these two related claims through a corpus-based contrastive analysis of 40,000 original and localized Web pages in Spanish. Given that all Web texts are localized using TM tools, the claim of increased quality and consistency is analyzed in contrast with Web texts spontaneously produced in Spanish. The results of the contrastive analysis indicate that localized texts tend to replicate source text structures and show higher numbers of inconsistencies at the lexical, syntactic and typographic levels than non-translated Web sites. These findings are associated with lower levels of quality in localized texts as compared to non-translated or spontaneously produced texts.

1. Introduction: Translation Memory tools in a digital age

In recent years the use of translation tools has become an imperative for translation professionals (Alcina, 2008; Bowker, 2002). While most tools are promoted in terms of their productivity, consistency and quality, less attention has been paid to the constraints they impose on the cognitive and textual process that the translator carries out (Reinke, 2004; Neubert & Shreve, 1992; Lörcher, 1991). In fact, if translation is understood as "a communicative event which is shaped by its own goals, pressures and context of production" (Baker, 1996, p. 175), which in turn will produce text with observable linguistic features different from text originally produced in any language (Baker, 1995; Baker, 1996; Kenny, 2001; Laviosa, 2002), it is logical to claim that the use of technology tools will leave a trace in translated texts that can be quantitatively observed using a corpus-based methodology.

In the context of corpus-based translation research, the seminal work of Baker (1999, p. 285; 1995) has placed the emphasis on social, cultural, cognitive and ideological constraints. Nevertheless, it has been argued that the introduction of Translation Memory tools (TM) has changed the nature of the task they intend to facilitate (Bowker, 2002), and consequently, the impact of technological constraints should also be taken into consideration. These technological constraints have been associated in previous studies to the reduction of the translation task to a mere "sentence replacement" activity (Bédard, 2001, p. 29), in which there is a partial decontextualization of the constituent segments that make up the holistic text (Bowker, 2006). Other scholars have argued that TM use leads to a translation process that tends to operate at a microtextual level (Shreve, 2006; Macklovitch & Russel, 2000), with clear implications in terms of style, coherence, cohesion or structural configuration (Heyn, 1998). These claims by translation scholars are somewhat related to the industry's assertion that TM tools lead to higher levels of quality, which according to Reinke (2004) is simply associated with the notion of increased *consistency*. According to companies marketing TM tools, given that pre-established terminology and repeated segments will be equally translated, the target text will display a more coherent and cohesive nature, and therefore higher levels of *quality*.

Nevertheless, several scholars have argued that the above-mentioned technological constraints might produce less coherent and cohesive texts. The rationale behind this claim is that translators might incorporate sentences from texts belonging to diverse domains or genres (Shreve, 2006), produced by several translators with unique styles (Bowker, 2006, p. 181) or that translators might avoid certain cohesive devices, such as anaphoric and cataphoric references, in order to promote future reuse (Heyn, 1998, p. 135). Additionally, it is fair to argue that the industry's rationale for promoting these tools cannot be fully supported in new translation modalities, such as software or Web site localization, given that these translations are always performed with TM tools. In these modalities, there would be no *tertium comparationis* against which to contrast their improved consistency or quality.

Consequently, it seems pertinent to propose that the quality benefits of TM tools could be evaluated through a contrastive analysis with those texts spontaneously produced in any language and therefore not subject to the technological constraints of a technology-driven translation process. Such is the approach taken by this paper: the corpus of texts that will be analyzed includes original Spanish Web sites alongside localized Web sites that have been subject to the pressures of translation as an industrial activity (Sager, 1989, p. 91). A second possible approach would be comparing a corpus of Web sites that have been localized using TM tools with a corpus of texts localized without them. Nevertheless, this would be virtually impossible, mostly due to the difficulty in identifying a large representative body of professionally localized Web sites following this latter approach.

Despite recent interest in the empirical investigation into TM use (Wallis, 2008; Gow, 2003; Reinke, 2004; Sommers, 1999; etc.), the above-mentioned claims on potential effects in the process and products have not been fully empirically researched. Therefore, the goals of this paper are twofold: on the one hand, it intends to research from an empirical perspective whether TM sentence-based processing has an impact in the final textual, pragmatic and discursive configuration of the target Web sites; on the other hand, it will investigate whether localized texts are more consistent than those spontaneously produced in any given language or sociocultural context. The first goal will be accomplished through a contrastive superstructural analysis of a comparative corpus of 40,000 original and localized Web pages. Following a genre-based model (Göpferich, 1995; Gamero, 2001; Askehave & Nielsen, 2005), a contrastive superstructural and macrostructural analysis of the corpus will be performed in order to observe whether localized Web sites maintain the textual structure of source Web sites. The second objective will be accomplished through a contrastive analysis of *inconsistencies* in localized Web sites identified through a previous study (Jiménez-Crespo, 2008a). These inconsistencies are lexical (analyzing intratextual denomintative variation, such as translated and untranslated borrowings), syntactic (addressing the user using formal-informal forms in the same text) or typographic (inconsistent capitalization of titles and neologisms).

2. Translation memory and the claim of improved quality and consistency

Translation memory tools have been used for over two decades. The number of publications that describe their possible uses in professional practice is steadily growing (L´Homme, 1999; Esselink, 2000; Austermülh, 2001; Bowker, 2002; Bowker, 2005; Corpas & Varela, 2003; Reinke, 2004; Freigang, 2005; Días Fouçes & García González, 2008), with several researchers focusing on TM evaluation and selection depending on the working environment (Höge, 2002; Zerfaß, 2002a; Zerfaß, 2002b; Rico, 2000; Webb, 1998) or the impact of TM use in translator training (Alcina, 2008; Kenny, 1999). Additionally, empirical studies on different aspects of TM use are steadily appearing (i.e. Wallis, 2008; O'Brien, 2007). Generally, most research into translation memory has adopted a process-oriented view, both from the tools' or users' perspective. Nevertheless, even when it has been previously suggested that TM tools bring about increased quality and consistency (Ahrenberg & Merkel, 1999), there is a scarcity of product-based empirical studies that compare texts translated using TM tools with those produced without them in order to validate some of these underlying assumptions.

2.1. TM tools benefits and the notion of *quality*

The use of TM has been generally associated to benefits in terms of quality, consistency, speed, improvements in the quality of the translator's experience or terminology management (O'Brien, 1998, p. 119; Webb, 1998, p. 20; Bowker, 2002, p. 117; Reinke, 2004; etc.). In particular, the evaluation of TM systems from an academic perspective has not concentrated on the claim of improved quality,[1] as this notion is controversial *per se* in Translation Studies literature (Wright, 2006; Bass, 2006). According to standards such as the ISO 9000, quality is defined as the ability to comply with a set of parameters predefined by the customer (Bass, 2006). These definitions have been criticized as it is theoretically and methodologically impossible to predefine the notion of *quality* in all translated texts: for this reason, common definitions of quality usually focus on the procedural aspects of processes as opposed to establishing what could be considered a *quality* translated text. Basically, such definitions govern procedures for achieving quality rather than providing normative statements about what constitutes quality (Martínez Melis & Hurtado, 2001, p. 274). The only standard that describes the properties of a quality translated text is the German norm DIN 2345. This norm defines quality as the property of a translated text that is complete, terminologically coherent, uses correct grammar, appropriate style and adheres to an agreed-upon style guide. Thus, it explicitly links the notion of quality to that of *coherence* and *consistency* normally used in TM marketing efforts.

In the case of Web and software localization, the notion of quality has also been associated by the Localization Industry Standards Association with a translated text that "looks like it has been developed in-country" (Lommel, 2004, p. 11), and therefore, it is fair to argue that a localized Web site would need comply to the set of expectations shared by the target discourse community, such as the conventional genre superstructure[2] and macrostructure (Nord, 1997). However, and as mentioned previously, the textual segmentation process primes the translator to consciously or subconsciously maintain the overall textual structure of the source document, ignoring that textual structure is culture-specific (Neubert & Shreve, 1992), and exemplars of a similar genre in two different cultures might show structural differences (Shreve, 2006; Gamero, 2002). In this sense, this paper agrees with Bowker (2002, p. 117) in that "The rigidity of maintaining the same order and number of sentences in the target text as are found in the source texts may affect the naturalness and quality of the translation." Therefore, it is assumed that a translated text that maintains the source text structure might produce a negative impact in the text receiver's appreciation of quality. The fact that translated texts maintain the source text organization has been previously put forward as a general problem in the evaluation of translated texts (Larose, 1998), and it has also been associated with the perception of lower quality by the receivers of target texts (Nobs, 2005). Thus, the first working hypothesis in this study is that:

> Hypothesis 1: The use of TM tools in the localization of Web sites will increase the tendency in translation to produce texts whose superstructure and macrostructure are somewhat different from that of spontaneously produced texts in the target language due to their sentence-based processing.

This hypothesis would be also based on previous scholars' assertions that the use of TM tools might produce the opposite effect of that touted; they might somewhat hinder the production of a *quality* target text (Wallis, 2008; Bowker, 2002; Bowker, 2006; Bédard, 2000; Heyn, 1998).

The second claim that this paper intends to investigate is that of increased consistency, a concept related to the linguistic notion of lexical and syntactic coherence (de Beaugrande & Dressler, 1981). Given that *coherence* is considered to be the most important standard of textuality in hypertexts (Fritz, 1999; Storrer, 2002), the following section reviews this notion and the importance of maintaining consistency in hypertext localization.

2.2. Texts, hypertexts and the claim of consistency

The notion of a unitary text in which translation activity is based is central in Translation Studies. From a text-linguistic approach, it has been defended that texts are the central defining issue in translation, and texts and their situation define the translation process (Neubert & Shreve, 1992). Nevertheless, the extensive use of TM tools has lead to a gradual disappearance of the single text as the operative unit in which the translation task is based. Several scholars have noted that the use of translation memory tools or global management systems (GMS) are forcing translators to work with disaggregated textual units that are not necessarily "the totality of communicative signals used in a communicative interaction" (Nord, 1991, p. 14),[3] or complete coherent and cohesive texts (Bowker, 2006). Instead, translators gradually process subtextual units that are part of a complete text that is sometimes unavailable (Mossop, 2005). From the perspective of the translation process, this has clear implications in terms of cohesion, coherence and contextual cues during source text comprehension and the subsequent textual production stage.

The decontextualization of textual segments is especially significant during the localization process (Dunne, 2006; Esselink, 2000), a translation modality that mostly deals with hypertexts. One of the main characteristics of hypertexts is the need to divide the global text into interrelated nodes or lexias that can be read on a computer screen (Landow, 1997). Due to this disaggregation of hypertexts in smaller subtextual units (the Web pages themselves or their different components such as banner ads), together with the fact that any hypertext can be accessed directly through any node and read in whichever sequence, it has been defended that coherence is their most important standard of textuality (Fritz, 1998; Storrer, 2002). This suggests that maintaining terminological coherence and consistency is crucial in order to produce high quality localizations.

In establishing coherence in hypertexts, it should be mentioned that each hypertextual page includes both *content text,* the new content that is included in each page and makes it an information and retrieval unit (Nielsen & Loranger, 2006), and *interface text*, the textual segments whose function is to structure the global unitary hypertext (Price & Price, 2002). Interface text can be identified as navigation menus, breadcrumb navigation menus, webmaps, and news columns, etc. It promotes global hypertextual coherence through lexical repetition found in all these textual segments[4] (Jiménez-Crespo & Tercedor, in press). Given that their main function is to structure the entire hypertext as a single textual unit,[5] TM tools would in principle assist the translators in maintaining the same translation for each of the terms associated to the hypertextual superstructure, such as the conventional lexical units: *contact us*, *about us*, *privacy policy*, etc.

Nevertheless, a previous study by the author found a high number of inconsistencies in navigation terminology in localized Web sites (Jiménez-Crespo, 2008a). These were mostly found when a source lexical unit can potentially be translated in several ways in the target language, such as "about us", which can be translated using two synonymous prepositions in Spanish: *acerca de nosotros* and *sobre nosotros*. These inconsistencies were also found whenever any segment of the overall hypertext included a reference to a specific page in the global hypertext, such as "Please refer to our *privacy policy* for more information [...]". In these cases, the problem resides in the fact that the sentence-based operation of TM tools does not fully allow for sub-sentence matches to be presented to the translator (Macklovitch & Russel, 2000; Gow, 2003). Thus, even when the translation of the lexical unit *privacy policy* might be stored in the TM database as a segment;[6] a sentence that contains a reference to this page might not trigger the previously stored translation. Thus, as pointed out previously by Macklovitch & Russel (2000), many repetitions might be subsentential and, therefore, difficult to locate while localizing Web sites.

Another case of recurrent inconsistencies attributed to difficulties in retrieving subsentence matches is the translation of borrowings and calques, such as *email*, *link* or *online*. In Spanish, the use of these loanwords from English is highly extensive (Cabanillas *et al.*, 2007), but nonetheless, the translator has to constantly decide whether to use the loanword or to insert the variety of possible Spanish neologisms, such as *correo electrónico* or *dirección electrónica*, *enlace - hipervínculo - vínculo* or *en línea* respectively. It would be expected that a Web site translated with TM and terminology management tools might consistently use the same choice, and that any inconsistency could be attributed to translators' behavior during the translation task. Thus, intratextual denominative variation in the case of borrowings and calques can constitute a valid variable in order to research whether TM tools provide higher consistency at the subsentential level than spontaneously produced texts.

Finally, another case of inconsistencies while translating into Romance languages entails differences in register as reflected in the use of formal and informal pronouns and verbal forms. In localization, the overwhelming majority of translations take place from English into other languages (Lommel, 2004), and in the case of Spanish, translators facing a direct appeal to the user have to constantly decide whether to use *tú* or *usted* forms (Jiménez-Crespo, 2008a). In these cases, given that this problem is only related to pronominal and verbal choices, potential matches in the TM database would be at the sub-sentence level, and therefore, the use of TM tools might not be useful in maintaining a consistent tone. This would lead to a syntactically and stylistically inconsistent target text.

After this brief description of potential inconsistencies, the second working hypothesis is that:

> Hypothesis 2: Due to the current inability of TM tools to effectively provide sub-segment matches and maintain consistency at certain levels, localized texts will display higher percentages of lexical, syntactic and typographic inconsistencies than texts spontaneously produced in a given language.

2.3. Web site localization and "pre-translation" TM mode

Before continuing with the description of the empirical study, it should be mentioned that globalized Web sites are normally updated using global management systems or GMS (LISA, 2007), a process that in TM terms has been identified as *pre-translation* (Wallis, 2008) or *batch mode* (Bowker, 2002, p. 112). In this case, whenever a Web site is updated, the GMS compares the entire text to the database of previous translations and extracts only those segments that do not have an exact match. This process might further accentuate the lack of consistency given that the target Web site is the product of an increasing number of translators with differentiated styles, preferences, etc. Additionally, it should be mentioned that in a previous empirical study the use of pre-translation has been preliminarily shown to produce lower levels of quality than normal interactive translations (Wallis, 2008).

3. Empirical study

The methodology used to test both hypotheses is based on the Spanish Comparable Web Corpus[7] made up of 267 original and localized corporate Web sites (Jiménez-Crespo, 2008a). This Web genre was selected as it has been previously identified as the most conventional digital genre (Kennedy & Shepherd, 2005). The Web corpus was compiled in the context of a wider research project that deals with the effects of the technological context of production of localized Web texts (Jiménez-Crespo, 2008a), and it consists of two sections: a corpus of original Spanish corporate Web sites (172 sites) and another corpus of all Web sites localized into Castilian Spanish[8] from the largest 650 US companies according to the Forbes list (95 sites). The corpus was downloaded synchronically during one single day in 2006. All texts were systematically selected from two directories, the Spanish Google Business directory and the Forbes list, so as to guarantee that the corpus would be representative of the textual population targeted. A detailed description of the corpus compilation process and composition have been given elsewhere (Jiménez-Crespo 2008a; 2008b; 2009), and therefore, only the most important characteristics will be highlighted in the following table.

Table 1: Spanish Web Comparable Corpus description

	Original Section		*Localized Section*	
	Total	*Average*	*Total*	*Average*
Web sites	178		95	
Web pages	19,102	111.5 per site	21,322	224.3 per site
Words in page body	4,945,103	258.87 page	8,871,512	416.07 page
Words total	8,659,856	453.34 page	12,562,894	589.50 page

In order to test the first hypothesis, a textual genre model was adopted in a modified form (Gamero, 2001; Askehave & Nielsen, 2005). Each thematic unit in a Web site represented in the navigation menu or sitemap, such as *contact us* or *about us*, is identified as a unique *move*[9] in the overall structure of the hypertext (Askehave & Nielsen, 2005; Jiménez-Crespo, 2008c). Moreover, each move is subdivided into *steps*, such as the conventional *history*, *location* or *mission* pages inside the section that describes the company in corporate Web sites. Each localized Web site will be analyzed and all entries in navigation menus and webmaps will be assigned to a move or step in order to quantify the frequency of use. This will provide a detailed statistical analysis of the frequency of use of all moves and steps. This methodology was previously applied to the corpus of original Spanish Web sites, providing a descriptive quantitative and qualitative foundation for this contrastive study (Jiménez-Crespo, 2008b; 2008c). By applying this same analysis to the localized section of the corpus, it will be possible to contrast the structure of localized texts using segment-based TM tools to that of original texts produced without them.

As for the second hypothesis, the intratextual analysis of inconsistencies requires a smaller sample of texts for a more controlled analysis. This led to the creation of a smaller comparable subcorpus made up of ten original and ten localized Web sites that were randomly selected and extracted. Each Web site will also be converted to .txt format and analyzed with the lexical analysis software Wordsmith Tools.

Once this smaller sample subcorpus is compiled and processed, each Web site will be subject to the following intratextual analysis: (1) consistency analysis of the all concepts associated with the hypertextual superstructure as represented in navigation menus or sitemaps; (2) analysis of intratextual denominative variation for borrowings and calques; (3) consistency analysis of the use of upper case letters in navigation menus and neologisms; and finally, (4) a consistency analysis of the use of formal vs. informal verbal and pronominal forms. The results from the original and localized texts will be compared and contrasted.

Table 2: Description of comparable subcorpus extracted from Spanish Web Comparable Corpus

	Original Section		*Localized Section*	
	Total	*Average*	*Total*	*Average*
Total Web sites	10		10	
Web pages	1984	198.4 per site	3141	314.1 per site
Words in body of pages	680,031	342.75 page	1,278,225	406.94 per page

4. Results

The results will be presented following the two distinctive stages in this study that correspond to each formulated hypothesis. The contrastive analysis of the textual superstructure will be presented first, followed by the intratextual consistency analysis designed to test the second hypothesis.

4.1. Contrastive analysis of the hypertextual structure

First of all, the contrastive quantitative analysis of the superstructure of original and localized Web sites shows that both textual profiles share the same number of possible moves or thematic units. In fact, all moves identified in the previous descriptive study on original Spanish Web sites (Jiménez-Crespo, 2008b; 2008c) appear in both corpora. This indicates that, to some extent, the internationalization of this Web genre has led to a similar number of possible moves and steps in original Spanish sites and those localized into this same language. However, the most significant finding relates to substantial differences in the frequency of appearance for several moves, such as *privacy policy* or *terms of use*. Given that, in principle, all texts are directed towards the same target audience and sociocultural context, this study assumes that any differences between both textual profiles can be attributed directly to the replication of the source text structure.

The following bar chart presents the contrastive analysis of the frequency of appearance for each move and step, and it clearly illustrates the superstructural differences between both textual profiles. It is organized according to the difference in the frequency between original and localized Web sites: the darker segment of each column represents the average frequency for moves or steps in original Web sites (FrO), the frequency of use in localized sites for the same move is represented by the total figure in each column (FrL), while the lighter segment represents the variable that reflects the difference in frequency (DF) between both textual profiles.

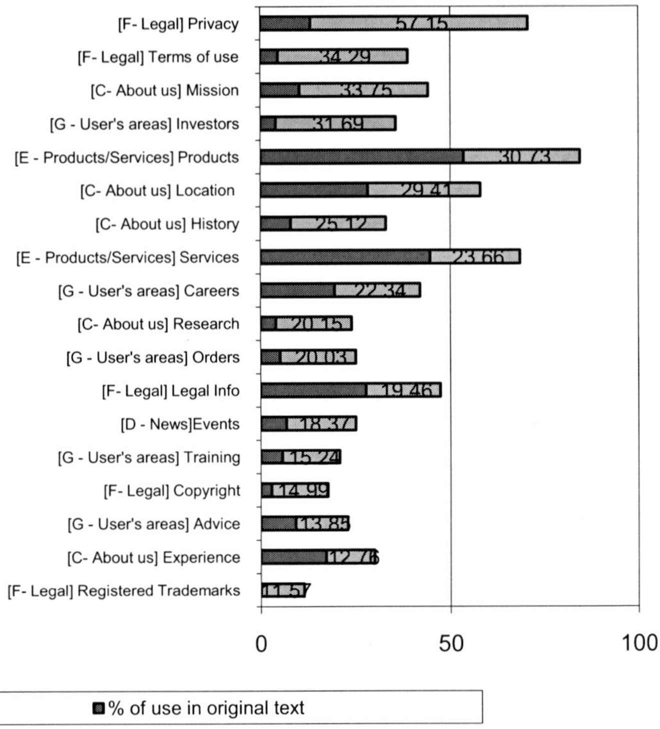

Figure 1: Superstructural differences between original and localized Web sites

The superstructural differences between both textual profiles are mostly concentrated in two moves: *legal* (F) and *about us* (C). In the latter move, it is of interest the higher frequency of the step that contains the values or mission of the company (DF=33.75%). This could be indicative of a conventionalized feature in US corporate Web sites reflecting the need to appeal to tradition and values in the US market. Nevertheless, and as shown by these results, this type of information is not conventionally offered in original Spanish sites (FrO=10.46%).

The most significant differences are concentrated in all moves or thematic units related to legal content, such as *privacy policy* (DF=57.15%), *terms of use* (DF=35.29%), *legal information* (DF=19.46%), *copyright* (DF=14.99%) and *registered trademarks* (DF=11.59%). It is fair to assume that the value of the variable DF reflects differences in the prototypical superstructure in this genre between the source and target sociocultural context, in particular, differences due to their legal systems. This finding is consistent with the results from an earlier study on corporate Web sites concluding that the most consistent difference between US corporate sites and other national sites was that in the former privacy Web pages were more frequent (Robbin & Stylianou, 2003). In fact, online privacy protection in the United States is self-regulated by companies under the guidance of the Federal Trade Commission, while this is regulated in Spain by the Spanish Data Protection Act of 1999. This means that US Web sites are required to explicitly formulate a full privacy policy, while Spanish sites simply indicate that their online privacy practices are in compliance with the above mentioned Spanish law. This can explain the high frequency (FrL=79%) of localized North American corporate Web sites including an independent privacy policy page while very few Spanish sites do (FrO=10.46%). These results prove that once US sites are localized, the structure of the source text is somewhat replicated in the target text. This indicates that the use of TM tools that operate at the page and sentence levels might promote or contribute to the *cloning* of the superstructure of source texts. This is consistent with what Larose (1998) refers to as *cloned texts*, that is, translated texts whose superstructure is fully maintained in the target text regardless of intercultural macrostructural differences for the same textual genre. Thus, the hypertextual page by page structure is somewhat maintained during the localization of Web sites, regardless of the conventional mental model of the genre structure shared by the target discourse community as represented by the Web sites produced by members of that community.

An additional analysis was performed in order to observe whether the macrostructure of pages containing legal information is also maintained in the translation process. Thus, it was observed that the average number of words in the pages with legal content was 2415.69 in localized sites, while the same average for original Spanish sites was 1074.94. This significant difference in the average number of words in legal pages (+224.72%) also points out the fact that the same sentence structure of the source texts could have been maintained. In this respect, it should be mentioned that the Web localization process is even more constrained that the translation of non-digital texts, as it requires the tag protection functionality offered by most TM tools. This additional issue could also discourage translators from seeking or implementing changes to the textual structures (as tags and/or programming code would also require restructuring).

4.2. Lexical, syntactic and typographic consistency

As mentioned previously, the consistency analysis at the lexical, syntactic and typographic levels was performed in the smaller comparable subcorpus consisting of ten original Web sites and ten localized Web sites. Following the progression noted in the methodology section, the description of the results will start with the contrastive study of lexical and terminological consistency.

4.2.1. Lexical consistency

The first analysis in this category involves the analysis of intratextual consistency for lexical units that denote a superstructural category in Web sites. This is represented in navigation menus, webmaps and page titles both at the top of the browser and at the top of the content itself. As an example, the analysis showed that in a single localized Web site the concept that denotes the move *contact us* is translated using four different lexical units; *contáctenos*, *contacte con nosotros*, *póngase en contacto con nosotros* and *contacto con nosotros*. Another example would be the translation of the concept *privacy policy* that is referred to in the same translated Web site as *política de privacidad*, *declaración de privacidad* and *normativa de privacidad*.

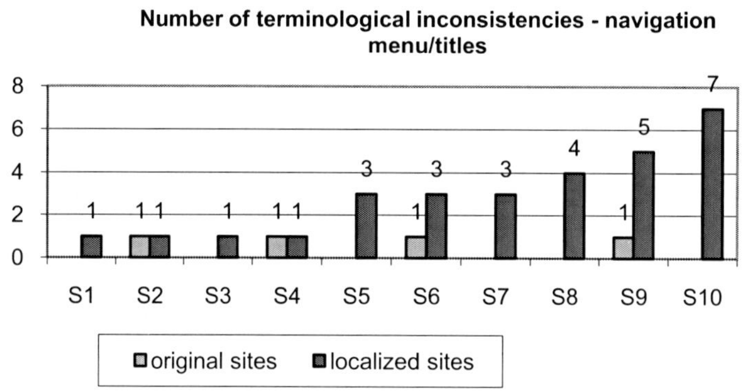

Figure 2: Contrastive analysis of inconsistent terminology for the same hypertextual concept in the same text

As shown in Figure 2, the contrastive analysis revealed that translated Web sites show a greater percentage of terminological inconsistencies in concepts related to the hypertextual structure of the site, mostly in cases in which the source lexical unit has several valid translations in the target language. In the localized section of the corpus, the average number of inconsistencies in superstructural terminology is 2.9 per Web site, with 100% of the Web sites containing this type of inconsistency. In original Web sites, the same analysis yields 0.4% of inconsistencies per site, with 40% of Web sites including this type of inconsistency.

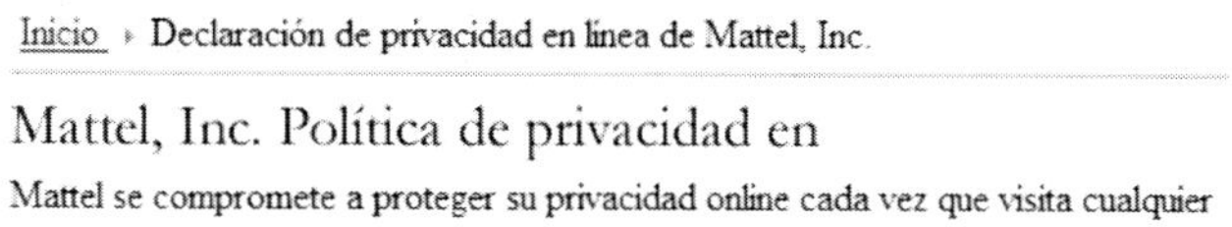

Figure 3: Example of intratextual denominative variation in the translation of "privacy policy" and "online". (Mattel Web site)

Thus, the results show that localized texts are on average less terminologically consistent than original Web sites, even when TM tools would in principle assist in providing consistent translation for these segments. This finding also points out that concepts related to the superstructure of Web sites might not be routinely standardized in terminology databases prior to the actual translation.

The second type of lexical inconsistency analyzed entails the presence of denominative variation in the loanwords and calques *link*, *online* and *email*. The following list illustrates the range of denominative variation found in the subcorpus for each concept. In this list, the use of quotations in order to indicate that the word is a neologism was identified as potential variation, together with the possibility of capitalizing the loanword or calque:

Email [9]: *correo electrónico, correo, dirección electrónica, dirección de correo, dirección de email, email, e-mail, E-mail, mail.*
Link [5]: *enlace, hiperenlace, vínculo, hipervínculo, link.*
Online [6]: *en línea, "en línea", online, On-line, on-line, "on-line".*

The point of interest for this paper is to observe which Web sites use two or more variants for each concept, and more importantly, whether localized sites are more inconsistent than original sites in this respect.

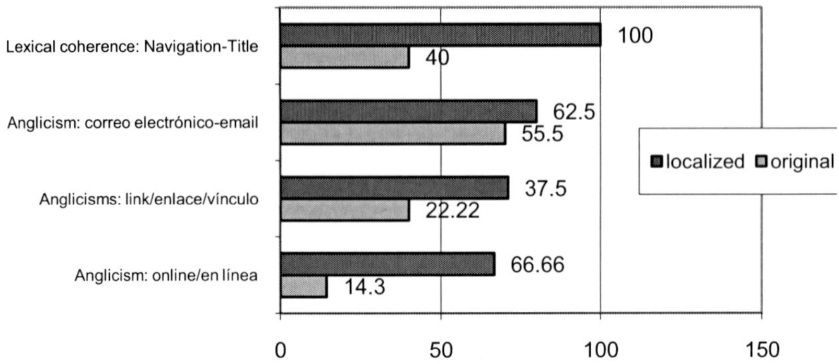

Figure 4: Analysis of lexical inconsistencies in Web sites

Figure 4 shows the contrastive analysis on lexical inconsistencies in which the bar represents the percentage of Web sites that include two or more variants for the same concept. It can be observed that localized sites consistently show higher levels of denominative variation in the same Web site when referring to the same concept. The tendency to use two or more variants for the same term is very similar in the case of the term *email*, with 80% of localized sites and 70% of original sites using the loanword. In the case of *online*, original sites are much more consistent in their use while localized sites show a high percentage of inconsistencies.

4.2.2. Typographic inconsistencies

The third analysis comprises the contrastive study of typographic inconsistencies, another aspect that TM tools cannot fully assist in controlling. In Spanish, capitalization in titles and listed items can be considered a typographic borrowing from English (Martínez de Sousa 2000). The analysis shows that 60% of localized sites use inconsistent capitalization in titles and lexical units in navigation menus, while only 10% of original sites show this type of inconsistency. Similar results are found in the case of inconsistent capitalization of the neologisms *web* and *internet*; localized sites also show higher percentages of sites that interchangeably use these terms both in upper and lower case.

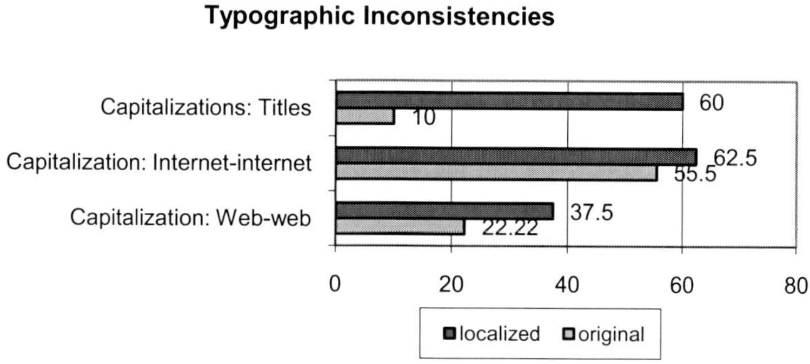

Figure 5: Contrastive analysis of typographic inconsistencies

Once again, it can be observed that localized sites show higher inconsistency levels than original Web sites.

4.2.3. Syntactic inconsistencies: politeness

The last analysis performed deals with the syntactic level. An intratextual analysis of each Web site was carried out searching for formal and informal second person pronominal forms such as *tú* / *usted* and *te* / *le* /*se*, possessive adjectives, *tu* / *su*, and verbal forms such as *haz click* or *haga click* 'click here'. Surprisingly, the percentage of Web sites that address the user both in the *tú* and *usted* form is higher in original sites (70%) than in localized sites (60%).

This finding would in principle contradict the second hypothesis in that original sites would present higher levels of inconsistency in the use of formal and informal markers. However, this can be explained in terms of the different audiences that a Web site might target, such as corporate or personal clients, and the subsequent variation on the power distance depending on the content of different sections of the Web site. In fact, it has been previously observed that Spanish corporate Web sites have a tendency to address customers formally using *usted*, but this tendency changes in the move *job–career,* as the targeted audience would potentially be part of the organization that released the text, and therefore, the power distance relationship would vary (Jiménez-Crespo, 2008a). Nevertheless, it should be noted that this analysis showed that original Web sites would switch between formal and informal tone depending on differences in the targeted audience of sections of the Web site (customer/future employee, regular customer/companies), while inconsistent localized texts would address the same user in both ways regardless of the user's status.

Following these three analyses at the lexical, typographic and syntactic levels, it can be clearly observed that localized sites are on average more inconsistent than original sites, and therefore, these results would in principle confirm the second hypothesis of this study: localized sites show higher levels of lexical, syntactic and typographic inconsistencies than texts originally produced in the target language. The results therefore demonstrate that, despite industry's claims, TM tools cannot fully control the different dimensions of consistency, a key quality issue in software and Web development (Nielsen, 2001).

5. Conclusions

During the last twenty years, TM tools have been widely promoted in terms of quality and consistency, while translation scholars have argued that technological constraints on the translation task might produce the opposite effect. The goal of this paper was to empirically investigate two related claims: whether sentence-based processing might promote or lead to the replication of source text structures and whether TM tools can guarantee the production of consistent texts. The empirical study was founded on the premises that technological tools would leave a trace that would be observable using a corpus-based methodology (Baker, 1995). Among several possible approaches, the study chose a comparable corpus methodology in which texts translated using TM tools were contrasted with texts originally produced in the target language. Two working hypothesis were formulated in this study. In the first case, the first hypothesis has been validated: original and translated texts from the same genre show significant differences in their prototypical superstructure. This has been explained in terms of the replication of the source text structure during a translation process subject to specific constraints (Baker, 1999, p. 285; Baker, 1995), some of which are related to the impact of TM use on the translation task. This effect has been observed not only in the higher frequency of certain thematic units that respond to source sociocultural norms and conventions, such as differences in the legal systems, but also in the higher number of average words in the same thematic unit, which could be due to a replication of the source sentence structure.

The second hypothesis related to lower consistency levels at the subsentence level was also validated: TM translated texts consistently showed lower levels of lexical and typographic consistency as compared to texts spontaneously produced in the target language. Again, it should also be noted that this effect cannot be fully attributed to TM use, but rather to combination with other factors, such as the presence of multiple translators, not following a pre-established style guide, or an inefficient editing process. Nevertheless, it has been clearly observed that current professional TM use cannot guarantee similar levels of consistency to that of original texts not subject to a technology-driven translation process. Nevertheless, in the case of the variable chosen to validate the syntactic consistency hypothesis – the inconsistent use of politeness markers – original Web sites were on average less consistent than translated ones. This was explained in terms of the specific communicative situation that defines corporate Web sites, as different sections of the Web site might be addressed at different audiences. A closer analysis found that translated texts were inconsistent when addressing the same user, such as a personal client, as opposed to original Web sites, which varied their politeness levels according to the type of user (such as personal clients or corporate clients).

As a final remark, it should be mentioned that the methodology used in this paper assumes that TM tools have changed the nature of the task that it intends to facilitate (Bowker, 2002). The differences observed between texts translated using TM tools and original texts could also be identified as a general tendency in translated digital texts or as a potential case of a new translation universal (Baker, 1995; Mauranen & Kujamäki, 2004) that would require further study. Thus, the revolutionary impact of TM tools on the translation practice might challenge some basic assumptions in Translation Studies, such as the individualistic character of translation or that translation necessarily entails an operation involving complete and unitary texts. This empirical study has shown that further research into the effects of TM in translation processes and the translation products themselves is needed. It is our hope that additional empirical investigations in this under-researched area promote the development of TM tools that could potentially account for domain and genre-specific intercultural variation or improvements in the retrieval of subsentential matches.

Bibliography

Ahrenberg, L. & Merkel, M. (1996). On translation corpora and translation support tools: A project report. In K. Aijmer, B Altenberg & M. Johansson (Eds.). *Languages in contrast. Papers from a symposium on text-based cross-linguistic studies* (pp. 185-200). Lund: Lund University Press.

Alcina, A. (2008). Translation technologies: Scopes, tools and resources. *Target*, *20*(1), 79-102.

Askehave, I. & Nielsen, A. (2005). Digital genres: A challenge to traditional genre theory. *Information Technology and People*, *18*(2), 120-141.

Austermühl, F. (2001). *Electronic tools for translators*. Manchester: St. Jerome Publishing.

Baker, M. (1999). The role of corpora in investigating the linguistic behaviour of professional translator. *International Journal of Corpus Linguistics*, *4*(2), 281-298.

Baker, M. (1996). Corpus-based translation studies: The challenges that lie ahead. In H. Somers (Ed.), *Terminology, LSP and translation: Studies in language engineering in honour of Juan C. Sager* (pp. 175-186). Amsterdam/Philadelphia, PA: John Benjamins.

Baker, M. (1995). Corpora in translation studies: An overview and some suggestions for future research. *Target* *7*(2), 223-243.

Bass, S. (2006). Quality in the real world. In K. Dunne (Ed.), *Perspectives on localization* (pp. 69-84). Amsterdam/Philadelphia, PA: John Benjamins.

Bédard, C. (2000). Mémoire de traduction cherche traducteur de phrases. *Traduire*, *186*, 41-49.

Biau, G., Ramón, J., & Pym, A. (2006). Technology and translation (a pedagogical overview). In A. Pym, A. Perekstenko, & B. Starink (Eds.), *Translation technology and its teaching* (pp. 5-20). Tarragona: Intercultural Studies Group.

Bowker, L. (2006). Translation memory and "text.". In L. Bowker (Ed.), *Lexicography, terminology and translation* (pp. 175-187). Ottawa: University of Ottawa Press.

Bowker, L. (2005). Productivity vs quality? A pilot study on the impact of translation memory systems. *Localisation Focus*, *4*(1), 13–20.

Bowker, L. (2002). *Computer-aided translation technology: A practical introduction*. Ottawa: University of Ottawa Press.

Cabanillas, I., Tejedor, C., Díez, M., & Redondo, E. (2007). English loanwords in Spanish computer language. *English for Specific Purposes*, *26*(1), 52-78.
Corpas Pastor, G., & Varela Salinas, M. (Eds.). (2003). *Entornos informáticos de la traducción professional: Las memorias de traducción*. Granada: Editorial Atrio.
De Beaugrande, R-A & Dressler, W.U. (1981). *Introduction to text linguistics*. London/New York, NY: Longman.
Días Fouçes, O. & García González, M. (2008). *Traducir (con) sofware libre*. Granada: Comares.
Dunne, K. (2006). Putting the cart behind the horse: Rethinking localization quality management. In K. Dunne (Ed.), *Perspectives on Localization* (pp. 95-117). Amsterdam/Philadelphia, PA: John Benjamins.
Esselink, B. (2001). *A Practical guide to localization*. Amsterdam/Philadelphia, PA: John Benjamins.
Freigang, K. (2005). Sistemas de memorias de traducción. In D. Reineke (Ed.),*Traducción y localización. Mercado, gestión, tecnologías* (pp. 95-122). Las Palmas de Gran Canaria: Anroart Ediciones.
Fritz, G. (1998). Coherence in hypertext. In W. Bublitz, U. Lenk & E. Ventola (Eds.), *Coherence in spoken and written discourse: How to create it and how to describe it* (pp. 221-234). Amsterdam/Philadelphia, PA: John Benjamins.
Gamero Pérez, S. (2001). *La traducción de textos técnicos*. Barcelona: Ariel.
Göpferich, S. (1995). *Textsorten in naturwissenschaften und technik. Pragmatische typologie-kontrastierung-translation*. Tubinga: Gunter Narr.
Gow, F. (2003). *Metrics for evaluating translation memory software*. MA thesis, School of Translation and Interpretation, University of Ottawa, Ottawa, ON.
Heyn, M. (1998). Translation memories: Insights and prospects". In L. Bowker, M. Cronin, D. Kenny & J. Pearson (Eds.), *Unity in diversity? Current trends in translation studies* (123-136). Manchester: St. Jerome Publishing.
Höge, M. (2002). *Towards a framework for the evaluation of translators' aids systems*. PhD thesis, Department of Translation Studies, Helsinki University, Helsinki.
Jiménez-Creso, M.A. (2009). Conventions in localisation: A corpus study of original vs. translated web texts. *Jostrans: The Journal of Specialized Translation*, *12*, 79-102. Retrieved August17, 2009, from http://www.jostrans.org/issue12/art_jimenez.php
Jiménez-Crespo, M.A. (2008a). *El proceso de localización web: estudio constrastivo de un corpus comparable de género sitio web corporativo*. PhD thesis, Departamento de Traducción e Interpretación, Universidad de Granada, Granada. Retrieved August 17, 2009, from http://hera.ugr.es/tesisugr/17515324.pdf
Jiménez-Crespo, M.A. (2008b). Caracterización del género 'sitio web corporativo' español: Análisis descriptivo con fines traductológicos. In M. Fernández Sánchez & R. Muñoz Martin (Eds.), *Aproximaciones cognitivas al estudio de la traducción e interpretación* (pp. 259-300). Granada: Comares.
Jiménez-Crespo, M.A. (2008c). Web genres in localization: A Spanish corpus study. *Localization Focus – The International Journal of Localization*, *6*(1), 4-14.
Jiménez-Crespo, M.A. & Maribel Tercedor, M. (in press). Theoretical and methodological issues in web corpus design and analysis. *International Journal of Translation.*
Kenny, D. (2001). *Lexis and creativity in translation. A corpus-based study*. Manchester: St. Jerome.
Kenny, D. (1999). CAT tools in an academic environment: What are they good for? *Target*, *11*(1), 65-82.
Larose, R. (1998). Méthodologie de l'évaluation des traductions. *Meta*, *43*(2), 163-186.
Laviosa, S.(2002). *Corpus-based translation studies*. Amsterdam: Rodopi.
L'Homme, M.(1999). *Initiation à la traductique*. Brossard, QC: Linguatech éditeur.
Lommel, A. (Ed.) (2004). *Localiztion Industry Primer, 2nd Edition*. Geneva: The Localization Industry Standards Association (LISA).
Lörscher, W. (1991). *Translation performance, translation process, and translation strategies A psycholinguistic investigation*. Tübingen: Gunter Narr.
Macklovitch, E. & Russell, G. (2000). What's been forgotten in translation memory. In J. White (Ed.), *Envisioning machine translation in the information future* (pp. 137-146). AMTA 2000: Proceedings of the 4th Conference of the Association for Machine Translation in the Americas; Cuernavaca, Mexico, October 10-14, 2000. Berling: Springer.
Martínez de Sousa, J. (2000). *Manual de estilo de la lengua española*. Gijón: Trea.
Martínez Melis, N. & Hurtado Albir, A.(2001). Assesment in translation studies: Research needs. *Meta 47*(2), 272-287.

Mauranen, A. & Kujamäki, P. (Eds.). (2004). *Translation universals: Do they exist?* Amsterdam/Philadelphia, PA: John Benjamins.
Neubert, A. & Shreve, G. (1992). *Translation as text.* Kent, OH: Kent State University Press.
Nielsen, J. & Loranger, H. (2006). *Prioritizing web usability.* Indianapolis, IN: News Riders.
Nielsen, J. (2002). *Coordinating user interfaces for consistency.* San Francisco, CA: Morgan Kaufmann.
Nobs, M. (2006). *La traducción de folletos turísticos: ¿Qué calidad demandan los turistas?*. Granada: Comares.
Nord, C. (1991). *Text analysis in translation.* Amsterdam:Atlanta, GA: Rodopi.
O'Brien, S. (2007). Eye-tracking and translation memory matches. *Perspectives: Studies Translatology, 14* (3), 185-205.
O'Brien, S. (1998). Practical experience of computer-aided translation tools in the software localization industry. In L. Bowker, M. Cronin, D. Kenny & J. Pearson (Eds.), *Unity in diversity? Current trends in translation* studies (pp. 115-122). Manchester: St. Jerome Publishing.
Price, J. & Price, L. (2002). *Hot text. Web writing that works.* Berkeley, CA: News Riders.
Reinke, U. (2004). *Translation memories: Systeme – konzepte – linguistische.* Frankfurt am Main: Peter Lang.
Rico, C. (2000). Evaluation metrics for translation memories. *Language International, 12*(6), 36-37.
Robbins, S. & Stylianou, A. (2003). Global corporate web sites: An empirical investigation of content and design. *Information & Management, 40*, 205-212.
Sager, J.(1989). Quality and standards: The evaluation of translations. In C. Picken (Ed.), *The translator's handbook* (pp. 91-102). London: ASLIB.
Shreve, G. (2006). Corpus enhancement and localization. In K. Dunne (Ed.),*Perspectives on localization* (pp. 309-331). Amsterdam/Philadelphia, PA: John Benjamins.
Somers, H. (1999). Review article: Example-based machine translation. *Machine Translation, 14*(2), 113-157.
Storrer, A. (2002). Coherence in text and hypertext. *Document Design, 3*(2), 157-168.
Swales, J. (1990). *Genre analysis. English in academic and research settings.* Cambridge: Cambridge University Press.
Wallis, J. (2008). Interactive translation vs. pre-translation in TMs: A pilot study. *Meta, 53*(3), 623-629.
Webb, L. (1998). *Advantages and disadvantages of translation memory: A cost/benefit analysis.* MA thesis, Graduate Division, Monterey Institute of International Studies, Monterey, CA.
Wright, S. (2006). Language industry standards. In K. Dunne (Ed.), *Perspectives on localization* (241-278). Amsterdam/Philadelphia, PA: John Benjamins.
Zerfaß, A. (2002). Comparing basic features of TM tools. *Multilingual Computing and Technology, 13*(7), 11-14.

[1] With the exception of Wallis (2008) that compared the quality of translated texts using interactive translation vs. pre-translation in TM.

[2] In this study, the superstructure of a textual genre is defined as the prototypical pattern that comprises a number of thematic or communicative textual sections whose hierarchical order is fixed to a certain degree (Göpferich, 1995, p. 127; Hurtado Albir, 2001, p. 495).

[3] Including graphics, typography, layout, animation sequences or functionality associated to each textual segment.

[4] Storrer (2002) identifies the function of lexical units in navigation menus as *global* and *local* coherence cues that assist users in navigating the hypertext by providing a the necessary coherence in order to identify a unitary text as such.

[5] Only in the case of hypertexts understood as a thematic, functional and textual unit (Storrer, 2002). E-texts, that is, printed texts simply uploaded to the WWW or linked on a Web site and hyperwebs, such as portals, do not share this characteristic (Jiménez & Tercedor, 2008).

[6] The lexical units in navigation menus or Web page titles cannot be strictly be defined as sentences (Bowker, 2002), even when TM systems consider them as a segment and stores their translation accordingly.

[7] In this study, a comparable corpus is understood as a representative collection of texts spontanously produced in one language alongside similar texts translated into that language (Baker, 1995).

[8] Only the *locale* Spanish-Spain or es-ES was selected in order to exclude the effect of dialectal variation in all Spanish varieties or cultural differences among the different areas in which Spanish is spoken.

[9] For our purposes, a *move* is defined as a "unit of discourse structure which presents a uniform orientation, has specific structural characteristics and has a clearly defined function" (Swales, 1990, p. 140).

BOOK REVIEWS

Díaz Cintas, J. (Ed.) (2008). *The didactics of audiovisual translation*. Amsterdam: John Benjamins. 263p.

The concept of interdisciplinarity has become part of contemporary mainstream academic research and has greatly contributed to a more multifaceted and enriched understanding of a variety of fields of research. However, with the concept of interdisciplinarity often come the risks of fragmentation and of trying to cover too many variables. Such risks loom especially when two or more fields of research interact to consolidate, reconceptualize and imprint past, present and future research. The field of audiovisual translation is no stranger to interdisciplinarity. As a distinct yet academically pliable field of research it uses insights from a multitude of other fields (e.g. linguistics, psychology, semiotics, technology) in an attempt to consolidate new findings both theoretically and practically. It is within the context of growing interdisciplinarity that Díaz Cintas's edited book *The didactics of audiovisual translation* and its accompanying CD-ROM can be read and used as a means of inspiration.

The clear link that Díaz Cintas tries to establish is the link between audiovisual translation on the one hand and the didactics of this highly unique form of translation on the other. With a total of 15 contributions divided into four distinct parts, Díaz Cintas and his contributors provide the reader with copious insights ranging from theory-related and conceptual information to practice-related exercises and materials for pedagogical interventions.

Part 1, entitled *Inside AVT*, sheds light on two areas which, according to Díaz Cintas, form the two prerequisites for any course on audiovisual translation: the semiotics of the audiovisual product and the importance of screenwriting in the training of audiovisual translators. In the first contribution (*The nature of the audiovisual text and its parameters*), Patrick Zabalbeascoa provides an analysis of the various constituent elements of audiovisual texts. Not only are the individual components of audiovisual texts described, but also the various intricate relationships between those components are highlighted. In so doing, Zabalbeascoa shows that the boundaries between the various components are not as clear-cut as one might expect and that areas of overlap can clearly be distinguished. In the second contribution (*Screenwriting and translating screenplays*), Patrick Catrysse and Yves Gambier turn the focus to screenwriting, which has become immensely popular but is nonetheless still largely ignored in AVT training programmes. The authors analyse screenwriting and highlight the various processes which can be found in screenwriting, all while making links to AVT. It is Catrysse and Gambier's view that insights into the various processes and strategies that professional screenwriters use can help improve the quality of both the translation process and the translated screenplay. In the third and final contribution in Part 1 (*Screenwriting, scripted and unscripted language: What do subtitlers need to know?*), Aline Remael investigates subtitles, which she describes as a highly special form of translation.

Her analysis distinguishes between film dialogue and impromptu speech (both forms of spoken language) and discusses the specific features of these forms of spoken language with regard to the creation of subtitles. In addition, Remael also focuses on the importance of developing students' insight into screenplays (especially the dramatic composition of screenplays) when training future subtitlers.

Part 2, *Hands-on experience in AVT*, turns the focus to the actual practice of audiovisual translation. With a total of seven contributions it is the largest part of the volume. In the first contribution in this part (*Subtitler training as part of a general training programme*), Jan-Louis Kruger highlights the need for so-called general language practice training as a basic requirement for training in specialised fields of translation such as audiovisual translation. The focus on such a solid foundation in general language practice training should be the first step towards specialisation. Consequently, Kruger believes that such general language practice training should be the foundation on which a training programme moves from general to more specific training. In the second contribution (*Teaching and learning to subtitle in an academic environment*), Jorge Díaz Cintas turns the focus to subtitling and discusses the variety of considerations that must be taken into account for setting up a subtitling module. He does this by considering both theoretical and practical aspects and by providing what he refers to as a "hands-on approach" to subtitling. The third contribution (*Learning to subtitle online: Learning environment, exercises, and evaluation*), provided by Eduard Bartoll and Pilar Orero, brings the practice of subtitling into the realm of 21st-century didactics by considering the feature of online teaching and its growing popularity. In their discussion of an online module offered by the Universitat Autònoma de Barcelona they share with the reader various aspects of this new form of digital technology. The fourth contribution is Anna Matamala's chapter on voice-over (*Teaching voice-over: A practical approach*), in which she addresses yet another mode of audiovisual translation. Matamala not only discusses the features used in the Universitat Autònoma de Barcelona's MA module on voice-over, she also provides exercises designed to practise features of this lesser known and less frequently taught mode of audiovisual translation. The fifth contribution is Frederic Chaume's chapter on synchronisation (*Teaching synchronisation in a dubbing course: Some didactic proposals*). The sixth contribution (*Training translators for the video game industry*), by Miguel Bernal-Merino, addresses issues at play in what is called the game localisation industry. The lack of academic focus on the translation of video games drives Bernal-Merino to discuss the current state of affairs in both the video game industry and academia. In so doing, the author promotes interaction between the industry at hand and academics with the suggestion of a specialisation module within the field of translation studies dedicated to translation of multimedia interactive entertainment software. The seventh and final chapter in this part (*Teaching audiovisual translation in a European context: An inter-university project*) is Fernando Toda's contribution to a project for teaching audiovisual translation skills to students from five European countries by means of joint, intensive courses in the areas of subtitling, dubbing and voice-over.

Part 3, entitled *AVT for special needs*, focuses on providing access to audiovisual media to people with sensory impairment. As such, it investigates two relatively new practices aimed at and providing such access: subtitling for the deaf and hard-of-hearing (SDH) and audio description (AD). The objective of this part is to highlight the practises of SDH and AD in an attempt to realise greater diffusion of the practices and, in so doing, to realise a reality in which truly everyone has access to audiovisual media. In the first contribution (*Training in subtitling for the d/Deaf and the hard-of-hearing*), Josélia Neves focuses on the specific features of SDH. Neves stresses the importance of considering these features when contemplating the set-up of SDH training programmes. SDH professionals are not only expected to have acquired general subtitling skills, but they are also required to master the skill of transferring messages intersemiotically, that is, from acoustic to visual codes. Insights into the specificity of this task will benefit any pedagogical considerations taken with reference to the practice of SDH. The second contribution (*Audio description: The visual made verbal*), provided by Joel Snyder, is similar to Neves's SDH contribution in that it also deals with pedagogical considerations, but this time the practice under investigation is that of audio description. Snyder takes a practice-inspired approach and outlines several ways in which AD may be presented, for example, in training programmes by means of a case study.

Part 4, *AVT in language learning*, moves the volume's focus to the potential of both intralingual and interlingual subtitles for facilitating both the foreign language learning process and the foreign language teaching process. In the first contribution in this part (*Using subtitled video material for foreign language instruction*), Jorge Díaz Cintas and Marco Fernández Cruz use the findings from various experiments designed to evaluate the role and impact of subtitled video material in the foreign language learning/teaching process. Díaz Cintas and Fernández Cruz's overall conclusion is that subtitled video material is indeed educationally beneficial in the foreign language learning/teaching process. However, they also point out that the use of subtitled video material is generally underweighted and advocate increased use of such material in the foreign language classroom. In the second contribution (*Tailor-made interlingual subtitling as a means to enhance second language acquisition*), Maria Pavesi and Elisa Perego flesh out the use and effects of subtitling in the foreign language process and consider a specific form of subtitles (SLA-oriented, interlingual subtitles) in what is referred to as incidental second language acquisition. The focus of this contribution is not on instructed second language acquisition but rather on uninstructed instances of second language acquisition and on creating subtitles for language learning purposes rather than on using subtitles to acquire foreign languages. The third and final contribution in this last part is by Vera Lúcia Santiago Araújo (*The educational use of subtitled films in*

EFL teaching). Santiago Araújo's contribution presents the findings of an experimental longitudinal project on whether subtitled films help foreign language learners of English improve their oral proficiency and how such films do this.

Although the 15 contributions cover an exceptionally wide range of topics and could, at first glance, be viewed as a prime example of the fragmentation that interdisciplinarity may lead to, Díaz Cintas provides a clear overarching structure into which the 15 interrelated contributions should be placed. This structure consists of four complementary parts, structured as follows: Part 1, *Inside AVT* (3 contributions), Part 2, *Hands-on experience in AVT* (7 contributions), Part 3, *AVT for special needs* (2 contributions) and Part 4, *AVT in language learning* (3 contributions). In turn, the four parts are nested within an overall structure that seeks to introduce and contextualize various didactic approaches to teaching (audiovisual) translation. What is new about Díaz Cintas's edited volume is its focus on both audiovisual translation (as a unique form of translation) and audiovisual translation training in all of its individual components. Díaz Cintas describes the goal of this volume as follows: "This selective compilation of 15 studies constitutes a rounded vision of the many different ways in which audiovisual programmes are translated and made accessible in different countries. By approaching them from a pedagogical perspective, it is hoped that this complex and dynamic area in the translation discipline, seen by many as the quintessence of translation activity in the twenty-first century, will make a firm entry into university curricula and occupy the space that is deserves in academia" (p. 18). Díaz Cintas's collection of contributions on the didactics of audiovisual translation shows unequivocally that interdisciplinarity need not lead to fragmentation. In addition, Díaz Cintas's edited volume demonstrates that interdisciplinarity that has been contextualised in a carefully considered overall structure can lead to productive insights that benefit the conceptual foundation of the discipline of audiovisual translations as well as those involved in the process of audiovisual translation training.

Jimmy Ureel – Department of Translators and Interpreters, Artesis University College, Antwerp

Ferreira Duarte, J., Alexandra Assis Rosa, & Teresa Seruya (Eds.) (2006). *Translation studies at the interface of disciplines*. Amsterdam/Philadelphia: John Benjamins. 207 p.

Translation Studies at the Interface of Disciplines est le fruit d'une conférence tenue à la Faculté de Lettres de l'Université de Lisbonne en novembre 2002 et intitulée *Translation (Studies) : A Crossroads of Disciplines*. L'ouvrage, qui entend participer au processus d'introspection dans lequel la traductologie est sans doute engagée à jamais, propose un échantillon de contributions regroupées selon trois axes ou parties : le premier engage une discussion sur la transdisciplinarité de la traductologie visant à ouvrir de nouvelles perspectives sur l'espace actuel de la traduction, le deuxième propose une réflexion sur l'importation, l'adoption, l'adaptation et la redéfinition de théories, de méthodologies et de concepts en vue de leur mise en œuvre dans l'étude de la traduction, et le troisième offre une analyse de l'interaction complexe du texte et du contexte en traduction.

La **première partie** s'ouvre sur une contribution d'Andrew Chesterman intitulée *Questions in the sociology of translation* (p. 9-27). Tout en passant en revue les différents cadres théoriques utilisés en sociologie de la traduction, l'auteur constate que peu de chercheurs se sont intéressés au processus de traduction considéré comme une série de tâches concrètes. Il propose de combler cette lacune en avançant la notion de *pratique* dont il donne une définition basée notamment sur celle du philosophe MacIntyre. Il formule alors une série de questions de recherche, liées à la notion de pratique, mais qui ne s'inscrivent pas aisément dans les cadres sociologiques proposés à ce jour. Il suggère de faire appel à la théorie de l'*acteur-réseau* des sociologues Latour et Callon, même si son application demanderait quelques amendements. Il plaide pour la collecte de données descriptives sur la sociologie de la pratique de la traduction dans des conditions et des cultures différentes afin de mieux comprendre la *causalité* et la *qualité* en traduction.

Yves Gambier, dans *Pour une socio-traduction* (p. 29-42), explique qu'il est "temps pour la traductologie de passer à l'étape de la 'socio-analyse' [...] et de développer sa réflexivité." Forte d'une telle démarche, la traductologie, avec sa pluralité d'emprunts, deviendrait ainsi une véritable « poly-discipline ». Gambier illustre son propos en interrogeant les rapports entre traductologie et sociologie. Il estime qu'entre l'approche culturelle et l'approche psychologique, il y a place pour une socio-traduction, à laquelle on adjoindrait une socio-traductologie. Il est "temps de dépasser certaines divisions traditionnelles [...] afin de mieux intégrer les traducteurs dans l'ensemble des producteurs langagiers, déjà légitimés ([...]), et les traductions dans la circulation des discours/textes ([...])."

Dans son article *Conciliation of disciplines and paradigms. A challenge and a barrier for future directions in translation studies* (p. 43-53), M. Rosario Martín Ruano explique que certains traductologues craignent actuellement que la discipline ne perde son caractère réellement interdisciplinaire : la traductologie a tant emprunté à d'autres disciplines que l'on observe aujourd'hui chez certains une volonté de *consensus*, d'*intégration*, de *conciliation*. Pour l'auteur, cette conciliation n'est pas la panacée et présente même des dangers de contradictions théoriques dont il donne quelques exemples. Vouloir concilier à tout prix, c'est nier le caractère complexe et pluriel de la traduction, c'est se priver d'une diversité d'approches nécessaires justement à la compréhension du phénomène de traduction.

On quitte la sphère sociologique avec la contribution de Gideon Toury, *Conducting research on a "Wish-to-Understand" basis* (p. 55-66). Comme son nom l'indique, l'article porte sur les méthodologies de recherche en traduction et, en particulier, sur le danger, selon l'auteur, d'adopter des cadres théoriques qui ne reposent en réalité que sur peu ou pas de preuves. Il illustre son propos en soulevant une série de questions à propos de la textualité en traduction, faisant par exemple référence à l'absence (parfois) de lecture du texte source en début de processus de traduction. Loin de nier les avantages de nombreux cadres théoriques d'un point de vue didactique, il entend ainsi révéler certaines faiblesses dès lors que l'on souhaite étudier empiriquement les comportements réels en traduction. Il conclut sur une série de recommandations à l'attention des chercheurs engagés dans des travaux empiriques, descriptifs et explicatifs.

La première partie de l'ouvrage se referme sur une contribution d'Annjo Klungervik Greenall, baptisée *Translation as dialogue* (p. 67-81). Comme ses prédécesseurs (Toury excepté), Klungervik Greenal rappelle que la traductologie est une discipline « patchwork », davantage pluridisciplinaire qu'interdisciplinaire. Pour renforcer son identité et son indépendance, une plus grande interdisciplinarité est nécessaire. Pour ce faire, on pourrait commencer par la possible *fusion* des deux tendances dominantes des XX et XXIe siècles, à savoir les perspectives linguistiques et culturelles. Les tentatives étant nombreuses mais non concluantes, l'auteur propose une alternative qui serait une véritable fusion de ces deux approches : le *dialogisme* du philosophe russe Mikhail Bakhtin. Avant d'aborder la notion de *dialogue*, il se penche sur la notion d'*hétéroglossie*, où la théorie de Bakhtin est déjà représentée. Ensuite, pour illustrer la manière dont langage et culture entrent (ou n'entrent pas) en dialogue, il prend l'exemple d'une traduction machine non réussie.

La **deuxième partie** de l'ouvrage débute par une contribution de Reine Meylaert, intitulée *Literary heteroglossia in translation. When the language of translation is the locus of ideological struggle* (p. 85-98). Alors que les recherches fonctionnelles sur l'hétéroglossie dans les œuvres littéraires originales ont une forte tradition au Canada, elles sont pratiquement absentes de la traductologie descriptive (*DTS*). Considérant la traduction comme un processus transculturel entre cultures aux relations de pouvoir inégales, l'auteur estime que son degré de pluralité linguistique peut être très chargé symboliquement. Dès lors, des études descriptives fonctionnelles de l'hétéroglossie dans les œuvres traduites pourraient changer le monolinguisme idéalisant de certains modèles de traduction et renforcer notre compréhension de la construction de l'identité littéraire et des dynamiques culturelles. Pour illustrer son propos, Meylaert met en avant quelques hypothèses inspirées de recherches menées sur des traductions de romans flamands en français dans les années 1920-1930 en Belgique.

On reste dans le domaine des *DTS* et de la traduction littéraire avec *Defining target text reader. Translation studies and literary theory* (p. 99-109) d'Alexandra Assis Rosa. Après s'être penchée sur les différents types de lecteurs tels que proposés par la théorie littéraire, elle s'intéresse aux types de lecteurs pertinents pour la traductologie et pour l'étude des normes de traduction, et souligne l'importance, en traductologie, de prendre en compte *lecteur réel* et *lecteur implicite* des textes traduits. Elle conclut en soulignant que l'application de ces notions n'est toutefois pas dénuée de problèmes et elle relève quelques objections.

On quitte le domaine littéraire pour celui du discours scientifique avec *Critical Language Study and Translation. The Case of Academic Discourse* (p. 111-127) de Karen Bennet. L'auteur met en avant la divergence d'approche des discours académiques en anglais d'une part et en portugais de l'autre, en offrant une analyse critique du discours de deux extraits représentatifs. Elle pose la question de la possibilité de traduire ce type de discours du portugais en anglais, tant les respectives visions du monde sont différentes. Ce type de traduction confronte le traducteur à un dilemme : refuser de traduire ou réécrire totalement l'article. Quel que soit la solution choisie, la configuration des connaissances telle que le conçoit la vision du monde portugaise est réduite au silence et l'auteur de reprendre le terme d'*épistémicide* du sociologue portugais Boaventura de Sousa Santos. Elle termine en plaidant pour une ouverture aux autres *voix* du discours académique.

Cette deuxième partie se termine par une contribution de Matthew Wing-Kwong Leung, intitulée *The ideological turn in Translation Studies* (p .129-144). L'auteur étudie l'intérêt d'un nouveau *tournant* idéologique en traductologie, après les tournants linguistique et culturel des dernières décennies. Après avoir expliqué le lien entre tournants culturel et idéologique, l'auteur se penche sur l'analyse critique du discours et sa pertinence pour le tournant idéologique de la traductologie. Il conclut en mettant en exergue les bénéfices potentiels de cette nouvelle orientation.

La **troisième et dernière partie** de l'ouvrage s'ouvre sur un article de Li Xia, baptisé *Institutionalising Buddhism. The role of the translator in Chinese society* (p. 147-160). L'auteur y explique que la traductologie, très *eurocentrique*, ne s'est pas ou peu intéressée à l'histoire (particulièrement riche) et à la pratique de la traduction en Chine, alors que le traducteur y a joué un rôle majeur dans la manière dont les attitudes face à la traduction et à la société dans son ensemble se sont façonnées. Li Xia passe en revue les premières activités de traduction en Chine avant de se pencher sur le rôle du traducteur dans la diffusion du bouddhisme en Chine, et en particulier sur le rôle du célèbre traducteur (entre autres) Xuan Zang. Ce faisant, il espère ouvrir la voie à une traductologie occidentale plus ouverte.

Subtitling reading practices (p. 161-168) de Maria José Alves Veiga nous emmène dans un tout autre domaine, celui de la recherche en traduction audiovisuelle au Portugal, et en particulier de la recherche sur le processus de lecture des sous-titres. Se basant sur un questionnaire diffusé parmi près de 300 élèves portugais âgés de 11 à 18 ans, l'auteur démontre que, si les jeunes sondés lisent peu sur support papier, ils regardent au contraire beaucoup la télévision et en particulier beaucoup de programmes sous-titrés. Par conséquent, ils *lisent* plus qu'on ne le croit. Par ailleurs, les jeunes sondés estiment que la lecture des sous-titres joue un rôle majeur dans le développement d'autres compétences, comme l'expression dans la langue maternelle par exemple. Puisque la traduction audiovisuelle semble jouer un rôle si important dans la vie des jeunes portugais, il est temps qu'elle trouve sa place dans la traductologie de leur pays.

On reste au Portugal avec *An Englishman in Alentejo. Crimes, Misdemeanours & The Mystery of Overtranslatability* (p. 169-184) d'Alexandra Lopes. L'auteur prend l'exemple de la traduction en portugais du roman *A Small Death in Lisbon* de Robert Wilson pour illustrer la complexité de la traduction d'un texte *trop traduisible* ('overtranslatibility'). Face à un tel texte, la réaction du lecteur portugais sera tantôt l'amusement, tantôt l'irritation. Pour Lopes, le choix d'une traduction littérale est malheureux : ici, le traducteur aurait dû s'interroger *aussi* sur ce qu'il vaut mieux *ne pas inclure* dans la traduction. En guise de conclusion, Lopes plaide pour plus de pouvoir pour le traducteur, ce qui lui permettrait plus d'audace mais lui donnerait aussi plus de confiance en soi.

L'ouvrage se referme sur une étude de cas sur les pseudo-originaux, de Dionisio Martínez Soler, intitulée *Lembranças e Deslembranças. A case study on pseudo-originals* (p. 185-196). L'auteur analyse quelques passages de *Lembranças e Deslembranças,* un recueil de poèmes posthume du poète espagnol Gabino-Alejandro Carriedo (1923-1981), dans lequel la version portugaise est présentée comme l'original, et la version espagnole comme la traduction. Martínez Soler y relève plusieurs éléments qui donnent à penser que certains poèmes ont été à l'origine pensés et écrits en espagnol. Il en conclut que l'ouvrage est non seulement un exemple de ce que certains appellent le 'translinguisme', mais aussi un cas d'auto-traduction cachée. Sans doute le poète Carriedo a-t-il voulu gagner en visibilité dans les deux pays, en vain toutefois semble-t-il. A moins qu'on ne retrouve la trace d'une version espagnole de *Lembranças e Deslembranças*, ce qui permettrait d'étudier le processus d'auto-traduction et d'écriture multilingue dont est née la version portugaise.

Isabelle Robert – Department of Translators and Interpreters – Artesis University College, Antwerp

Lewandowska-Tomaszczyk, Barbara & Marcel Thelen (Eds.) (2008). ***Translation and Meaning. Part 8. Proceedings of the Łódź Session of the 4th International Maastricht-Łódź Duo Colloquium on "Translation and Meaning", 23-25 September 2005.*** **Maastricht: Zuyd University, Maastricht School of International Communication, Department of Translation and Interpreting. 441p.**

In her review of the preceding volume, i.e. Volume 7, of this series of proceedings of the International Maastricht-Łódź Duo Colloquia on "Translation and Meaning", which have taken place every five years since 1990, Leona Van Vaerenbergh announced that the areas of translation and meaning would again be present in Volume 8, the proceedings of the Łódź session, but with a "focus on the theoretical aspects" (2008, p.282). While it is true that the largest section of Volume 8 is, indeed, **Section II** 'The *theory* of translation' (my italics) and that it contains the works of ten contributors, numerous other topics in this volume resemble those in number 7. In addition, Volume 8 also includes a section with the vaguer title 'Translation Studies' (**Section III** in 7) and appears to include additional theoretical articles. Moreover, many of the remaining sections run parallel to those in Volume 7: **Section III** 'Media translation and interpreting' (cf. 'Audiovisual Translation' in 7), **Section V** 'Translation strategies and translation training' (cf. 'The training of translators/interpreters' and 'Translation strategies' in 7), **Section VI** 'Lexicology and terminology' and Section VII 'Language corpora and translation' (cf. 'Terminology/terminography' and 'Corpora/lexicology/lexicography' in 7) and **Section VIII** 'Translating literature' (cf. 'The translation of literature' in 7). All this goes to show that there is not much difference between Volumes 7 and 8. This is also confirmed by a look at the sections that are new in Volume 8: **Section I** 'Translation and cognition', **Section IV** 'Contrastive studies between pairs of languages and translation' and **Section IX** 'Translation quality management'. However, together with the sections on lexicology and terminology (**VI**) and language corpora and translation (**VII**), these new sections are the shortest of the volume, with only one, two or three papers each. Such short sections surely follow from a type of decision questioned by Van Vaerenbergh (2008, p. 280) and again raises suspicions about the breadth and depth with which the subject is treated.

The contents of the volume reveal a conglomeration of different author nationalities, although, as evident from the list of contributors, the majority are Polish. The myriad nationalities of contributors is further reflected in the examples presented in the texts. Unfortunately, as someone who does not know the Polish language, many of the examples are lost on me for lack of a back-translation into the language of the article itself. For slightly over a quarter of the total 41 articles, that language is German; another quarter of the contributions are written in French and the rest are in English. Although I am not in a position to judge the quality of the German and French, the varieties of English in this volume are hard to pinpoint, unless they can be grouped under what Mary Snell-Hornby called "Globish American British (GAB)" in her presentation at the CETRA conference in Leuven in August 2009. Increasingly, editorial work seems to suffer from the time pressures under which academics must work, and this volume is not an exception: readers are, therefore, advised not to expect British or American English, but to have an open mind to different types of EFL, or English as a Foreign Language (i.e. the type of English that is being collected either in the International Corpus of Learner English or in VOICE, the Vienna Oxford International Corpus of English).

As with the previous volumes, Lewandowska-Tomaszczyk and Thelen have taken the trouble to compile a multilingual index, which is useful if readers want to know something about the topic. However, if readers are seeking every piece of information that the book holds about a particular topic, they should look at the topic's translations in the index (e.g. both *translation competence* and *translatorische Kompetenz* are included in the index, but each refers to a different article). In addition, such readers should also leaf through the book itself. The reason for this is that a random test showed that the index is not complete: readers wanting to know more about studies based on *questionnaires* will be guided to Zaliwska-Okrutna, but not to Tomaszkiewicz, and readers interested in discussions of *(un)translatability* will be referred to Bogucki and Dynel-Buckowska, but not to Al-Salman, Tomaszkiewicz, or Plusa.

Leaving language and technical matters aside, the volume does present a broad range of ideas. The editors present the colloquium and its theme in the introduction and describe the articles individually in a survey that follows the categorization and order of the sections in the book itself (pp. X-XII). Since any categorization built on different criteria rather than just a single one inevitably leads to discussion, the division into sections of Volume 8 can be questioned in the same way that Van Vaerenbergh (2008) questioned the sections of Volume 7. Indeed, in looking at the section titles of Volume 8, one sees that some papers have been grouped together because they address a particular *element* of the translation situation, like the type of translated text in **Section VIII** 'Translating literature'. Other studies constitute a section because of their *aim* (**Section II**, The theory of translation), and others because they describe a similar *mode* of translation (**Section III** 'Media translation and interpreting). Such diversity of criteria in one and the same volume cannot but raise questions about the consistency of the categorization. Readers might, for instance, wonder why two articles that deal with a similar topic – Potok-Nycz and Sypnicki's 'Quelques observations sur la traduction des *stéréotypes*' (my italics) and Dyoniziak's '*Stéréotype*, sens, traduction, approche générale' (my italics) – have not been brought together more closely, or why the contribution 'Implicature blocking strategies and translation problems' (Razmjou) has not been classed under 'Translation and cognition'. However, the field of translation studies has become so broad, and its topics and approaches so diverse, that a single categorization is bound to fail to pay respect to all features that a set of translation studies articles share with one another.

In brief, while readers can find one-line summaries of all articles in terms of the sections and themes offered by the editors at the beginning of Volume 8, this review will present a different categorization, with slightly different one-line summaries, because of the different focus adopted.

The survey below is based on a single criterion which is actually most relevant to Lewandowska-Tomaszczyk and Thelen's volume: the type of meaning which the article focuses on. Admittedly, most translation studies do not discuss or analyse only one type of meaning, so my classification should be seen as one that reflects those meanings that play the most central role in the discussion. The types of meaning that I distinguish (described in more detail in Vandepitte 2008) are as follows: propositional (or semantic or referential) meanings, such as predication, modification, quantification, reflexivity, embedding and coherence, and messenger-related (or pragmatic) meanings, such as the states of affairs to be communicated (cf. Lederer's synecdoche, 1976, p. 13ff), the propositions and the attitudes taken towards them, the addressee envisaged and how the messenger's knowledge about the addressee affects choices of expression, and, finally, the information that is conveyed about the messengers themselves.

In her discussion of the translation of culture-specific references (e.g. *macarons* and *sandwiches*) both in the real world and a fictional one, Mitura explores *predicational* meanings. Those constitute the main departure point for Zaliwska-Okrutna's outline of areas of cognitive and neurocognitive translation research and for Dybalska's analysis of the dubbed version of a film. Similarly, arguments are the main subject in Podhajecka's account of difficulties encountered in the compilation of a dictionary of lexicography and Lewandowska-Tomaszczyk's exploration of the differences between lexicology and terminology. A more contrastive-linguistic approach is taken by Kubacki in his examination of techniques to translate German deverbal nouns into Polish.

Both *predication and modification* are dealt with by Al-Salman, who discusses the translation of potentially ambiguous words and idioms (e.g. *the cranes were transported to Paris*) within a language acquisition and learning framework, and by Ríos Castaño, who looks at how intersemiotic translation of a text or a play into a film may change activities and personalities of characters. In her presentation of the problems encountered when translating iconic structures (onomatopoeia, repetition, etc.), Pieczyńska-Sulik points at similarities between the referential world and the language used.

Quantification is a topic that is not touched upon by this volume. However, a discussion of *reflexivity* is present, albeit only in Wertheimer's exploration of the translation of displasionable terms (such as *red* in *'Red' means red).* Similarly, only one article deals with *embedding*: Senczyszyn examines what the audience can derive from *the way the information is structured* and studies the effect of 'conceptual division' on the audience. Finally, the only contribution to investigate *coherence* is Gumul's analysis of the rendition of conditional conjunctive cohesive markers in consecutive and simultaneous interpreting.

As for pragmatic meanings, Filar examines perspective from a cognitive-linguistic viewpoint and analyses the parts of a particular *state of affairs* described in source texts and translations. Tomaszkiewicz points not only at intertextual references in films that may go unnoticed by an audience in the target culture, but also at connotations that are national (*patriotyzm* has a positive value for Polish people) and thus investigates *attitudes* that messengers may have towards certain *propositions.* Connotations are rife with stereotypical expressions, the central topic in Dyoniziak's contribution. And many high-frequency words have connotations or 'semantic prosody', the topic of Oster and Van Lawick's corpus-based contribution on phraseological units. Jereczek-Lipińska's political discourse analysis of blogs that vulgarize the Treaty of the Constitution of the European Union reveals the negative values that readers associate with certain words (e.g. *bank* and *competition*).

The messenger's (or translator's) *knowledge of the addressee envisaged* is central to Mazur's classification of translation procedures in terms of the globalization-localization dichotomy. It is also the topic of Jarniewicz's 'poetics of excess', which explains how literary translators fill in source text indeterminacies and produce translations with fewer lacunae. The metaphor is a construction that always relies on the addressee's knowledge, a subject taken up by Tamjid within a cognitive-linguistic framework. Within a more pragmatic yet still cognitive framework, Razmjou discusses the implicature-blocking strategies which the source text writer has employed and how a translator can deal with those. Every interpreter or translator plays an important role as addressee and their knowledge plays a central role in anticipating the source text messenger, the topic of Bartłomiejczyk's article.

Whereas the previous contributions mainly consider envisaged or required *background knowledge* of a translation audience, Dynel-Buczkowska's topic, namely, the effect that translated humorous passages (e.g. *as wound as a Timex*) may have on their audience, deals with the messenger's knowledge of the addressee in terms of its role in the *audience's reaction* to a certain message. Similarly, Heltai explores explicitness and explicitation and looks at its effect on the reader. Translators may make judgement errors with respect to the functional or dynamic nature of their translated utterance; such errors are called 'relative errors' by Paprocka in her survey of translation errors categories. Gajewska, in her contribution on business letters and their translations, addresses politeness phenomena.

The final type of meaning, information about the *messengers themselves*, is present in Płusa's reflections on Nietzsche's view of adequate translatability and in Feinauer's discussion of ideology in literary translation.

Finally, there is a set of articles that are difficult to assign into my classification, because they are of a more general nature: Blaskowska describes the job of an animator-interpreter among foreign exchange students; Bogucki discusses the translation unit; Borowczyk relates how inexperienced translators have used different understanding strategies; Étoré seeks to demonstrate that the translation process is governed by antonymic couples; Gawłowska looks for causes of consecutive interpreting errors in psycholinguistics and cognitive psychology; Jurewicz investigates oral features in consecutive interpreting such as self-corrections; Quentel adopts a sociolinguistic view in his survey of translation problems that arise with Celtic languages; Sitarek presents a typology of false friends, taking into account their frequencies; Thelen proposes a quality management and quality control system for monitoring the translation process and the translation service; Tirkkonen-Condit and Mäkisalo present the design of a subtitle corpus that covers various languages; Walkiewicz discusses the role of paraphrase in translation; Zaliwska-Okrutna inquires into (neuro)cognitive aspects of translation; and Żmudzki sets up a communicative model of consecutive interpreting.

This collection of proceedings is a clear continuation of the preceding volumes. For conference proceedings, editors have different options: they can present a particular interpretation of a conference and group together those contributions which communicate that interpretation; they can present a peer-reviewed qualitative selection of the contributions; or they can give everyone interested in writing an article the opportunity to present their work. Clearly, the editors have chosen the third option (and have done so for a long time). An additional result of the present volume is that it more than likely presents a comprehensive survey of Polish translation studies today.

Bibliography

Lederer, M. (1976). Synecdoque et traduction. Traduire : Les idées et les mots. *Étude de linguistique appliquée* 24, 13-41.

Van Vaerenbergh, L. (2008). Thelen, Marcel & Barbara Lewandowska-Tomaszczyk, (eds) (2007). Translation and Meaning. Part 7. Proceedings of the Maastricht Session of the 4th International Maastricht-Łódz Duo Colloquium on "Translation and Meaning", 18-21 May 2005. Maastricht: Zuyd University, Maastricht School of International Communication, Department of Translation and Interpreting. 517p. [Review]. Looking for Meaning: Methodological Issues in Translation Studies. Linguistica Antverpiensia. New Series – Themes in Translation Studies, 7/2008, 280-282.

Vandepitte, S. (2008). *Translating Untranslatability. English-Dutch, Dutch-English.* Ghent: Academia Press.

Sonia Vandepitte - University College Ghent/Ghent University

Martínez Sierra, Juan José (2008), *Humor y traducción: Los Simpson cruzan la frontera.* En: Collecció "Estudis sobre la traducció", núm. 15, Universitat Jaume I. 271p.

La globalización - Macdonaldization (p. 92) - es un hecho y el mundo de la traducción no escapa a sus efectos. La emblemática familia creada por Matt Groening cruzó la frontera española en 1991. A los españoles les gustan los Simpson o mejor dicho, les gusta la versión doblada de la serie hasta tal punto que expresiones como "multiplícate por cero" o "¡mosquis!" han pasado a formar parte del léxico común (p. 50). La clave del éxito de Los Simpson estriba en un tipo de comicidad culturalmente específico. "Los Simpson se tambalea entre aquello sobre lo que se mofa y aquello que al mismo tiempo reproduce. (...) El mismo sistema que ataca es el que hace posible que el show sea un negocio tan lucrativo" (p. 191). El escopo principal de la actividad traductora consiste pues primordialmente en la (re)producción del efecto humorístico buscado en la versión original (p. 40). Y esto confronta al traductor con una serie de problemas que no son fundamentalmente lingüísticos sino de índole cultural ya que el humor se conceptualiza de manera diferente en cada sociedad (p. 95), en parte porque se basa en un conocmiento previo compartido entre emisor y receptor (p. 123). De ahí que el traductor se conciba esencialmente como experto intercultural (p.99) "no sólo bilingüe sino también bicultural" (p. 234).

Ahora bien, los excelentes índices de audiencia que tiene la serie en España llevan a Martínez Sierra a suponer que el humor audiovisual resulta traducible (p. 233). Eso sí, la conjugación de palabras, imágenes, música, efectos especiales, sonido, colores, etc. le invita al traductor a degustar un "delicado cóctel de compleja composición" (p. 132).

El volumen que aquí se reseña - resumen de una tesis doctoral - se enmarca en el ámbito de los estudios de la traducción audiovisual. Más en particular, Martínez Sierra se propone "desde un enfoque discursivista e intercultural, desarrollar una metodología descriptiva para el estudio contrastivo de la traducción del humor en textos audiovisuales que conduzca a la identificación de tendencias de traducción" (p. 172).

El libro se articula en siete capítulos. Los contenidos teóricos de los cinco capítulos iniciales se ofrecen al lector de forma escalonada y lógica, sentando las bases para el planteamiento empírico de los capítulos sexto y séptimo. El libro se destaca por una claridad y una coherencia asombrosas. En ningún momento el texto se desvía del hilo argumentativo claramente explicado en la introducción y recogido en las primeras líneas de cada parte. Enlazando con la imagen del libro como plato suculento saboreado con "un instrumental exquisito (...) como cubertería fina" (prólogo, p. 14), diría que las porciones teóricas perfectamente equilibradas y fácilmente digeribles (capítulos 1-5) dejan sitio para un excelente postre de chocolate (capítulos 6-7, conclusiones) que, como suele ser el caso, sabe a más.

El capítulo 1 versa sobre la idiosincrasia de los textos audiovisuales cuya traducción presenta una serie de características propias que la definen como una actividad traductora "a medio camino entre el código restringido (el del discurso oral espontáneo) y el elaborado (el del discurso escrito)" (p. 35). En el capítulo 2 Martínez Sierra se ocupa de la rama descriptiva subrayando la importancia de una base empírica de ejemplos reales que evite caer en la teorización más absoluta (p. 83). Se introducen y se definen los términos estrategias de traducción, tendencias traductoras y normas de traducción (p. 82).

El capítulo 3 ofrece una visión panorámica de los Estudios Culturales e insiste en la relación entre la cultura y el humor. Todos los humanos tenemos sentido del humor pero nos reímos por distintas razones (Klopf, Murcock, Rabadán, p. 95). En el capítulo 4 se trata la cuestión del humor de forma más pormenorizada. Para que un chiste tenga éxito se requiere un conocimiento previo compartido entre el emisor y el receptor (p. 123), lo cual dificulta la labor del traductor. Basándose en Zabalbeascoa, el autor llega a una tipología de elementos humorísticos de los chistes (p. 153). Siguiendo por este camino, en el capítulo 5 se relaciona la traducción del humor con algunas cuestiones de carácter pragmático: las máximas conversacionales, la intencionalidad y el foco contextual (Agost p. 156). El capítulo 6 va dedicado a la descripción del análisis y de la metodología seguida. El capítulo 7 es un capítulo clave en el libro puesto que incluye la aplicación práctica de las distintas posturas más bien teóricas a un corpus de 365 chistes, recogidos de cuatro episodios de Los Simpson. Tras un escrutinio minucioso de la carga humorística de los chistes, el autor nos presenta los datos cuantitativos y cualitativos mediante tablas y fichas para luego identificar una taxonomía de tendencias traductoras. Entre ellas se destacan las siguientes: i) una clara tendencia a conservar el humor de los chistes, ii) en caso de pérdida de la carga humorística, una voluntad de limitarla, iii) el recurso a otras modalidades traductoras, como la subtitulación, iv) el carácter compuesto de los chistes tanto en el texto de origen como en el texto meta, v) una tendencia hacia las soluciones extranjerizantes y vi) al mismo tiempo una tendencia a evitar el uso de elementos sobre la comunidad del sistema cultural meta (p. 243).

Con todo, en el presente volumen Martínez Sierra ha realizado un excelente trabajo de observación y de descripción. Su análisis muestra de manera científica - sin dejar de ser ameno - cómo los chistes de la serie han cruzado la frontera del idioma y de la cultura. Es más, nos alcanza las herramientas y la metodología necesarias para analizar cualquier tipo de humor en cualquier texto audiovisual. Y es precisamente ahí donde reside la originalidad de su acercamiento al humor, el autor no ofrece un análisis subjetivo de un caso particular sino una propuesta de análisis interdisciplinaria, aplicable tanto a la tarea del traductor como a la del analista. Todo ello viene ya acertadamente formulado en el prólogo y se ve confirmado en cada una de las 271 páginas que cuenta el volumen.

Anne Verhaert – Department of Translators and Interpreters, Artesis University College, Antwerp

Milton, John & Paul Bandia (Eds.) (2009). *Agents of Translation.* Amsterdam/Philadeplphia: John Benjamins. 329p.

In this volume, Milton and Bandia present thirteen case studies in which translation is used as a way of influencing the target culture and furthering literary, political and personal interests. In the introduction, they examine key concepts related to agency in Translation Studies, including patronage, power, habitus and networking. In their view, agents occupy an intermediary position between a translator and an end user of a translation. This volume, rather than focusing on the functional role of the agent, emphasizes "their role in terms of cultural innovation and change" (2009, p.1). Agents can challenge the dominant system, political as well as literary, and put forward an alternative one.

In the first case study, Georges L. Bastin takes us to Latin America and investigates the role of Francisco de Miranda (1750-1816) as an intercultural forerunner of emancipation in Hispanic America. In this particular case, the actual role of translation is that of having contributed to this emancipation movement, to the creation of a national and continental identity and to the construction of a new culture. Miranda represents "the very model of a politically committed translator and agent of translation, who sees translation as a weapon of emancipation and therefore does not hesitate to manipulate the original by adding or subtracting from the original everything he considers (ir)relevant to his readership" (2009, p.39).

The second case study focuses on the influence of the *Revue Britannique* on the work of the first Brazilian fiction writers in the 19th century. This French revue was an important mediator or agent of British ideas and cultural forms, adapted to contemporary French critical opinion. Brazilian society was in search of a history and literature, and, through translation, modern ideas and new cultural forms were brought to this particular part of the new world and were subsequently adapted to the local culture's own needs.

In the third study, translation is studied as a form of representation, examining Fukuzawa Yukichi's (1835-1901) representation of the 'other' in 19th-century Japan. Yukichi introduced Western civilization to Japan through his translations and agency. Uchiyama studies the translation of *Nations around the world* (a book on geography) and some editorials written by Yukichi. In these works, the latter represents the civilized West and uncivilized 'others', a representation that in Japan has had lingering effects on the formation of stereotypical images of other cultures.

In the fourth contribution, Denise Merkle studies the publishing company Vizetelly & Company as (ex)change agent and looks at the modernization process of the British publishing industry in Victorian times. Vizetelly & Co was one of the most innovative publishers of the time, and its challenging of dominant norms and confronting the British public with foreign literature were undertakings that proved not to be without risk.

The fifth case study deals with the 'Libraries' of the British publisher Henry Bohn as a form of translation within the margin in the Victorian Age. Bohn was an example of a publisher who was successful in keeping difficult (classical) works in circulation and avoid censure (by staying clear of the most incendiary material). O'Sullivan attributes this to "the degree to which his policy of widespread but restrained expurgation kept him ostensibly within the margins of Victorian decorum" (2009, p. 126).

In the sixth paper, Semircioğlu discusses the case of Ahmed Midhat (1844-1913), an Ottoman agent of translation. Semircioğlu's main argument is that cultural and literary items from a 'model' culture may be transferred by means of free agents of translation to a receiving culture in a variety of culture-specific ways, especially to a culture undergoing profound transformation. By studying paratexts that accompany the translations and reflect the cultural and literary constraints of the target language system, the author reconstructs the translational norms underlying the texts.

In the seventh article, Tahir-Gürçağlar focuses on the interactions between politics, culture and translation and the personal history behind the turbulent career of the Turkish cultural agent Hasan-Âli Yücel (1897-1961). He was an important cultural agent in Turkey at a time when the nation-in-the-making was trying to replace religion as the uniting sentiment with a common language and culture. As a cultural agent he was active at different levels, as a writer, politician, teacher, etc. He created institutions, such as the Village Institutes for education and the Translation Bureau, which helped Turkey in its initial phase of Westernization/modernization.

Outi Paloposki, in the eighth contribution, looks into the different kinds of agency for which two important Finnish translators of the 19th and 20th centuries were responsible. Paloposki names three kinds of agency: textual, paratextual and extratextual. The translators advised publishers about what to translate, thereby introducing unknown authors to Finnish audiences.

The ninth article offers a case of translation at the service of history. Paul Bandia describes the struggle of Cheikh Anta Diop (1923-1986) to unearth Africa's prestigious historical past and traces its relation to ancient Egyptian civilization. Diop emphasized the importance of translation practices in shaping the discipline of African history.

In the tenth case study, Bradford discusses the agency of poets and the impact of their translations in Argentine literary magazines. Until the 1970s, the French ideal was used to validate local production. Three groups of poets, aided by imported texts, challenged those pre-existing conventions in Argentine poetry. Bradford explains how certain literary magazines dealt with translation and how they contributed to moulding Argentines' taste in translation discourse by enforcing certain poetics and constraining others.

The eleventh chapter discusses the role of Concrete poets Haroldo and Augusto de Campos in bringing translation to the fore of literary activity in Brazil. Médici Nóbrega and John Milton introduce the de Campos brothers, who became important agents of translation in Brazil via introducing unknown authors, influencing literary changes in the Brazilian canon, criticizing and promoting translations and introducing a theoretical approach to literature in which translation played a central role. They made translation a respectable and desirable field to work in and brought it to the forefront of literary studies.

The twelfth study focuses on the theatre translator as cultural agent. Christine Zurbach looks at the collective agent Centro Cultural de Évora (CCE), a theatre ensemble in Portugal. Their intervention corresponds to Even-Zohar's 'cultural planning' as the aesthetic choices of the programmes led to importation of theatrical and cultural models already established in France (1950-1970). Translation is seen as a decisive element in the importation of a foreign theatrical model. The CCE made efforts to change the cultural direction after the fall of the dictatorial regime in 1974 and worked for the abolition of political censorship.

In the thirteenth and final study, by Francis R. Jones, embassy networks are examined in the Bosnian post-war context. Translations are not instigated and produced by a lone translator but by a network of agents. According to Jones, an embassy network is a combination of Actor-network, activity and social game theory and illuminates how people act together to produce translations, how they are motivated and how they are influenced. Jones distinguishes three types of poetry translations in post-war Bosnia and gives detailed information about the actors, the locations (origins and workplaces of the actors) and illustrates it with a case study.

Agents in translation offers an encompassing view of the multiple facets of agency. This agency is considered from very different angles, ranging from those of publishers' to translators', from politicians' to theatre ensembles'. The thirteen studies offer insights into the significance of agency in implementing changes in the literary, social and political context of a target culture.

Sara Verbeeck – Department of Translators and Interpreters, Artesis University College, Antwerp

Pöckl, Wolfgang & Michael Schreiber (Eds.) (2008). *Geschichte und Gegenwart der Übersetzung im französischen Sprachraum.* Frankfurt am Main-Berlin-Bern-Bruxelles-New York-Oxford-Wien: Peter Lang Verlag. 200 p.

Les actes de la section "Histoire et actualité de la traduction dans l'espace francophone" du cinquième congrès des francoromanistes allemands (septembre 2006) abordent, derrière quatre parties au découpage moyennement convaincant, deux aspects principaux de la traduction en langue française: d'une part l'étude de quelques exemples tirés du passé ou du présent, d'autre part et surtout le phénomène de la traduction des "petites" littératures.

Dans ce recueil, Michael Schreiber propose un excellent survol de la traductologie en France dans les cinquante dernières années. Cette synthèse qui mérite de devenir une référence obligée pour tous les apprentis traductologues lisant l'allemand fait bien ressortir les lignes de force, depuis la stylistique comparée jusqu'à Pierre Bourdieu en passant par Mounin et Cary, l'école de Paris et Ladmiral, Meschonnic et Berman. On retiendra notamment les réflexions finales sur la faible réception de la traductologie française à l'étranger (p. 56): moins que des raisons linguistiques (la prédominance de l'anglais), ce serait la faible reconnaissance ("keine wirkliche Kanonisierung") des études de traduction en France qui pourrait expliquer son écho jusqu'alors modeste hors de l'hexagone.

Trois études de cas illustrent ensuite différentes étapes dans l'histoire de la traduction en langue française. Tatiana Bisanti présente avec beaucoup de rigueur et de clarté la traduction de Gl'Ingannati publiée par Charles Estienne en 1543. Elle montre que le traducteur n'applique pas un seul principe dans la transposition des références culturelles, mais choisit au cas par cas. De l'article de Gisela Thome sur la traduction de livres pour enfants (Cornelia Funke, Jürg Schubiger et Peter Härtling), on retiendra surtout les réflexions sur le traitement des images, l'étude normative des textes publiés nous paraissant de moindre intérêt.

Enfin, l'article de Norbert Bachleitner sur les différentes traductions de Ulysses de Joyce en français et en allemand n'offre pas simplement un excellent aperçu de la question, mais aussi une prise de distance salutaire par rapport à certains enthousiasmes de la critique française. La mise en parallèle de la traduction collective publiée en 2004 sous la direction de Jacques Aubert et de la version individuelle, que le grand traducteur allemand Hans Wollschläger (mort en 2007) a publiée en 1981, apporte des éléments précieux pour une réflexion sur le concept de retraduction, les mêmes caractéristiques semblant se dégager des deux versions secondes. Même si la situation de départ est différente (la première traduction allemande était déplorable tandis que la version française d'Adrienne Monnier demeure digne de respect), grammatique et style subissent une évidente modernisation. Et quand il n'y a pas erreur (comme trop souvent dans la traduction de Goyert en allemand), les diverses traductions mettent surtout en évidence la nécessité de choisir qui s'impose aux traducteurs face à la complexité, la polysémie et la profondeur psychologique de l'original sans qu'on puisse parler de progrès ou de supériorité.

Prenant du recul par rapport au marché de la traduction moderne qui, comme le remarque finement Jörn Albrecht, ressemble à maints égards à celui du Haut Moyen Âge où quelques langues fortes écrasaient une multitude de langues faibles, les francoromanistes allemands se concentrent par ailleurs sur la médiation des littératures en situation d'infériorité. En reprenant la distinction de Roman Jakobson entre traductions intralinguale, interlinguale et intersémiotique, Jörn Albrecht aborde ainsi la question de la traduction entre deux dialectes (Mundarten) de poids différent à partir du cas particulier de l'occitan. Cet exemple, comme celui du souabe ou du bavarois par rapport au Hochdeutsch, permet de se demander à partir de quel degré d'autonomie la traduction ne paraît plus nécessaire ou, pour le dire autrement, à partir de quand l'arrêt de mort des langues minoritaires est signé.

Wolfgang Pöckl, quant à lui, propose un panorama éclairant de la réception française de la littérature autrichienne du XXe siècle, laissant entrevoir un stéréotype qui se vend à l'étranger tandis qu'à l'intérieur des frontières de la langue allemande la définition d'une littérature autrichienne demeure tout sauf aisée, comme le rappellent les exemples de Kafka ou Canetti. Depuis le "mythe habsbourgeois" de Claudio Magris jusqu'au "pays merdique" de Jacques le Rider, on voit se dégager un ensemble de clichés et de légendes qui permettent la diffusion de quelques auteurs phares (Handke, Bernhard, Jelinek), déjà bien étudiée par divers chercheurs. La province autrichienne, en revanche, reste négligée dans l'étude des transferts littéraires: les contacts culturels entre l'Autriche et la France restent conçus comme des contacts entre Vienne et Paris.

Enfin, les articles de Frank Wilhelm sur la traduction au Luxembourg et d'Irene Weber Henking sur plusieurs générations de traducteurs suisses apportent des informations intéressantes sur le travail de médiation dans les pays plurilingues. Le marché du livre français apparaît aux yeux de Wilhelm comme "fort protectionniste et peu ouvert à des auteurs-traducteurs inconnus à Paris" (p. 95) tandis que Weber Henking souligne que les droits de traduction de Robert Walser ayant été achetés à Suhrkamp par Gallimard, les éditeurs helvétiques (notamment les éditions Zoé de Genève) doivent se contenter de miettes. Pour être connus en Suisse romande, les auteurs suisses allemands (non seulement Walser, mais aussi Jeremias Gotthelf par exemple) doivent même passer par l'étranger.

La plupart de ces contributions évoquent le rôle essentiel de quelques personnalités fortes et influentes (Richard Thieberger pour Fritz Hochwälder ou Marthe Robert dans le cas de Robert Walser), de la revendication identitaire et de la politique (la renaissance du provençal ou les traductions de Gottfried Keller dans la deuxième moitié du XIXe siècle), d'institutions (l'Institut d'Études Occitanes, l'Institut autrichien, le Centre d'Études et de Recherches autrichiennes, Pro Helvetia ou la fondation ch) et de l'autotraduction (Frédéric Mistral ou George Erasmus) dans la médiation des littératures de langue minoritaire.

Deux articles consacrés à la traduction des classiques français en allemand sortent du cadre strict annoncé par le titre. Celui de Gabriele Blaikner-Hohenwart consacré à la pièce Bérénice de Molière d'Igor Bauersima et Réjane Desvignes (2004) n'en reste pas moins une contribution de valeur sur une forme extrême de traduction pour la scène au début du XXIe siècle. L'ensemble constitue par conséquent un état des lieux dense et riche qui prouve la vitalité des études sur la traduction en français du côté germanophone.

Frédéric Weinmann - Lycée Hoche, Versailles

Alphabetical list of authors & titles with keywords

Aranberri-Monasterio, Nora and O'Brien, Sharon Evaluating RBMT output for –ing forms: a study of four target languages
Keywords: Machine Translation, -ing words, controlled language, post-editing source text, automatic evaluation metrics, Machine Translation evaluation correlations, IT domain, commercial machine translation, RBMT 105

Babych, Bogdan, and Hartley, Anthony Automated error analysis for multiword expressions: using BLEU-type scores for automatic discovery of potential translation errors
Keywords: automated error-analysis, multiword expressions, BLEU, automated metrics, concordance, concordance-based evaluation of Machine Translation, MT-tractability 81

Bowker, Lynne Can Machine Translation meet the needs of official language minority communities in Canada? A recipient evaluation
Keywords: Machine Translation, recipient evaluation, official language minority communities, official bilingualism, rapid post-editing, maximal post-editing 123

Daelemans, Walter, and Hoste, Véronique Evaluation of Translation Technology
Keywords: evaluation, machine translation, translation tools.......... 9

Estrella, Paula, Popescu-Belis, Andrei, and King, Maghi The FEMTI guidelines for contextual MT evaluation: principles and resources
Keywords: MT evaluation, contextual evaluation, quality models for MT, contexts of use for MT, evaluation plans, web-based interfaces, FEMTI 43

Fernandez Costales, Alberto The role of Computer-Assisted Translation in the field of software localisation
Keywords: Localization, software localization, CAT evaluation, translation technology 179

Jimenez- Crespo, Miguel A The effect of Translation Memory tools in translated Web texts: evidence from a comparative product-based study
Keywords: Web localization, TM evaluation, corpus-based evaluation, product-based evaluation, monolingual comparable corpus, coherence, terminology 213

Macken, Lieve In search of the recurrent units of translation
Keywords: translation memory systems, sentence-based translation memory systems, chunk-based translation memory systems, text types, fuzzy matches, bilingual concordances 195

Mihalache, Iulia Social and economic actors in the evaluation of translation technologies. Creating meaning and value when designing, developing and using translation technologies
Keywords: translators' communities, knowledge communities, collaborative environments, collaborative translation tools, multi-user technologies, technology adoption, technology use, translators' attitudes, translators' perceptions, innovation transferability.............. 159

Vandeghinste, Vincent Scaling up a hybrid MT System: From low to full resources
Keywords: MT evaluation, contextual evaluation, quality models for MT, contexts of use for MT, evaluation plans, web-based interfaces, FEMTI 65

Way, Andy A critique of Statistical Machine Translation
Keywords: Statistical Machine Translation, Phrase-Based Statistical Machine Translation, Corpus-based Machine Translation, Rule-Based Machine Translation, Example-Based Machine Translation, Machine Translation Evaluation, Syntax, Machine Translation ....
17

Alphabetical list of contributors & contact addresses

Aranberri-Monasterio, Nora
Dublin City University
School of Applied Language and Intercultural Studies
Centre for Translation and Textual Studies
Dublin 9, Ireland
e-mail: nora.aranberrimonasterio@dcu.ie

Babych, Bogdan
University of Leeds
School of Modern Languages and Cultures
Centre for Translation Studies
Leeds LS2 9JT
United Kingdom
e-mail: bogdan@comp.leeds.ac.uk

Bowker, Lynne
University of Ottawa
School of Translation and Interpretation
70 Laurier Ave East, Rm 401
Ottawa, ON K1N 6N5
Canada
e-mail: lbowker@uottawa.ca

Daelemans, Walter
University of Antwerp
Computational Linguistics - CLIPS
Prinsstraat 13, Building L
2000 Antwerp
Belgium
e-mail: walter.daelemans@ua.ac.be

Estrella, Paula
National University of Córdoba
FaMAF
Haya de la Torre s/n
Ciudad Universitaria
5000 - Córdoba
Argentina
e-mail: pestrella@famaf.unc.edu.ar

Fernández Costales, Alberto
University of Oviedo
Escuela Universitaria Jovellanos
Laboral - Ciudad de la Cultura
Calle Luis Moya 261
33203 Gijón, Spain
e-mail: albertofernandezcostales@gmail.com

Hartley, Anthony
University of Leeds
School of Modern Languages and Cultures
Centre for Translation Studies
Leeds LS2 9JT
United Kingdom
e-mail: a.hartley@leeds.ac.uk

Hoste, Veronique
University College Ghent
LT3 Language and Translation Technology Team
Faculty of Translation Studies
Groot-Brittanniëlaan 45
9000 Ghent, Belgium
e-mail: veronique.hoste@hogent.be

Ghent University
Department of Applied
Mathematics and Computer Science
Krijgslaan 281 (S9)
9000 Ghent
Belgium

Ghent University
Department of Applied
Mathematics and Computer Science
Krijgslaan 281 (S9)
9000 Ghent
Belgium

Jiménez-Crespo, Miguel A.
Rutgers University, The State
University of New Jersey
Dept. of Spanish and Portuguese
105 George St
New Brunswick, NJ 08901
USA
e-mail: miguelji@rci.rutgers.edu

King, Maghi
Université de Genève
TIM/ISSCO
École de Traduction et d'Interpréta-
tion
40 Boulevard du Pont-d'Arve
1211, Genève 4
Switzerland
e-mail: Marga-
ret.King@issco.unige.ch

Macken, Lieve
University College Ghent
LT3 Language and Translation
Technology Team
Faculty of Translation Studies
Groot-Brittanniëlaan 45
9000 Ghent
Belgium
e-mail: lieve.macken@hogent.be

Mihalache, Iulia
Université du Québec en Outaouais
Département d'études langagières
283, boul. Alexandre-Taché,
bureau F-1046
Case postale 1250, succ. Hull
Gatineau QC J8X 3X7
Canada
e-mail: iulia.mihalache@uqo.ca

O'Brien, Sharon
Dublin City University
School of Applied Language and
Intercultural Studies
Centre for Translation and Textual
Studies
Dublin 9
Ireland
e-mail: Sharon.obrien@dcu.ie

Popescu-Belis, Andrei
Idiap Research Institute
Centre du Parc
Rue Marconi 19
CP 592
1920 Martigny
Switzerland
e-mail: andrei.popescu-
belis@idiap.ch

Robert, Isabelle
Artesis University College
Department of Translators and Interpreters
Schildersstraat 41
2000 Antwerp
Belgium
e-mail: isabelle.robert@artesis.be

Ureel, Jimmy
Artesis University College
Department of Translators and Interpreters
Schildersstraat 41
2000 Antwerp
Belgium
e-mail: jimmy.ureel@artesis.be

Vandeghinste, Vincent
Katholieke Universiteit Leuven
Faculty of Arts
CCL Centre for Computational Linguistics
Blijde Inkomststraat 13 (bus 3315)
3000 Leuven, Belgium
e-mail: vincent.vandeghinste@ccl.kuleuven.be

Vandepitte, Sonia
University College Ghent
Faculty of Translation Studies
Groot-Brittanniëlaan 45
9000 Ghent
Belgium
e-mail: sonia.vandepitte@hogent.be

Ghent University
Department of English
Rozier 44
B-9000 Ghent
Belgium

Verbeeck, Sara
Artesis University College
Department of Translators and Interpreters
Schildersstraat 41
2000 Antwerp
Belgium
e-mail: sara.verbeeck@artesis.be

Verhaert, Anne
Artesis University College
Department of Translators and Interpreters
Schildersstraat 41
2000 Antwerp
Belgium
e-mail: anne.verhaert@artesis.be

Way, Andy
Dublin City University
School of Computing
Glasnevin, Dublin 9
Ireland
e-mail: away@computing.dcu.ie

Weinmann, Frédéric
74 rue destailleurs,
59000 Lille
France
Email: fredericweinmann@yahoo.fr